INDIE FILMMAKER PRODUCER'S GUIDE

The Nuts and Bolts
of
Independent Film Production

In Memory: Kayla

*During the writing of this book, our very dear family
pet, Kayla, died at the age of 12. She passed on her own, with-
-out me having to raise a hand. She did it her way. She had been
bravely battling arthritis and diabetes and was blind. Although she
had lost control of her bodily functions, we learned how to have
patience from her for those less capable, and we never ever condemned her
for her mishaps. My wish is that if there is a great beyond that awaits us,
that she finds her way to the great Rainbow Bridge and waits for us there.
Till then, goodnight my sweet little girl.*

INDIE FILMMAKER PRODUCER'S GUIDE

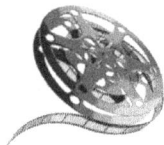

The Nuts and Bolts
of
Independent Film Production

YOUNG FILMS & PUBLISHING LLC

Book cover design by Jackie Young

Authored by Jackie Young

Edited by Jill Lewellen Pomerantz

ISBN-10: 0977432858
ISBN- 13: 9780977432851

Printed in the United States of America
10 9 8 7 6 5 4 3 2 1

To those with the guts to be independent film producers...

A SPECIAL THANKS TO

*My children, Nick and Christina, and my Granddaughter,
Meara. You are the bright stars in my movie
called life.*

Table of Contents

Table of Contents

Table of Contents

FOREWORD

"I believe that filmmaking - as, probably, is everything - is a game you should play with all your cards, and all your dice, and whatever else you've got. So, each time I make a movie, I give it everything I have. I think everyone should, and I think everyone should do everything they do that way."

- Francis Ford Coppola

Some wise words from a great director. I have a word that every indie producer should include in their vocabulary: **care**. Care about the story that you tell. Make sure it is the very best and that it evokes emotions from the audience. Care about the cast and crew, about getting every scene in focus, and that the acting is the very best. Caring about what you do means taking the extra time and effort to get it right. This attitude of caring must be passed on and embraced by those under us and as producers, we need to lead them. Find ways as the producer to do things better each time you go into production on another film. Look for methods that help create better films. Never assume because you don't have the budget or stars that you wished for that you shouldn't still shoot for the very best. Never settle when you can always bring the bar up a little higher.

Jackie Young

INTRODUCTION

I was prompted to write this book when I found myself in long conversations with other up and coming producers who wanted to know the ins and outs of film production from someone who had been in the trenches of independent filmmaking. No, I'm not a big Hollywood producer and no you haven't seen me and probably won't see me at the Academy Awards accepting any awards. I'm just a typical filmmaker who has been through all of the bumps and grinds of trying to break into the system and just make films. However, I have made inroads for Young Films in the industry and have learned a lot of the dos and don'ts (I believe). I've certainly beat my head against the wall enough times in this business. I won't bore you with too much of my background so that we can get into the details of producing films, but I will give you some info on me just the same. I started out as a screenwriter over 20 years ago and after becoming frustrated with not being able to get my screenplays produced, decided to produce my own short film. That was in 1997.

As an engineer by trade, I have always tried to apply processes and methods to the madness of filmmaking and some have worked. We followed the short film with an international co-production of a romantic comedy feature film in Canada in 2001. I will speak about these co-productions later in the book and what to watch out for when doing them. One of the tricks I learned from engineering was to take away lessons learned from projects. On each film project that I'm involved with, I try to identify what worked and what didn't work and to find ways to fix the problems. Naturally, you hope this leads to better and better films as you progress from one film to the next. It does, to a certain degree. However, filmmakers seem to be doomed in repeating these problems on every project. Later, I will go into how these are inherent in low budget filmmaking and how in essence we create our own problem.

Anyway, I took a break from films after the co-production to focus on publishing our brand of books called "Read-A-Movie" with my brother Dan. The concept was interesting and we published several books under that banner for several years. After my father passed several years ago, my brothers, who are members of our film company, talked me into possibly producing another film, this time, a horror film. The film was started in 2010 but the production ended up being delayed until 2011. In total, we spent three years on the film from preproduction to distribution. Although distribution isn't complete, we do have markets for the film and believe we are on the way to seeing profits. Of course, profits from indie films are always questionable as we will discuss later in the book. We discovered during the production of our last film how much the technology and landscape of film production had changed since our last film in 2001 and found ourselves on a very steep learning curve to catch up with what was going on in the industry. This technology and this new landscape will be discussed later in the book.

On the films, I have had the honor of participating as screenwriter, executive producer, producer, director, editor, composer, and as manager of Young Films, LLC. I do not have a formal film degree but do have a Bachelors of Science Degree with an emphasis in Technical/Information Management from Bellevue University. I also have over 4 years as a member of the Nebraska Writers group and was the coordinator of the Nebraska Screenwriters for over four years. I have written over 40 screenplays in all genres and am the author of "How to Write a Screenplay in 3 Days: The Marathon Method." I am also the publisher and contributing writer to the Read-A-Movie book series.

As the title of the book, "Indie Filmmaker Producer's Guide" suggests, the book is written from the film producer's perspective. Although I will cover many more aspects of film production than just producing the film, this is the main perspective. The producer is the person who spins up the film from every aspect. Without the producer, the film goes nowhere. Sure, the other elements such as a screenplay, actors, director, etc. are important, but the producer is the key to ramping up a picture. The other aspect, mentioned in the sub-title, "The Nuts & Bolts of Independent Film Production" is the attempt to provide a book that is useful for the independent filmmaker. When I first began my filmmaker journey, I could not find a book that told me what I wanted to know – how to make movies. There was every conceivable book on the market, except the one I needed. I try to cover everything I know about indie film production from A to Z and provide valuable insights into where it's easy to make mistakes or lessons learned from my experiences.

Young Films LLC is comprised of me and my family (immediate and extended). Yes, others are involved in the production of our films, but at the core of our company is our family. We all pull together to make feature films. So, in this book, you'll find that theme throughout. Do you have to make films with your family? No. But can you? Sure, and it can be fun as well, stressing at times but still fun.

If you are familiar with screenplays, you know that typically screenplays are written in three acts: Act I is where we introduce our characters and the main conflict that will drive the story. Act II is where the conflicts play out and the action happens. Act III is where everything gets resolved... or it doesn't. Film production is similar. Preproduction is like Act I where we get introduced to all of the elements of film production and everything will play a role in the story (movie) being told. The production phase is where the principal photography happens, the capturing of the conflict as images and sound. Act III is where everything we've captured during production is assembled into a final product and all issues with that final product must be resolved.

Therefore, this book is laid out in three phases of production. The first part of the book deals with the preproduction phase, followed by the production phase, and then the post production phase. There is also a film distribution section that follows. Although standard film production involves the first three phases, typically it is handed off to a distributor who takes control from there.

However, as I mentioned earlier, the landscape has changed for film producers and this is one of the big changes. More and more filmmakers are doing self distribution rather than handing it off to distributors. Young Films LLC did just this, handling a lot of the distribution for its latest film. There are, of course, pros and cons to this, but we felt that it was important enough to have a dedicated section to the topic.

The intent of this book is to provide the aspiring filmmaker with the information and lessons learned from our adventures in filmmaking so that they have a better understanding of all of the phases and are aware of all of the elements involved. At the same time, the intention is to impart to the filmmaker what we've learned about the process while imparting some tips and tricks they can use to make their adventure easier and more productive in order to create a better quality film. Hang onto your hats and let's get started!

A final note before we get started. I wrote this book with the intent of the book being printed in full color. However, the costs to produce a full color print version would have put the price out of the price range of most indie filmmakers (Around $ 50.00 as opposed to $ 20.00). So some discussions on colorization may not be clearly understood from viewing black & white photos that were meant to be presented in color. However, indie filmmakers will have the choice of a prinited book (B&W interior) or an e-book (full color interior).

PRE-PRODUCTION

I have a great idea for a film, what's the first thing I should do?

I can't tell you how many times I've heard this from people who know that I'm in the film business. I always tell them to start by writing it down and expanding the concept into a story line. From there, a screenplay can be developed. If the person with the idea can't write the screenplay, it can be handed off to someone who can. If you are willing, there are many screenplay books on the market that teach format and character development. Once you have a screenplay developed, then you either need to seek out a producer who can put all of the pieces together for the production or consider producing it yourself. This book will walk aspiring film producers through all of the processes of film production. Figure 1 shows a sample page from a screenplay that I wrote. You can see that a screenplay follows a different type of format than fiction. A screenplay is a visual guide or blueprint of the film. It's composed of location, character, character descriptions and character narrative that visually depict each scene of the film. Only information on how the story is visually told should appear, unlike fiction where everything must be visualized by the reader.

The screenplay becomes the heart of production. It is the story, the film. However, from a production standpoint, it spawns a wealth of required resources and assets that need to be attained and organized into a smooth running production with a budget, schedules that need to be adhered to and commitments that need to get accomplished. The length of the screenplay will drive the cost of producing the film. For every minute of film that's shot, there are associated costs so this can drive up the budget. Typically, screenplays should be from a minimum of 90 pages to a maximum of around 105 pages. Figure approximately one minute of running time for each page of screenplay. Therefore, a 90 page screenplay equals a 90 minute film.

So develop a screenplay based on that idea. Then pitch the

screenplay to a producer for development. This is actually harder than it sounds. Most major studios today will NOT accept unsolicited screenplays from writers. You can, however, pay an entertainment lawyer to act as middle man to pitch your screenplay. The costs will be around $350. If you do this, find an entertainment lawyer in LA. You can also shop your screenplay at numerous web sites on the Internet where you may land an independent film producer looking for a film project. Be advised that most don't pay and will defer any form of payment to you. Welcome to independent film. The other option is to develop and produce the film based on your screenplay yourself. This book will help you with the latter. For help on writing screenplays, look for my book mentioned earlier on Amazon.com or go to www. youtube.com and search on "read-a-movie screenwriting" to watch my free screenwriting tutorials.

```
photos are all the same.

                    CHIEF
          So what's this?

                    MATTE
          That's the signature of your killer.

                    MATTE
          That's the latest.

She nods towards the wall.

                    MATTE
          The rest are from across the
          country for the past twenty
          years. And wherever James Harrison
          was, the bodies followed.

The Chief examines the photo then hands it back.

                    CHIEF
          The lab showed me this. They said it
          was a bad print.

                    MATTE
          It's not a bad print.

                    DEPUTY
          What is it?
```

Figure 1- Example Screenplay Page

How To Find A Screenplay And Options

If you are not a writer but feel confident as a producer, screenplays can be found on the web at numerous web sites such as http://www.inktip.com/ and http://www.screenplaycontests.com/market/ to name a couple. Typically, production companies will **option** the screenplay from the writer. An option is a legal agreement between the production company and the screenwriter that allows the production company to try to bring some funding to the project and get the film spun up. Usually the option runs anywhere from six months to a year. At the end of the period, the option can be renewed to continue trying to get the film into production. Options usually pay $5K to $10K for each period. Of course, everything is negotiable so it's up to the producer and screenwriter to strike a deal. Keep in mind that the option ONLY allows the producer to work with the screenplay to get the film spun up. If the producer actually gets it spun up, another negotiation needs to take place during which the producer and screenwriter settle on a purchase price. The option price is totally separate from the purchase price.

Elements Of Film Production

The first job as producer is to calculate what the cost of producing the film is by making casting/crew decisions and breaking down the script into production elements. We'll start with the breakdown because this is more important to the indie producer. This breakdown of the script will also become useful to the Production Manager (PM) later on when they are put in charge of managing all of the resources. The PM job is a critical position during film production and I would not suggest filming without an experienced PM running the show.

The best approach to take when breaking down the costs of the screenplay is to visualize each scene without any resources, i.e. with the actors naked. Everything must be removed from the scene except the naked actor. Now, slowly start putting back everything into the scene and cataloguing it: their clothes (wardrobe), their guns (props), the cars in the background (vehicles), the coffee shop in the background (location), the passersby (extras) in the background, the snow falling (snow machine or SFX in post), the cuts and black eye from the fight (makeup and special effect makeup). You get it, right?

Everything in a scene MUST come from somewhere. It must be bought, rented, created, or added in post. These are all resources that must come from somewhere and become a part of the budget. You not only must decide what resources are needed for which scenes but for how long. Again, for an indie producer with limited budget this is critical. If I only have one scene with the expensive limousine, then I only want to rent that limousine for half a day at the most. I don't want to pay for a full day when I don't need it.

Filmmakers should also be aware that when considering the production of futuristic or period films, that costs may soar in trying to create that era on film. Everything in the camera's eye must be controlled and only props and vehicles from that era should be in frame. Otherwise, the illusion is lost. This can increase a film's budget drastically. This may explain why indie filmmakers tend to set films in current time. Filmmakers experience less worry and fewer costs when not trying to recreate a bygone or future era.

Experienced filmmakers who are savvier and have a track record, should consider **attachments** (stars, directors, cinematographers) when budgeting the film. As we will discuss later, indie filmmakers without these attachments face the problem of getting distribution for their film. To put it plain and simple, when there are no attachments, distributors are left without any marketing angle for the film and will turn it down. There are exceptions, but this is the general rule.

For most indie filmmakers, their limited budgets don't account for any attachments. Not that they shouldn't approach stars and directors for attachment to the project, it's just unlikely they will get brand name recognizable attachments for their film. Again, welcome to indie film.

How much does it cost to make a movie?

Film budgets vary from a few thousand dollars to hundreds of millions. It depends on, as we mentioned, your track record, your connections, attachments, and the type of film you're shooting. Realistically, indie films (non-studio) budgets can be as little as a few thousand dollars (if you own your own equipment or can borrow it) to a few million. Naturally the larger the budget you have to work with, the more attachments you can afford and most likely the better quality film produced. Figure 2 shows a high level budget graphic developed for an investor proposal. You'll notice that a lot of the budget is shoved out towards the back end of the film development. This provides for marketing and advertising funds for self distribution. This relates to the discussion earlier about filmmakers distributing their own film. We will talk later about film distribution in more detail, but now wrap your head around the concept of a producer having a vision for film production just as the writer has a vision for his story, a director a vision for how he tells that story, and an editor a vision of how it should be told. The indie film producer's vision should encompass not only film production, but what the plan is for distribution when post production is complete. When a film producer's visions only take them to the end of post, you end up with a product that has no method to reach its potential customer. Think bigger!

Pre-Production

- Star Attachments: $ 90K for 3 actors ($ 25K each) to lockdown contract
- Location Insurance/E&O Insurance = $ 20K
- Locations/Costumes/Props = $ 20K
- Young Films Studio Building/Rental office furniture/big screen for one month - $ 10K
- Film Web Page
- Design/Maintenance - $ 2.2K
- Pre-production activities $ 15K
  - o Location Mmgt
  - o Auditions
  - o Contracts

Total $ 157.2K

Production

- Star Attachments: $ 90K for 3 actors ($ 25K each) balance of payment for work
- Star lodging – For 4 actors, 3 weeks = $ 16K
- Food for 20 people for 28 days = $ 16,800
- Crew of four for 4 weeks = $ 12,800
- Makeup for 4 weeks $ 3,200
- Young Films crew of 10 for 4 weeks = $ 20K
- DP (Rob) 4 weeks = $ 20K
- Tracking and dolly vehicle $ 7K
- Camera boom = $ 7K
- Red One/Lenses rental = $ 15K
- RV Rental - $ 3K
- Equipment truck - $ 3K
- Transportation - $ 3.5 k

Total $ 217.3K

Post-Production

- Song for soundtrack - $ 60K for 3 hit songs
- Editing of film - $ 20K
- Iain Kelso – Score = $ 20K
- Animation at beginning of film – $ 1,500
- Graphic Artist - $ 4K
- MPAA Rating - $ 3K

Total $ 108.5K

Distribution Costs

- Printing costs – Posters for theaters - $ 10K
- DCP development - $ 12K
- VPFs for 100 theaters -$ 100K
- Advertising film release $ 400K (60K-trailers at Cinema, 5% on Web Advertising)
- TV Show Promotions $ 40K
  - o Travel. Lodging, food for 2 or 3 actors
- PR Person $ 15K
- Develop Trailer for film $ 5K

Total $ 582K

Total Film Budget $ 1065K

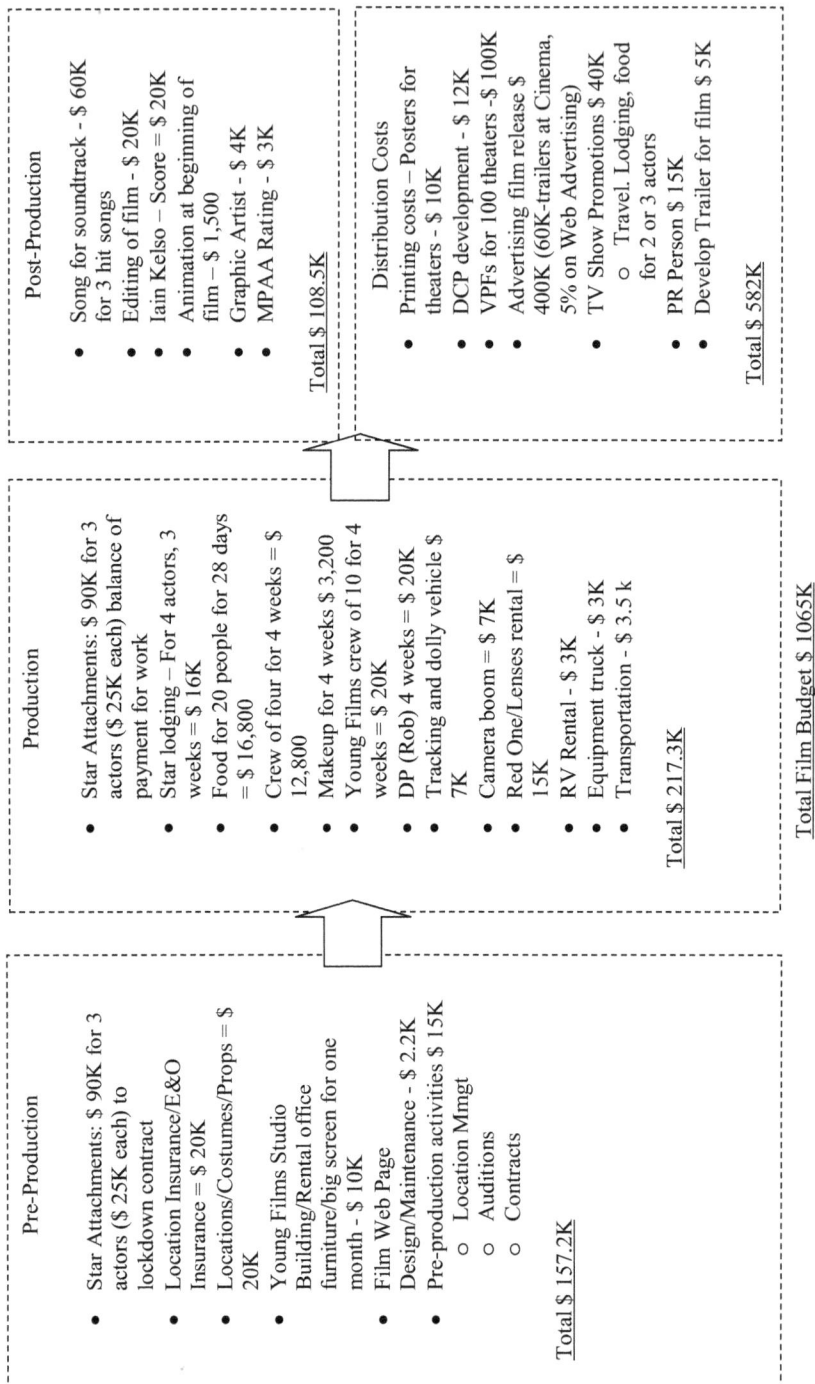

*Figure 2-**High Level Budget Diagram***

The totals in Figure 2 give a possible investor an idea of how funds will be used in each phase and shows that the filmmaker (producer) has looked past production activities and given extensive thought to marketing and making profits. Figure 3 shows a portion of a detailed budget where the producer will document all expenditures and expenses during all production phases. It consists of **above-the-line** and **below-the-line** expenditures. Above-the-line items include individuals such as the screenwriter, producer, director, casting director and actors. Below-the-line consists of the rest of the crew and expenses associated with the making of the film. It will include all money paid out and **deferred payments**.

Deferred pay is money that will be paid out when producers realize profits. Yep, you guessed it; this doesn't happen on the majority of films. Lots of us are still waiting for that deferred payment. The trick to this is to get this concept to work by doing the right things during production that will make the film profitable and get everyone a paycheck, a mighty goal in this business. Without deferred salaries, most indie films would never get made. The question becomes in indie filmmaking, how much actual cash do you need to produce the film? What the film actually costs on the books is totally different because that will include all of the deferred salaries. There are enough hungry writers, actors, and crew members out there that are chomping at the bit for the next film to come along. It could be the film that breaks them into the business. If not, it's another film under their belt and a film they can add to their portfolio.

Now for the good news. With the latest technology that includes high definition (HD) CMOS digital camera technology, multi-CPU rendering capability and advanced special effects software now on the desktop editing work station, the indie filmmaker is a lot closer to realizing their film vision for a lot less than what it used to cost. My first film was shot on Super 16 MM and cost $30,000 for an 11 minute short film. In 2001, during post production of our first film, using an HD digital camera, it cost over $25,000 dollars for the editing of the HD film. There were only a few post production houses that could do HD editing at that time. Today, HD editing is available on the desktop.

Young Films LLC	Title: Paperhearts			Producers: Jack Young		
Director: I Jack Young	**Writer:** Jack & Dan Young					
Acct #	Description	Amount	Units	X	Rate	Subtotal	Total

Acct #	Description	Amount	Units	Rate	Subtotal	Total
100-001	**STORY**		deferred	8,000	8,000	8,000
100-002	**SCREENPLAY PURCHASE**					
	purchase		deferred	125,000	125,000	125,000
				Total for 100-001		**133,000**
110-00	**PRODUCER**					
110-01	**EXECUTIVE PRODUCER**					
	Jack Young		deferred	12,500	12,500	12,500
110-01-01	Sales Agent / Distributor		deferred	0	0	0
	TBA - @ negotiated % of sales					
110-02	**PRODUCER**					
	Jack Young		deferred	12,500	12,500	12,500
	Dan Young		deferred	12,500	12,500	25,000
110-03	**ASSOCIATE PRODUCER**					
	TBD	0	contract	0	0	
	tax	0		0	0	0
110-04	**Location InsuranceFees**					
	TBD		Allow	25000	25,000	
				Total for 110-00		**50,000**
120-00	**DIRECTOR**					
120-01	**DIRECTOR**					
	Jack Young	4	Week	7,500	30,000	
	fringes	0	deferred	0	0	30,000
120-02	**CASTING FEES**					
	t.b.d		Allow	500	500	500
120-03	**DIRECTOR'S SECRETARY**					
	TBD	3	Weeks	150	450	
	taxes	0.15	Allow	450	67.5	518
				Total for 120-00		**31,018**
130-00	**CAST**					
130-01	**PRINCIPAL PLAYERS**					
	Elderly Male Lead # 1	3	Weeks	12,000	36,000	
	fringes	0.17		36,000	6,120	42,120
	Elderly Male Lead # 2	3	Weeks	12,000	36,000	
	fringes	0.17		36,000	6,120	42,120
	Elderly Male Supporting	3	Weeks	12,000	36,000	
	fringes	0.17		36,000	6,120	42,120

*Figure 3-**Example of a Detailed Film Budget***

What a film costs to get made is very subjective. As I mentioned, a lot can be deferred, but there are essentials in filmmaking that can't be avoided, such as the camera, lenses, sound recording equipment, lighting, and an editing platform. The rest is negotiable. In later chapters we will discuss these essentials.

For now, if this is your first film, consider some things that will naturally keep your costs down. Select a screenplay that is character driven (characters in a dramatic situation or conflict) and doesn't include any major special effects, car chases, explosions, or alien spacecraft battles. Try to keep your locations to a minimum. However, do NOT try to shoot the entire film in a single location (like your basement). We'll discuss an approach to locations later and it definitely does not include your basement. Select a screenplay that is set in current time. Remember our discussion on period pieces and futuristic settings? This can cause your budget to balloon out of sight. Focus on story, acting, and cinematography to tell an engaging story.

Once you have a screenplay, look at each scene as we discussed and take a very methodical and analytical approach to the budgeting of it. Identify each element in each scene and determine where you can acquire it and what the associated costs are. Most items can be priced on the Internet or Amazon. Document this and move on to the next item. When you have completed every scene in the screenplay, then total up the entire costs. Add this total with the costs for acquiring the essential film equipment (we'll talk equipment later on). We will also talk about locations, feeding actors, acquiring location insurance, and other items that will add additional expenses to your budget.

How To Finance Your Film

Of all of the issues that indie filmmakers face this is the most daunting one. Without a budget, the hopes of making a quality indie film are crushed. If you move ahead and try to produce the film without funding, you will be forced to make decisions that could affect the quality of the film. There are several ways to finance film production. These are:

- Personal finance
- Crowd funding
- Investors

- Banks

First, I'd like to inject a story that will drive an important point home. For me, there is absolutely nothing more exciting than getting up at the break of dawn and leaping out of bed and heading to the set to shoot a film. There's nothing (well, maybe except a smile and a kiss from my granddaughter) that gives me that same feeling. I love filmmaking and am passionate about it. Let me give you two examples of my passion.

When a driver backed into my old Ford Taurus and smashed in the back fender, the insurance company totaled it. It's a 1995 and has fairly low miles. So, the cost of repairing the car was more than the car was worth. It was not pretty, but it was drivable. I needed funds to wrap up a distribution deal for VOD, so I took the money and guess what? I didn't fix the car. I put the money into my film. Why? Because I'm passionate and I can drive the bomb like it is if it will allow me to chase my dream. That's passion. On another occasion, my wife noticed that my leather coat was falling apart so for Christmas she bought me a very expensive new leather coat for $400. I have to admit it was nice, but at the time I needed film money, so guess what? Yep. I'm still wearing my old beat up leather coat…and driving the bomb. But I'm passionate about filmmaking. So what's the point? If you really love this, examine the choices that you make. Perhaps, you can find ways to accrue funds to make a low budget film after all. Here's something you may not know. When Sam Raimi was making the first *Evil Dead* film, they were so short of funds during production that they would set up in the aisle of a grocery store and show customers what they had shot so far and ask for additional funds so they could continue shooting. I don't think I need to tell you where that got him. So that's option number one, personally finance your film. I have personally financed all three films that I have produced. However, I plan on changing my ways and using investors. I borrowed money from my 401K plan to support my habit. Not that I would advise anyone to do that, but it is an option.

Another way is crowd funding (maybe Sam was ahead of his

time here). This has become very popular among filmmakers and has funded quite a few films to date. Places like Indiegogo, Kickstarter, and others provide a way to get funding for their film project. The solicitation is set up for a predetermined amount of time, like say three months, during which the production company offers potential contributors perks such as DVDs of the film, posters, roles in the film, etc. for contributing to the film. Usually, soliciting in amounts from $5 to as much as $10K, the type of perk grows in value with each value of the contribution. However, some crowd funding sites may require that the funds not be issued if not reaching the goal and they do charge a percentage of the gross that you raise (around 5%). Be sure to check all rules when using these sites.

I have personally not used crowd funding but it sounds like a great way to raise funds. The interesting part is that the contributors do not end up owning any share of the film or are not owed back the funds they contribute. I have heard of some film projects that have star attachments raising up to $2 million dollars using this approach.

Investors make up a large portion of independent film funding. I've known of a couple of indie films that have had upwards of over half a million and $2 million that was raised using investors. First of all, let's be clear that investing in independent films is a very risky business. As the old adage goes, if you cannot afford to lose it, don't invest in it. This is particularly true with investing in film. However, I truly believe that smart filmmakers can help to reduce that risk for investors. Throughout this book, I will discuss ways that you as a filmmaker/producer can reduce the risk involved with completing a quality film and making it marketable. When soliciting investors for millions of dollars, risk plays a large part of whether you can close the deal or not. So how can a filmmaker reduce risk for investors, you may ask?

One way is attachments. Investors figure that if an actor or director has a recognizable name, there is some assurance that there is a market for the film and thus will get their investment back. Additionally, probably the one greatest risk reduction factor that an investor will look at is the track record of the producer/filmmaker.

Did their last film make money? This carries as much weight as attachments. Unfortunately, most first-time filmmakers will not be able to make that claim. I have, however, seen investors invest in films solely based on attachments, so it does carry weight with investors. But if you pitch to investors, be ready to answer the question, what did you make on your last film?

Another way to reduce risk for investors is to take advantage of federal and state tax breaks for film investment. Section 181 of the federal tax code was extended in January 2013 during the Fiscal Cliff Bill to extend through 2013. Section 181 will have to be extended again to be available after 2013. This code states that investment in a motion picture shot in the US is 100% tax deductible for the investor in the same year invested. Under Section 181, an investor may deduct the money which is invested in a film or television production from his or her passive income earned in the same year. Productions with budgets below $15,000,000 and up to $20,000,000, and which have at least seventy-five percent (75%) of its production completed within the United States, qualify under Section 181. Investors can be either individuals or businesses.

Many states currently have tax breaks set up for filmmakers to include Illinois, New Mexico, Louisiana, New York, and North Carolina. Illinois is one of the leaders with a 30% tax break for film producers. So, in addition to the Section 181 tax deduction, if the feature film is made in one of these states it is eligible for rebates or transferable tax credits. The film producers can pass this subsidy onto the investors upon release of the rebate. As an example, if a $1,000,000 movie is shot in Illinois and every penny is spent in the state, the state of Illinois will issue a 30% tax rebate, worth approximately $333,000. If shooting in a low income area, another 15% percent tax break is available through the state of Illinois. A total 45% tax break can be realized depending upon the geographic area that the film is shot in. The Illinois tax break refund money can then be passed onto the investors. This is a way to reduce risk for the Investor. Depending on the investor's tax bracket and the percentage of the production funds spent in Illinois, investors can see a tax break anywhere between 50%

and 70% on their investment. It's suggested that the producer verify the type and amounts of tax breaks available to investors using a certified public accountant (CPA) and make this information available to investors.

But the point here is that by offering or informing the investor of these tax breaks, and knowing how they work, you can offer to reduce their risk by 30%, 40%, and maybe even 50%. That's a sizable reduction in their risk. So this combined with attachments, gets you almost there (maybe the whole way), but combined with a track record on a "profitable" film, you can close the deal for that $2 million budget. Of course, you'll need to lay this out neatly in an investor prospectus or what most people call a business plan.

Major studios (i.e. in LA) use banks to finance major motion pictures. Typically, motion pictures that have major star attachments and track records of producing successful films will lock in deals with major distributors guaranteeing distribution. Studios use this as a form of collateral against the financing. There's more to it, but you get the general idea. However, you'll quickly find that when you talk to banks in the Midwest, they are not even aware that banks get involved in financing motion pictures. The issues of banks not understanding filmmaking as a business may just be a communication issue.

During the limited theatrical release of our last film, we did have a bank involved but to a limited degree. They were waiting in the wings ready to provide rotating credit up to $50K for opening additional theaters. I believe by educating local banks on how the film business works we can build financial partners for funding more and more of film production. The key to this partnership is developing better film production models for indie films that more resemble the models used by major studios in Hollywood.

In conclusion, I'd like to talk a little bit about an approach to funding that I call **hybrid funding**. Hybrid funding combines methods of film funding. If you haven't noticed there seems to exist a sort of catch 22 for funding films. Investors don't want to fund projects that don't have attachments because attachments assure some level of success in the marketplace. BUT without funding how do you secure actors? The answer may be in the form of hybrid film funding. Using crowd funding, it's possible to mount a solicitation campaign to raise the funds to secure the attachments. Once the funds are raised, it can be used to secure the attachments. Now, along with the star attachments, the indie film producer can go to investors with the attachments and pitch the rest for the production for funding.

The Investor Prospectus

The feature film **investor prospectus** should answer every question that a prospective investor will have about your film project. If it doesn't, you won't get your funding. I recently completed a prospectus for a film that we are trying to produce called "Paper Hearts." As we discuss important topics that should be included in a pitch to investors, don't be alarmed if you see topics that you aren't familiar with. I will attempt to cover all of these in this book so that when you get to these topics in your pitch, you'll know more about the subject matter.

Not only does the prospectus make the case for the film by telling them about the story we want to tell, the actors we'd like to attach, the funding needed, but it breaks down the budget per phase and discusses our approach to production and distribution. It gives that "full" producer's vision that we discussed earlier. Data for similar projects (genre, budget, etc.) can be attached as appendices in support of the investor pitch.

When pitching these types of investment proposals, plan on pitching a group of investors (up to ten) with a target goal of each investing a large chunk of the required funding. The investors need to be wealthy enough to absorb these losses if things do not go well for the film. Also look for investors who also have an interest or love of films. The producer should also seriously consider shooting in states that provide tax breaks and passing on those kickbacks to investors to reduce the risk they will carry by investing in the film. This then becomes a selling point for the production of the film.

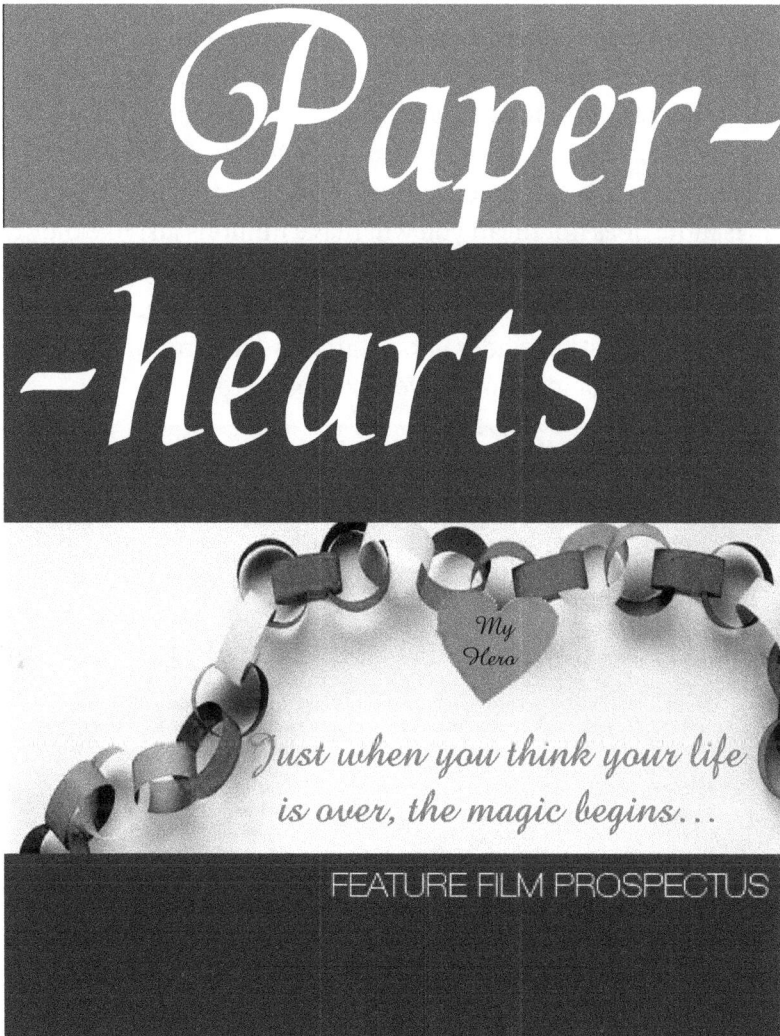

*Figure 4-**Prospectus for Paper Hearts Film***

Not all investor proposals are written in the same way. Some proposals that already have star or director attachments may focus on their accomplishments and what they bring to the project. My proposal does not have these attachments, although we had planned on having at least a few star attachments to make the film marketable. Instead, it focuses on our understanding of the filmmaking process from beginning to end and provides some creative solutions to issues with independent film thus reducing the risk for the investor. However, when you write yours, do not make the mistake of making leaps in logic and conclusions like comparing your indie film to another successful indie film. Drawing the conclusion that because theirs was indie and yours is indie does not mean you will make millions just like they did. All films are different and anything can happen in this business. If you want to show movie statistics, the MPAA Theatrical Market Statistics (try to get the latest) provides good statistics on trends in the theater. Below is a list of topics in our investor prospectus.

FEATURE FILM PROSPECTUS

DISTRIBUTION

Paperhearts

"Investors have an active role in our profits scheme rarely offered to investors!"

Theatrical Release

One of the biggest challenges for a filmmaker is to achieve a theatrical release of their film. Most independent filmmakers will four-wall a theater to release their film. This means basically that they are PAYING the theater to show it and usually it's very expensive and is usually only a one or two night showing. It is NOT an official theatrical release by any means. Young Films has had an actual limited release of its last film "The Darkening" at theaters and understands the process of achieving theatrical release. Young Films has developed solid contacts that have asked us to come back for the release of our next film. Yes, Rave Cinemas, where we did a limited release at 4 theaters for 2 weeks, has asked us to bring our next production to them.

Many filmmakers are happy to get a DVD release or to have their film shown at festivals. Here's the beauty of theatrical release. The theaters payout in 30 days! That's right. By taking the film directly to the theater, Young Films cuts out the middle man, the distributor, who gets a whopping 30 % of the profit from the theaters. Young Films positions itself to receive 45% of the box office receipts and has no middle man to share the profits with. So Young Films is not only a production company, we are the distributor as well. Young Films is willing to share 2.5% of its net profit from theatrical release with each investor (2.5 % for each $ 100K). Each $ 100K investor will receive the entirety of their investment back from film profit then receive 2.5% of the theatrical release net profits.

Other Forms of Distribution

Young Films has established relationships with companies that distribute films in all types of media. One such company is Gravitas Ventures which provides Video On Demand distribution throughout North America and is the largest supplier of VOD products in the country. Young Films already has a deal in place for Gravitas to provided its last film in VOD format to all of its content providers across the country. We also have contacts at Lions Gate and other distributors that can distribute films

*Figure 5-**Distribution Discussion***

- **Summary** – Introduce yourself, your company, others involved, and your credentials if you have any.
- **Synopsis** – Sell them on the story your film will tell. Spend the time on a summary of the story that will grab them.
- **Cast/Stars** – Stress the importance of attaching recognizable stars whether they are A list, B list, or C list stars. Discuss who you have in mind for the parts and any letters of intent you may have. Give them a chance to visualize the actor in your film that you've just excited them about.
- **Distribution** – Discuss the forms of distribution that you have in mind for the film. This should include whether you plan on seeking a distributor or doing it yourself. Discuss any plans for theatrical release, cable, DVD, video-on-demand and other options. If self distributed, discuss any plans for getting an MPAA rating, handling virtual print fees (VPFs) for theatrical release, creating the digital content packages (DCPs) for distribution to digital theaters, developing film posters, and the distribution approach for the video on demand (VOD) markets.
- **Genre/Rating** – Discuss the genre and rating of the film you are proposing. Investors will have their name attached to the project and if it turns out that they are offended by the theme or rating, they will not be happy campers. Investors need to understand what they are signing up for. Certain genres and ratings also do better at the box office. Show backup data for this in the appendices.
- **Marketing** – Discuss your marketing approach. If the plan is to turn the marketing over to distributors that allow them do everything, that's fine, just tell them that is your strategy. If you are marketing it yourself, provide enough details so it sounds like you understand how to get it done. Sound confident. Discuss marketing approaches to include social media, television, radio, newspaper, and theater advertising.

- **Tax breaks** – Since not every state in the union offers tax breaks, all of this may not apply to your film. However, keep in mind that tax breaks that can recover a substantial portion of the investor's funding can be very attractive. If your state doesn't offer tax breaks, consider shooting in other states that do.
- **Schedule** – A schedule shows an investor that you have a detailed plan for accomplishing the principal photography. It not only shows how the scenes are scheduled to be shot, but also shows that you understand where resources such as extras, vehicles, etc. are needed in support of the shooting.
- **Budget** – In our plan, we show the budget to the investors from a couple of perspectives. One, we show them how the funds will be appropriated during each phase of production and we show them a typical standard form used to capture the film's entire budget. Our example budget shows only a portion, but keep in mind, you'll need to have a completed budget for the entire film that includes ALL expenses to show the investors should they request it.
- **Preproduction** – List and be prepared to discuss the major tasks that will be accomplished during the preproduction phase and any associated costs. These include items such as:
  - Finalizing optioning/purchasing the screenplay
  - Securing star attachments (letters of intent)
  - Writing actor agreements
  - Liability insurance (minimum $1 million of liability insurance)
  - Securing locations
  - Securing costumes and props/vehicles for production
  - Securing HQ location/furniture if required
  - Develop film web page for film
  - Location management (scouting)
  - Auditions of cast
  - Conducting rehearsals

- o   Development and review of contracts
- o   Arranging meals & transportation
- o   Attaining permits for factors such as street closings
- **Production** -   List and be prepared to discuss the major tasks that will be accomplished during the production phase and any associated costs. These include items such as:
  - o   Star wages
  - o   Catering
  - o   Crew wages
  - o   Makeup and special effects makeup
  - o   DP wages
  - o   Film equipment rentals
  - o   Tracking and dolly vehicle equipment
  - o   Camera boom
  - o   Red One/Lenses rental
  - o   Digital Workflow (Set & Editing)
  - o   RV rental
  - o   Equipment truck
  - o   Transportation
- **Post Production** - List and be prepared to discuss the major tasks that will be accomplished during the post production phase and any associated costs. Identify whether you will be doing the editing, scoring, etc. or if it is outsourced. If it is outsourced, who have you identified and what are the associated costs? These include items such as:
  - o   Film editing
  - o   Songs for soundtrack
  - o   Sound track scoring
  - o   Automatic dialog replacement (ADR)
  - o   Foley work
- **Domestic release** - Discuss any plans for theatrical release domestically and how you plan to promote the release of the film.
- **Foreign release** – Discuss any plans for a foreign release.

- **Budgeting** – Discuss the plan for ensuring that a detailed budget is completed for the film showing exactly how the investor funds will be spent. We show an example for one in our plan. The producer may want to have a complete budget as a backup should the investors want to see more details.
- **Payouts** – The producer should have a clear plan for paying out all of those involved in the film production. Investors will want to see where they are in the pecking order for payouts.
- **Closing** – Summarize your pitch in the closing and reinstate any major selling points to the investors.
- **Appendices** -   These contain any supporting and research data that helps the investor better understand the current film market or supports your statements and conclusions such as:
  - Film sales – What are current distributors buying which could relate to your film project?
  - Film production numbers – These can provide investors with an overall picture of the current industry.
  - Video on demand (VOD) – Since VOD is probably the hottest market for indie films, this provides additional data on what's happening in that market. Try to find the latest data on VOD. Unfortunately, at the time of this proposal, there wasn't any good number available. Check for current numbers.
  - Screens – This feeds into the new landscape for indie filmmakers. The conversion to digital theaters has opened doors to the indie filmmaker. Get the latest number on digital screens. This is how your product can be marketed all across America and worldwide.
  - Risk – The producer MUST have a dedicated slide for discussing risk. First of all, indie film is a very risky business. Secondly risk is what you need to get the investor past If you think that marketing (finding your customer) is the biggest risk, tell how you have a person that specializes in marketing. Look at every option to

reduce that risk, find a creative solution to reduce it, and close the deal.

o   Trailers – Trailers deserve a dedicated slide because it is how the movie is sold. Data supports the fact that trailers are effective. Communicate this to the investors and how you will take advantage of this.

o   Indie sales – Show how some indie films have fared in the past. Never hurts to reinforce this with the investor.

o   Track record – I include this as an appendix because it is extremely important to investors. If you have made profits from film production, this indicates to the investor that you can create products that return profits. If you don't have a track record, perhaps you should begin with a smaller film and develop that statistic first. It IS that important.

o   Why Illinois? – (or other location) Discuss how you chose where to shoot and why. The investor wants to know that you've given this some thought and why you decided to choose the shooting location. If you don't know why, then you haven't done enough research.

Once you have your investor prospectus written, be sure to have it reviewed by friends or relatives that have business backgrounds to fine tune the final. If you do not have a brick and mortar business establishment, consider holding the investor pitch at a local hotel conference room or at a restaurant party room for privacy during the meeting. If you can afford it, make refreshments and snacks available. Have the investor prospectus printed in color and bound by someone who will do a professional job, like *Kinko's*. Make enough copies for each investor and the presenter. It's not required to develop PowerPoint presentation slides, although it looks more professional.

Dress and conduct yourself professionally for the meeting. If you have previous films or film related products that you have developed, arrange for a big screen to show samples to them. If you get the investors interested in your pitch, set a deadline by which you'll need commitments. Set a preproduction start date and a tentative shoot date. Let investors know these dates and when you would need the commitment. If they commit, they will want to see a contract from you. Be prepared to provide one at their convenience.

Company Structures

Okay, here's the thing. Just because you Photoshop a cool logo and name for your production company, doesn't make it legit. It's only recognized by the state and federal government if it is legally formed and registered with the state that your company resides in. Otherwise, for legal and tax purposes, your company does not exist. If you plan on making money or claiming expenses against the company, you'll need to make it a legitimate company. Company structures also provide liability protection so that everything you own isn't up for grabs from someone who files a lawsuit against you.

If you create a legal entity under which you conduct your film business, that "entity" is responsible for those dealings with clients and other entities. My company is filed under the state of Nebraska as a Limited Liability Company (LLC). This is one of the most popular structures. It provides liability protection from my personal assets and is reasonably easy to form/create. I did mine myself. Costs may vary from state to state, but figure on spending several hundred dollars to set up an LLC.

There are numerous sources on the web that discuss how to do this and many companies out there that will do this for you for a fee. Another important point in setting up a company structure is that it provides your company with a tax ID. You will need this when doing business with other businesses. They will ask for this.

Once you have your LLC (or other structure) established, go to your bank and set up a business checking account for your newly formed company. You do NOT want to mingle business dollars with personal dollars. Also make sure to have at least one annual meeting with any members of your company. If your company is ever called into question during a lawsuit, even a legally formed LLC can be called into question as to whether it is actually a real business entity, a dedicated bank account and annual meetings with members can be enough to validate the legitimacy of the LLC. Since film production companies deal extensively with copyrights, licensing rights, and a variety of other licensing and liability issues, do not get into film production until you have formed a legally recognized entity. This formal entity will be the one entering into agreements and contracts with the actors, screenwriters, producers, directors, businesses, and other production companies to produce the film. As with any other business venture, if you aren't sure if what you're doing is legal, seek out advice from a licensed lawyer or entertainment lawyer in your area.

Where To Now?

Okay. So at this time we're just getting our ducks in a row. You have a legitimately formed company and have acquired or are writing a screenplay to produce. At this point, you probably don't have enough information to write that investor prospectus, but that's fine. At the end of reading this book, we have hopefully touched on all of the subjects and if we haven't given you the information you need, we have at least told you where to find it.

Script Breakdown

To get started, you'll need to know about every single element that is required for the production. This breakdown will tell you:

- How many actors you need
- What locations need to be secured
- What SFX scenes are needed
- Any special props needed
- Vehicles needed
- The length of the shoot
- Any special camera equipment needed

- Wardrobe needs
- Stuntmen or stunt women required
- Overall budget of the film

As I mentioned earlier about breaking down the script, every scene must be stripped naked and then examined for every single item to be acquired or purchased. The script breakdown also will provide the director with a detailed list of all of the required shots for a complete film. We'll examine a few scenes from *The Darkening*, the last film that Young Films shot to illustrate the process.

We're going to run through the scenes from the producer perspective in an initial effort to identify the number of actors needed, the number of locations needed, and any special requirements. Later in the book, we'll take a more in-depth look at each scene from the production manager perspective to not only further identify these requirements but to develop a detailed shooting schedule from which the film will be shot.

Note the highlighted areas in Figure 6. These all point out items for production consideration. First, we have the "Harrison" house. This is a required location. There are interior (INT) and exterior (EXT) shots, so we'll need to be able to shoot outside and inside of the house. Since this is a horror film, the location scout should keep this in mind and find an older larger house that has some creep factor and that would maybe look good on a DVD cover or on a poster. The producer should go through the entire script and make a list of locations, and list whether interior and exterior shooting is required. Additional notes can be added to better describe the location for the location scout to use.

The second and third highlights on the page are the names of the two principal characters. The producer should go through the script and write down ALL characters, principal and other. The screenwriter will normally give us information on these characters when they first introduce them (age, etc.). Therefore we now know that both actors (playing James and Kristy) are needed for this particular scene. We also should know that they will need wardrobe, makeup, and hair for this scene. Since James has a scar on his neck from when he was attacked as a youth, he will also need special effects makeup. A SFX makeup person and assistant will need to be a part of the crew.

```
door wide and briskly steps across the room to a table
covered with a sheet.

                    JUDY
          Hi. Thought I'd come early and make
          sure the utilities were on.

INT. HARRISON HOUSE - LIVING ROOM - AFTERNOON

James and Kristy step inside. The furniture is covered with
SHEETS and the rest of the belongings are DUSTY.

                    JUDY
          Give me a call when you get it
          cleaned up.

Judy lays the KEYS on the table and turns to leave.

                    KRISTY
          Thanks. I'll walk you out.

Judy leaves the keys on the TV. Kristy accompanies Judy
outside as James notices a sheet on the floor covering a
long object. The object now resembles the body of his
mother.  He approaches.

EXT. HARRISON HOUSE- AFTERNOON

Kristy follows Judy out of the house.

                    JUDY
          Is he okay? Looks like he
          saw a ghost. Of course if I had
          seen what he saw in that house,
          you couldn't drag me back in.

Judy looks up at the house and walks away

INT. HARRISON HOUSE - AFTERNOON

James is bent down staring at the sheet that seems to cover
a body.  He moves forward (Camera Angle from floor) towards
it.

James reaches down to the sheet and forces himself to take
the edge of the sheet. He throws it back. It's his mother's
CORPSE, with rotting flesh.
```

*Figure 6-**Example Page from Script***

The next highlight "furniture" tells us that if the location doesn't have furniture, then we will need to do set preparation. On our last film, we found a vacant house to use for our location and had to bring furniture in and make the set.

The next two highlighted items are "sheets" and "dusty belongings." This adds more to the set and these are just additional props and set decoration that needs to be done.

The next highlight "Judy" is the name of the real-estate lady who had the keys to the old house. This is another actor to add to the list. She'll also need wardrobe that suggests she's a real-estate person. Add a briefcase to the prop list for her. She also leaves a set of keys on the table, another couple of items for the prop list.

The next highlight is the "TV." Since this is an old house where James lived as a boy and has been gone over twenty years, most likely the TV is not a modern HD TV but an old tube type. This will need to be added to the prop list.

The next highlighted item is the "corpse with rotting flesh." First, this is played by James' mother. So we need to make sure that we have this actress on our list. Secondly, our SFX makeup person will need to do corpse makeup on her. I would start a separate list of SFX shots required and add these two (scar and corpse) to that list. The SFX person will need to know all of the SFX shots so he/she can estimate latex and other materials cost.

For each film, I develop a battle plan (See Appendix E in back for a complete copy). In it, I list all elements needed for production such as actors, locations, equipment and identify issues that need to be addressed. It's a great place to dump all of my thoughts and strategies for the film. The following lists are from my last battle plan. You'll see things that will hopefully give you ideas for your film.

Props:
- Black raincoat and hat
- Coveralls for Kyle (Need to purchase)
- Dulled butcher knife (purchased and dulled)
- Vacuum cleaner – old-will cut cord (have in storage)

- Lazy eye and cauliflower ear for Kyle (Discuss with makeup person)
- Scar for James on neck – noticeable but not very prominent (See above)
- Raincoat for young James (Need to buy)
- Older bike that Kyle has thrown off bridge
- Blood – Kyle bleeds a pool on floor (See makeup person)
- Flickering lights – used throughout film (Need to work this)
- Lightning effects – machine or in post? (Need to purchase)
- Prop pills and bottle for James in bathroom scene and for his dad's suicide scene
- Ned's handgun – 357 Magnum (Chrome), Sig Saur 9MM pistol, Colt 25 caliber pistol
- Police uniforms
- Handcuffs. Bought 2 pair of chrome ones. Need to buy cheap pouches for handcuffs? (purchased)
- Cloth or sheets for the Harrison house that's been abandoned, also need dust, maybe cobwebs
- Pictures of James and his dad/mom for house – need to take early on with actors (Need to arrange)
- Fake newspaper reports of murders (Need photo of Karen to get fake newspaper. Need to order online.)
- Camera for news team (Have Dan talk with his contacts at radio.)
- News team van Channel 3 or 6 insignia for van and possibly microphone?
- Have insignia for microphone (Square – white. Need printed label to go on it, i.e., NEWS 3)
- Gothic clothes for Brad – have Charlie Manson t-shirt and black pants.
- Packing boxes – Kristy is packing old stuff from Harrison house (Who to get?)

- Paint cans and supplies – few scenes where they're painting some rooms in house
- Fake diploma and degrees to hang on doc's office (Where to get?)
- Bound doll
- Hair aging for Kyle – white aging spray for Kyle when he's older (See makeup person.)
- Costume for palm reader – Bandana, scarves, necklaces, large earrings – other?
- Mystic Shop sign or just a "Palm Reader" sign for a new age shop
- Mini tape player – doctor uses
- Luggage – the Doctor's wife is leaving on trip – she'd have very nice luggage
- Black gloves – doctor and Frank both wear these (find)
- Plastic baseball bat – James uses a bat to beat Kyle to death – Found a plastic bat (Louisville Slugger style) painted to make look like wood.
- Funeral ceremony – need a casket and the green material or carpet on the ground
- Photos of Robin – used on newscast, probably high-school picture (get photo to use)
- Photos of the Doctor, James, and Brad used for ID when they have the witness – these are supposed to be from the DMV so they should look bad (get these from actors)
- Dolls – Karen has a massive collection of dolls in her bedroom where she's murdered
- Full length mirror – Karen is exercising in front of the mirror when she's murdered
- Posters and Goth stuff for Brad's apartment (ideas?)
- Rope that killer uses to kill with
- Forensic case – CSI has one at crime scene
- CSI badge

- Fake Doctor's office key – the one that gets stolen
- Fake badges for Sheriff and deputy
- Fake calling card – deputy gives one to Kristy
- Towel – James uses while talking to police
- Small caliber fake gun – The doctor pulls a gun at end (purchased)
- Food tray – prison style – used at end of film (purchased)
- Police gun – fake – James steals from dead cop (purchased)
- Police line tape – used at scene where cops are killed (borrow from police?)
- Chief's radio – does he have one with him? (borrow from police?)
- Umbrella – The doctor's wife has when she comes home (girls?)
- Flashlight – Chief has when he goes into the Doctor's office
- Smock and stethoscope (purchased)

The major locations are:

- Harrison house – residential neighborhood.
- Harrison apartment – this is where James and Kristy live when the film opens.
- Café – Ned and Robin meet here.
- Hardware Store – where James and Kristy see Robin, who is the first victim.
- Doctor's office- must have a lobby area with desk. Separate office for doctor with door.
- Police station – interrogation room, visitation room, front desk, hallway, briefing room where they discuss case, front of building master shots. The Freeport Police Chief has already agreed to allow us use of the old police station. Dan and I are meeting with him in September to

take a tour of the building to see what has to be done.

- Prison – visiting room. Master shot of Joliet to establish that Doctor is visiting a prison. We have talked to the Illinois Correctional POC and they don't have an issue shooting the master shots if we can have a law official there. Dan to see if we can get someone from Freeport. Also need to talk with them about shooting a scene inside. (Jack)
- Downtown street – Where James and Kristy are walking when they see Mystic shop. Freeport Police said that we can close a street online for $10. Must do two weeks before shooting.
- Mystic Shop – (convert a new-age shop) where they meet a Madam who tells James to trust himself.
- Phillips home – an upper class home ($300 to $500k) where the doctor and rich wife live. Dan has POC (young doctor) who sounds like he's open to idea. Need to meet and give him the details. Need Location Agreement signed.
- Bar – (interior/exterior) Where Robin and friends go the night she's murdered. The bar owner has already agreed to our using the bar for shooting. We just need to give them a date and get a Location Agreement signed.
- Robin's murder scene – supposedly not far from the club – off beaten path. The County Police Chief has already said this is not a problem. However, we will need to get a police volunteer to come out to control traffic. We need to find one that will do it for credit and free copy of movie.
- Chief's brother's house – exterior only. Chief tells brother of Robin's murder
- Cemetery # 1 – Robin's funeral. Need to follow up. We were told that we could get this for free. We need to have further conversations with them about using a casket.
- Karen's (interpreter) apartment – kitchen, bedroom,

hallway scenes
- Brad's rundown apartment – decorated in early Charley Manson – should be dirty, cluttered, etc.
- Airport (exterior) – Doctor meets his rich wife at airport scene. Need to follow up on this.
- Miller's Crossing – (actually bridge now) where Kristy is taken at end. We have permission to do this but we need to clear shooting on the bridge at night. Need to follow up and get a Location Agreement signed.

So once you have identified ALL actors, all locations, and all props needed, you can begin casting of your film and scouting locations. For each location identified, the location scout should take photos of the possibilities and review these with the producer, director, and DP. You'll need to identify where all the props are coming from. Are they borrowed, rented, or purchased? You'll need a total of costs on props for the budget. Later we'll talk about how all of these elements come together in the shooting schedule.

Contracts

As a legitimate business entity, everything that you do with others should be done through a formal agreement or contract. If you don't, you leave yourself open for a lawsuit. Agreements and contracts bind the terms and conditions of the agreement between your company and other parties. If you have a signed and legal agreement or contract between you and someone else, it is also more likely that person or entity will deliver to you what you have agreed upon. Without this, it can't be enforced.

First of all, I'm not a lawyer and most filmmakers I know aren't lawyers either. So if you aren't a lawyer and don't have a brother in law that is a lawyer, how do you write contracts? The next best thing is for you to get a copy of Mark Litwak's book "Contracts for the Film & Television Industry." It's worth its weight in gold. It's loaded with contracts that will give you a basis to start with.

A contract is usually between two individuals or entities. Usually both sides are expecting something. One side may be expecting a service and the other side the money for providing that service. It's always a give and take situation. I always try to think in the simplest terms, although most contracts seem to be written so that you don't understand what is being negotiated. Always look at the contract as a way to get exactly what you want, no less, and no more. Don't ask for anything that you know you don't need. It just muddies the waters. Always try to be fair and straightforward if possible.

In film, filmmakers must legally be able to use images and sounds in a variety of markets (theater, TV, DVD, VOD, etc.) and put those into a variety of products both domestically and worldwide forever. At the same time, you must give something back to the right or license holder. That can vary from offering a deferred salary to an agreed amount upon commencing production. Most indie filmmakers don't have a lot of budget so they will offer deferred salaries to stars and crew and a courtesy DVD of the film for portfolio use. Many actors and crew members who are trying to break into the business understand this. However, your intention as a filmmaker should always be to make a profit from the production and to share those profits with those that help make your dream come true.

Always remember that ANYTHING that appears in front of the camera (actor, product, location, extra) should have a paper trail for those rights. This includes the screenplay. Anything that is used in post production (editing) whether it's visual or audio MUST also have a paper trail connected to it. Any music, special effects, footage, photo, music score, ANYTHING, must be traceable to a piece of paper giving you permission to include it. Those pieces of paper (agreement or contract) MUST detail how it will be used and to every extent possible that will give you the freedom to not just create products but to use any of those pieces (music, images, likenesses) however you need to market and promote it as well. You will need contracts for the following:

- Investor agreement or contract
- Actor agreements or contracts
- Crew member agreements or contracts

- Producer contract
- Director contract
- Director of Photography contract
- Production Manager contract
- Location agreements
- Music agreements or contracts (local bands)
- Master & Sync Rights contracts (published songs)
- Score music rights
- Product release from product owner (products that appear in film)
- Extra release
- Editor agreement or contract

Most of these can be written as a **Work for Hire** contract and the producer acquiring all rights, allowing them to file for the copyright of the film as the **author**. This just means that you pay a person to perform a certain task for you and you're willing to pay a certain amount for the work. Some contracts will actually have a percentage on the back end as a part of the negotiations, such as name brand writers, actors, or directors. Sometimes giving a percentage of profits on the back end of the film may be the only way to involve those that are experienced or well known. As a general rule if you are going to give away percentages on the back end, adhere to a **tier based** payout system. This is a system with tiers (levels) of how money (profits) gets paid out.

Deferred salaries should be paid out first. These are considered deferred expenses of the film. Secondly, stars that were offered a percentage are paid (again, an expense of getting it made). Investors, those who contribute the funds to get it produced, should be paid out third. What's left is the profit of the film company. When looking at giving away percentages on the back end, always try to keep the total percentages below 50% of the total net profits. Don't give away the farm, just a few acres.

Contracts that involve large funds or that have a lot at risk will normally include an arbitration clause. Basically this defines how an issue that arises with the contract will be arbitrated or resolved.

Contracts may call out an agency or special committee that would be assigned the task of the arbitration of the issue. The best thing to do is to write contracts that are fair, clearly define the deal, and are straightforward and clearly understood by both parties.

If you are a filmmaker considering a co-production with another production in a foreign country, be aware that a co-production contract is extremely important. Also be aware that some foreign countries will require the production company (residing in that country) to be the "owner" of the film to qualify for certain government sponsored grants and tax breaks to the production company. This means that all rights must be granted to the foreign production company and they must file with their own government sponsored copyright office as the author of the work. Make absolutely sure that you have an entertainment lawyer review the co-production contract and are in agreement with all terms before moving forward.

When writing contracts for indie films and trying to establish salaries, don't just pull a number out of your hat, check current SAG rates for indie films in your budget range and what the daily rates are. Look up current wages for screenwriters (story and screenplay) and what others (directors, production manager, cinematographer, crew, etc.) in the industry working on indie films are being paid. If you have to defer their salary, defer wages that reflect what's currently being paid in the industry.

When a film has been completed, the producer must file a copy of the film, along with paperwork, with the U.S. copyright office to get the copyright on the film. The central question that the copyright office will asks is "who is the author of the film?" What they are asking is who owns the film? Unlike manuscripts that automatically have copyright attached to them upon completion, to own a film, you must have a stream of rights given to you by the writer, actors, musicians, directors, etc. This stream of rights gives you that ownership.

Just because you make a film, you do not automatically have the rights to it unless of course you wrote it, shot it, starred in it, did the music, did EVERYTHING and have nothing in the film that requires rights. Most likely this is not the case. So to claim ownership as to what the copyright office calls the "author", make sure you have been delegated all rights you require through some form of contract.

Every filmmaker has heard of the dreaded **Errors & Omissions (E&O) insurance**. If you bring your film to a legitimate distributor, they will ask if you have E&O insurance. E&O is insurance that covers every right and license for the film production that you may have not included. It's based on the assumption that you made every best effort to completely cover all rights and licenses required. You know, the ones we've been discussing, actors, directors, locations, music, footage, products, etc. This is where things can go south on you very quickly. If you haven't done all of the agreements and contracts and say that you have, and something goes wrong (like an actress turns against you and wants to get paid her deferred salary and realizes she never signed a contract). You've got problems.

The distribution company has the right to hire a lawyer to resolve it and send you the bill. If you've ever hired a lawyer, you can imagine the bills that will arrive with your name on them. If there are bigger problems like copyright infringement, things can get even worse for you. So, at the end, when you are looking for distribution, whether or not you took the time to get contracts on everything will come back to haunt you and could even shut down any attempts at distribution. For our last production, although I wrote all of the contracts, I delegated the responsibility to my sister Brenda to make sure everyone signed a contract because Brenda is meticulous at everything she does. Assign the task to someone who is meticulous and will get the job done.

I have included sample contracts in Appendix C. These are just examples. Filmmakers should always seek out professional advice from licensed lawyers or entertainment lawyers whenever there is a question about rights or licensing elements of production.

Getting Actors

This may be the trickiest part of filmmaking and also the most exciting part at the same time. For without actors, your story can't be told. Actors can make or break your film. There are actually several approaches to getting actors for your film. A lot also depends on your budget. In fact most of it depends on this. If you're lucky to have a great script and funding, you're smart to at least attach one or two name recognizable stars.

For indie film these don't need to be A-list actors like Tom Cruise, but can be B-list or C-list actors that the audience will recognize. If they are recognizable stars, they will most likely belong to the Stage Actors Guild (SAG) union. Don't get shook up yet because the SAG has indie film rates available for lower budget films. Rates for very low budget films can be as low as a couple of hundred a day (modified low budget) depending on the budget.

Of course these are minimums and you would still have to negotiate for the actual salary you'll have to pay them. Unless you have connections with others in the business and are able to work directly with the actors (most of us don't) then you have to work through the actor's manager or agent. In the past, you could call SAG and get the actor's representing agency (Like Creative Artist Agency (CAA)) where you could contact their manager or agent. Today, you must fill out a form and submit for approval to access a database of actors (called iActors) to contact their representative. Let me warn you about contacting them. You must have funds in place to call them. This is usually the first question they will ask you, "do you have funds in place?" If you answer "no," the conversation is over.

Today, many actors working in Hollywood are open to the idea of independent film work. If it's a great script, there may be an interest. If they are interested, have them sign a letter of intent. See Appendix C. If you're like most indie film companies, you probably will have very limited funds for actors. That's understandable. But there are things you can do as a producer to sweeten the pot for these actors. You can offer them a back-end deal where you offer them a piece of the film (2%, 5% or 10% of the gross profits) to entice them.

Also try to be smart as to how you'll utilize the star if they become interested. Work the shooting schedule so that all of their shots are done first and you only tie them up to do their scenes for a few days. Of course, if they have a lead role, this may be more difficult. However, if they only have a bit part, this is workable. Be careful though. If the role is too thin, they may not be interested.

However big the part is, try to arrange the shooting schedule so they aren't waiting around and wasting their time for the little that you're paying them. Make the role attractive to them and reduce their time on the set if possible. If you decide to bring a SAG actor into your production, make sure that you can mix SAG and non-SAG actors on the set or you'll have to go one way or the other (all SAG or all non-SAG). Discuss this with the actor and a SAG representative. Be aware that when working with SAG actors there are specific union rules about pay and other expenses that you have to contribute to the SAG union. The SAG site is at http:// www.sagaftra.org/production-center/theatrical/signatory-information. You'll note that you'll need to become a signatory to hire SAG actors and that you need to be a legitimately formed company (back to that again) as well. Such things as a chain of titles on the screenplay (agreement/ contract assigning the producer the rights) and a list of non-SAG actors (if mixing non-SAG and SAG) are also required.

When budgeting the film, if using a SAG actor, make sure you expense for everything from travel arrangements to hotel accommodations, to food per diems and any other SAG expenses into your budget. Be prepared to do quite a bit of research and reading on the SAG site before considering SAG actors. Be sure to find the appropriate type of agreement for the budget of your production. The SAG site has a variety of agreements based on the budget and type of film. These are:

- Theatrical
- Low budget
- Modified low budget
- Ultra low budget
- Short film
- Student film

Working with SAG actors requires a lot more paperwork and obviously more expenses, but it strengthens your film with higher caliber actors and makes the film a lot more marketable during distribution.

SAG OR NON-SAG

Okay, here's where most of us that are doing indie films find ourselves. If this is your first film and it's a no-budget or very low budget film, you probably don't have the resources for including name recognizable stars or SAG actors. Don't worry. Films have gotten made without these and some have done well. It will, however, make the road to distribution tougher to travel and make marketing the film more difficult. Here's my take on actors. Although it's important, let's put marketing of the film aside for a moment. Every actor at some time in their career was an unknown and had to prove themselves. Someone had to give them their first break. Someone had to be their mentor and guide them through that performance that got them into the business. Just like the show *American Idol*, there are many talented actors out there all across the United States, when given the opportunity and some guidance, could become stars. Many of the biggest stars in Hollywood's history were discovered sitting in a café or were found during an audition. If you choose to not use seasoned actors from Hollywood, then you must develop an eye for talent, acquire that talent and nurture them into being that actor you need for your film. I believe that the talent is out there. It just has to be discovered. So build your own stars for your film!

On my first film (a short) I worked with an international casting director that split his time between London and the U.S. I hired him to work with me in casting my short film in Omaha, Nebraska. I would suggest that if you live in a big enough city that has a fairly large actor community and playhouse, that you seek out a casting director and hire them to assist in finding local talent. Believe it or not, most are reasonable in what they charge. Besides, they love their craft and most are willing to help discover talent. Here are the secrets that I learned from the casting director. While holding auditions, rate each actor on the following five attributes:

- Acting ability
- Looks
- Body movement in front of the camera

- Voice

What is acting ability? Believe it or not, acting sometimes gets in the way of acting. Doesn't make much sense, does it? What I'm saying is that when you ask someone to act a part, they think that they need to turn a switch on that turns them from being their everyday normal self to "acting" like someone else. It then becomes obvious that they are acting or over-acting. Acting is at its best when it doesn't appear that they are acting. In other words, they appear perfectly natural, but with a different name and identity. It's a natural ability to become someone different. That's what you are looking for. The actor must take the words and attitude of a character and make them their own. The better that they can do this, the more stars you should give them.

What do looks have to do with it? A lot, since film is a visual medium, and looks play a very large part of the visual experience. It's critical that you record auditions to see if the camera "likes them." Some actors look great on film (or in the lens) and they just have a great look. Others just don't look good through the lens. Me, I try to stay behind the camera, because I know the camera doesn't like me. Sometimes it's not that the person isn't attractive, it's just the way their facial features look through the lens. It's very subjective.

Body movement is also important. Some people are just not comfortable in front of the camera and will seem stiff in their body movements. The actor must be relaxed and seem natural in front of the camera. This is another important reason to have the camera running during auditions so you can capture their body movement across the lens.

Voice is one half of the illusion of film. Some of the most memorable actors have great voices like James Earl Jones (Darth Vader) and John Wayne that adds to their persona. I've seen auditions where the actor looked great in front of the camera and had good body movement but the minute they spoke you knew it was over. They had the wrong voice. Voice is important. Again, it's subjective, but it's all part of looking for that all round star persona that you need for your film.

Prepare for the auditions by making sheets with spaces for the actor's name. Next to each actor's name add the four attributes listed above. For each attribute give the actor a star rating between one star and five stars. Give them one star if they at the bottom of the spectrum (not very good), three stars if they are average, and five stars if they are stellar. Make sure that you have a good camera (similar to what you'll be using on the set) and record all of the auditions. You'll want to review these at a later time when auditions are completed.

ACTOR NAME:_____

ROLE: _____

Acting Ability_____
Looks   _____
Body Movement   _____
Voice   _____

Notes:_____
_____

During our last film, we discovered an attribute that wasn't originally included when assessing actors. It was the ability to follow directions. We found actors that fit the bill on all of the above, but when told to do something, they would choose to do it another way or not the way they were being told. They couldn't follow directions. If an actor cannot or will not follow directions, you do not want them on the set. So the set of criteria to judge actors on becomes:

Acting Ability   _____
Looks   _____
Body Movement   _____
Voice   _____
Follows Directions _____
Notes:_____
_____

You'll find that some will have the acting ability and look good on film, but their voice just doesn't fit the character. Or you'll find that some are very stiff with their body movements on camera and just don't look natural. In reality, what we discovered was that most people (90%) auditioning for film can't act, or can't act very well. If you use these criteria to evaluate the auditioning actors, it will help you find the actors that can carry your film. Never ever just pick a bunch of friends or people you know and think they can pull it off. This is the biggest mistake young filmmakers make. Search out and discover talent. Use a methodology that assists you in identifying those who have talent and those that don't.

Using Child Actors

When working with child actors there are laws for filmmakers to adhere to. They must have a form from the state (Work Release Form) completed and their legal guardian must sign their contract. Work release forms can be attained from the state or the school that the child attends. There are also rules about the hours you can work them and how late.

Auditions and Local Talent

Auditions are critical to discovering local talent for your film. Audition for ALL speaking parts. Any role in the film that has lines should be auditioned for. Because even a small scene with limited lines by a bit player, if bad, will stick out like a sore thumb and ruin the film. It will pull the viewer out of the illusion you have created.

If you have limited funds, like most indie filmmakers do, auditions can be held at numerous places that are free or at little cost. The point being, do NOT hold auditions at your house. It's not professional and nobody auditioning will take you seriously. On our first film, we held auditions at a local high school. Since we were looking for mostly teenagers, this made perfect sense. My twelve year old daughter handed out forms (most didn't have headshots) for them to fill out and my sixteen-year-old son ran my camera for me. I have always involved my family in my filmmaking. It's fun for them and they learn a little about the film business. Besides, they can say they knew so and so star when they were upcoming and unknown if they ever make it. My daughter met Chris Klein who was standing in line auditioning for our film and at that time an unknown teen.

Anyway, auditions can be held anywhere that is public and has a lot of space. Make sure you have enough room though. For our short film, we had a couple hundred teens turn out. We had them lined down the hallway of the high school. Be ready in case you have a major turn out. If it's possible, try to hold auditions where there is seating. Auditions take time and a lot of people auditioning may be there for a while. If you hold auditions during the summer, make sure you have bottled water available for those who are there a while.

I've noticed that one of the best ways to get the word out for film auditions is the radio. Local radio stations are glad to air a spot for film auditions in the local area. For the spots, be prepared to explain what the film is about without giving away too much but enough to get people excited about the film. Also be prepared to identify the roles you are trying to fill. Describe the age of the character and a little about them. Like he's a bookworm, or he's a jock, or she's the girl next door, etc. Give them enough about each character so the actor can connect or identify with the role. Provide information as to when the auditions run and where. Fliers can be posted at local colleges and universities as well. A web site that promotes the film and the auditions is also effective. Sides can be posted in PDF format on the web site and the web site promoted on the radio spots. This is highly effective.

On the day of auditions, make sure you have a sign-in sheet that collects info on each potential actor to include their name, age, email and phone number just in case you need to contact them. For each part you are auditioning, provide **sides** for each actor. Sides are individual scenes pulled from the script for each part. Pull scenes from the script that will test their acting ability. Using a highlighter, highlight the character's name in the scene for which they are auditioning. You should print out at least twenty or thirty copies of each side for auditions. Make sure to have a printer or copy machine available in case extra sides are needed.

After auditions are completed, the director and producer should review all possible candidates for the film. Those that are chosen to be the best are included in the call backs. The call backs will give them another opportunity to showcase their skills and allow you to narrow it down to the final cast for the film. If the auditions fail to provide the actors of the caliber that you need, you will have to schedule another set of auditions and perhaps widen the search to find the right actors.

Most of the time actors will come to the auditions having read the sides for a particular actor and be set on auditioning for that specific character. This is always a great place to start, but keep other roles in the film in mind when auditioning. If the actor doesn't fit that part, have them tryout for additional roles in the film. You may be surprised to find a perfect fit. Solicit friends and family or others involved in your indie film project to help out during auditions. The more organized it is, the smoother it will run. If you have a big turnout, and you aren't organized, it will reflect badly on your film company and not present a very good initial impression of your company.

I'd also suggest having your screenwriter present at the auditions. As the screenwriter on all of our film productions, I find it invaluable to hear the actors saying the lines. In just about every occasion, it has resulted in screenplay rewrites. Although the lines may sound great on paper, during auditions (and rehearsals) you may find that the scene doesn't work. The screenwriter must realize that it's nothing personal, but in the interest of creating the best film, it just makes sense that all scenes work at their very best.

After you have selected your actors, I'd suggest getting them all together for a meeting. I like meeting at a restaurant or some place public. Here's where I always give what I call my "big speech." I do this for a couple of reasons. First, with low budget indies, there is most likely no funds to pay actors, instead, payments will be deferred. so it is important to let them know this before going any further, and it sets the tone for the film production and their expectations. What I tell them is the truth that this is a low budget film with limited funds and that for actors the wages are deferred. It's no surprise that most of them have heard this before. BUT, I follow with my commitment to them that I will do my very best to make this a good film and to make them look their very best in front of the camera. This will be something that can take them to the next level and they can proudly include in their portfolio. Now these cannot be merely words. You must follow through and deliver. I have never had anyone stand up and say "I'm out of here" on me. They all stay committed and I also stay committed until the end and I keep my word. Give them your word you will do your best and do it. That's usually enough for actors trying to break into the business.

Conducting Rehearsals

Here's something that can improve the quality of the independent film without adding cost – rehearsals. The effect of rehearsals on actors varies with the needs of each actor. I've seen actors who could be given a line and ten minutes later nail it on the head without any preparation. I've also worked with actors who needed time to get their head wrapped around it. It's best to make the time in the schedule for rehearsals to ensure that your actors are strong enough to carry the film.

As with auditions, the producer needs to arrange a place that actors can rehearse for an extended period. Make sure the place has access to bathrooms and snack/drink machines if possible. Consider bringing in snacks and drinks if necessary. Arrange for some seating and an open space where actors can act out the scenes.

Rehearsals should start with a table top reading of the full script. Arrange for a large table where all of the main actors can be seated. The producer, director, and screenwriter should all attend and take notes during the rehearsal. Afterwards, they should meet and discuss any issues with the chosen actors and with the story or script. If performing scenes where an actor required for the scene is not present, the producer should ask another actor that is present to sub in so the rehearsal can continue. As the rehearsals progress, it helps to add props and costumes to get the actors in the mode. It also helps to have a little fun during rehearsals. At one rehearsal, I showed up dressed in full police gear to include a weapon, cuffs, full uniform, hat, and sunglasses. I interrogated the actors about the local events associated with the screenplay story and asked the actors questions that the actor had to answer while in character. This helped them to think like their character and they had fun doing it.

As the rehearsals progress, the producer and director should feel confident that the selected actors are capable of carrying the film. If there are actors that are weak, a strategy must be developed to strengthen their performance or replace them. Remember, that at this time. We are still working on contracts and have not yet signed the actors. Do not sign contracts until you are 100% sure that the actors you have chosen can perform in front of the camera as needed. The actors will most likely bring up the issue of contracts. Let them know that they are being worked and once you are comfortable with the actors, bring them in for signing. We will discuss writing contracts later in the book.

As with anything else sometimes things don't always go as planned. During our rehearsals on our last film *The Darkening* (a horror/suspense film) we found ourselves in a dilemma with some of the actors in that we didn't feel that some of the performances were up to what we needed for a feature film. We needed to develop a strategy to break through to the actors to bring their performance up. A couple of issues were hindering their progress and not that it applied to all, but most of them. As my brother Dan, the producer, and I watched, we felt that the dialogue was not as natural as we needed and we didn't believe that the actor believed in what their character was saying or doing. It needed to be stronger, but how could we break through to them. As Dan and I discussed this, we came up with a couple of ideas that could perhaps solve our problems. The first idea was to stage a fight between Dan and me with actual scripted dialogue.

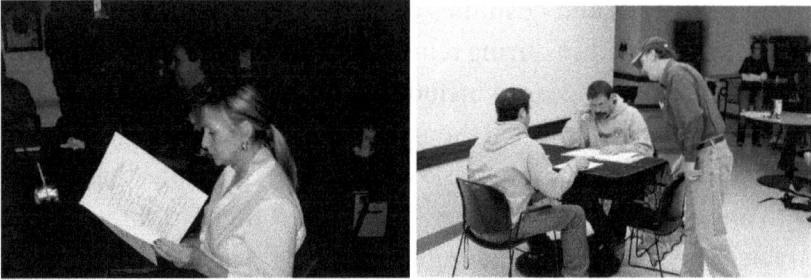

*Figure 7-**Actors Studying the Script***

*Figure 8- **Myke and Dan Recording Auditions***

We would actually stage a scripted argument during the rehearsal in an attempt to suck them in and believe that it was real. Of course, we also realized that if we didn't do it convincingly enough, we would look pretty stupid. If it worked, we could perhaps break through to them with a lesson on believability. The second lesson wasn't as daring. I sat with each actor and had a casual conversation. On an agreed signal, they would add one of their character's lines from the script. The intent was to bypass the switch in their head that flips when they go from natural and casual dialogue to saying lines from a screenplay. This was intended to help make their screen dialogue more natural sounding.

During the next rehearsal, we sprang our trap on our captive audience. As Dan fiddled with the camera (he recorded all rehearsals) I become irritated and this led to an all out heated argument resulting in Dan quitting production and walking out. As Dan walked away, my sister Brenda stood up and yelled "cut." You could hear a pin drop in the room. The cast had bought in 100% and believed everything that had been said. Later on, while reviewing footage on the camera, it had captured the faces of the cast and every single one of them had their mouth open in shock and with a look of "there goes the film" on their faces.

It had worked. I then stepped back to the front of the room and told the cast that if Dan and I could do something that you believe, and we're not even actors, then you can do something on the big screen that EVERYONE will believe. From that point on, the performances improved to the point where we were confident that they could carry the film. If you can get your actors to believe 100% in their character and deliver natural dialogue, you're half-way home!

Remember that rehearsals are a great place to test drive the screenplay and story you are telling. Either a scene works or it doesn't. This is probably most important for indie filmmakers since they probably don't have access to the high-end caliber screenwriters in Hollywood. Screenwriters should be at every rehearsal and pay attention to what is working and what isn't working. Another added benefit to rehearsals is the discovery of talent. The screenwriter may discover an actress in a bit part who is amazing and needs her role expanded. That's exactly what happened to us during rehearsals of *The Darkening*. The screenplay had a small bit part for a forensics person. It was one scene. However, when we latched onto our actress for that role, we soon discovered that she was amazing and needed a meatier part. So, as the screenwriter on the film, I went home and wrote more lines for her. Producers need to think on their feet in indie film production and take advantage of every single opportunity that adds production value to their film. Take advantage of rehearsals to hone the film into the best that it can be.

Other Casting Decisions

Here's a clever idea for aspiring indie filmmakers. Search out people in the media through friends and acquaintances such as radio and television personalities for small bit parts in your movie. People in the media love the silver screen and will jump at the chance to pop up somewhere in it. When it comes time to publicize your film they will be in the forefront to help promote it. Just be careful about giving out lines. Remember that a few lines to someone who can't act can quickly ruin a film. If it's a horror movie, let them play a dead body. Also seek out a local band if you have any club or bar scenes. Lots of local bands have devoted fans that would pay to come see the band in a movie. You never know, you could even arrange for them to write some music for your film.

Crew Choices

Probably the biggest mistake that an indie filmmaker can make is thinking that they can do everything themselves. Just as with studio films, indie filmmakers should make the attempt to departmentalize the different areas of film production and look for talented individuals for those areas. Most indie films, because of budget limitations, have small crews and crew members performing in multiple roles. There are several principle roles on film production where it is important to get the right person.

> **Producer** – The producer brings all of the elements together for film production and will hire the key players such as screenwriter, director, cinematographer, production manager, sound engineer, actors, location managers, makeup, editor and crew. They also will seek out funding (executive producers), write the contracts and pursue distribution. An experienced film producer will obviously make production go a lot smoother. If you are a first time producer, you have a learning curve ahead of you and

hopefully this book will help.

Director - The director captures the vision for the story on film in concert with the director of photography (cinematographer) and guides the actors through their scenes and their performance on screen. The director does more than just shout "action" and "cut." The director must ensure that the actors bring the proper emotion and urgency to each scene and know where in the character arc (if there is one) they are in each scene. The producer should seek out an experienced film director, if possible, for the film. I stood behind the director on every shot on two films before I felt confident to take the helm myself.

Director of Photography (DP) – For indie films, the DP is usually the same guy behind the camera (cinematographer). He makes the decisions on how the film will look such as lighting and framing. If he's the same guy behind the camera, he also determines the camera settings. The producer should seek out an experienced DP or a talented photographer who understands, or can learn, the mechanics of the shots required for film.

Production Manager (PM) – The PM is probably the most underrated role but yet one of the most critical on the set. Without a PM, a set can be nothing but total chaos. The PM manages all resources and assets needed for every single minute of film production. The PM runs a production schedule that is developed in conjunction with the producer and director. The production schedule breaks down the shooting script into a timetable that covers the entire shooting period and all locations.

Line Producer – The Line Producer (if you have one) manages the budget for the below the line items. In larger films with investors, they will track the budget and provide reporting to the investors on whether the film is over or under budget. For films that are very low budget or no budget, the producer would most likely pick up the role of the line producer because of reduced staffing and resources.

If you have an expanded indie crew, other important crew members include:

Focus Puller (1st Assistant Camera) – For more complex cameras, they may be equipped with an additional piece of hardware called a follow focus that is mounted around the lens. The follow focus adjusts the lens focal plane during actor movement on the set. The focus puller sets marks on the follow focus wheel for each mark that the actor hits on the set. This keeps all camera movement on the set in focus.

Clapper/Sound Slate (2nd Assistant Camera) – This person slates the film. They update the slate with the current scene number and take number.

First Assistant Director (AD) – This person works with the PM and director to keep the film shooting on schedule. This role is easily trainable. You just need someone who is organized and can manage tasks.

Digital Imaging Technician (DIT) - The DIT is a new position on the film crew created by the birth of digital film production. They are the expert on the set on the digital camera but their main focus is managing the wealth of data that can be created, especially when shooting in 4K resolution or higher. Data must be continually managed and archived.

Script Person – The script person can help to create the director's cut by notating the take (print) that the director prefers during shooting. They also update the script during shooting for any changes. The updated script becomes the final and can be used for any closed captioning requirements.

Continuity Person – Continuity is one of those things that some film buffs love to watch for. From scene to scene there must be continuity between costumes, makeup, scars, props (glasses half empty), and position of other items on the set. On indie sets, one of the crew may fill in for this role. On our film, my sisters took pictures of actor's wardrobes in each scene and scars so they could be matched in later shots.

Sound Engineer – On the indie set, this is the person running the digital field sound recorder. They ensure that the recorder is set to proper recording levels during capture of audio.

Boom Operator – This is the person that holds the microphone boom during shooting on the set.

Gaffer – The guy who heads up the electrical on the set. On indie films, he's the guy that knows how to connect up to 220 VAC for heavy duty lighting and electrical breakout boxes. For indie films that power their equipment with 110 VAC, this position isn't really needed.

Grips - The guy who puts up the lighting at the direction of the DP. They can add gels and adjust barn-doors at the direction of the DP. They also setup large screens and hold up bounce cards and light reflectors/absorbers.

Makeup – Usually for makeup, you'll need a makeup lead person and a group of assistants under that person. Many times with a large cast, more than one makeup person will be working at a time. Contact your local cosmetology college for free support on your film. Many of these colleges offer students credit for working on a feature film.

Transportation Captain – This person drives actors from location to location or will chauffer them to and from the set if they require transportation.

Equipment/Prop Master – On an indie set this person may not only be in charge of all props but also oversee all of the equipment in the equipment truck. They will also drive the equipment truck from location to location.

Swing Gang – The swing gang works under the equipment/prop master and helps to unload and load equipment from the equipment truck. On indie films they will also help to stage dolly tracks.

For our last production, we not only recruited crew from the local area (DP and sound) but I also involved my family. My brother Dan acted as producer. One sister, Brenda, did production management while another sister acted as first assistant director. Another brother, Tom, acted as equipment/prop manager, and my other brothers Bill and Jerry both helped as grips for the DP. Bill also subbed in for transportation while Dan and Brenda both also subbed in for sound on the set. If you don't have a large family like mine, you can post fliers at local colleges that teach theater and/or broadcasting to solicit crew members. College students love to work and gain experience on real feature films. Everybody on an indie film set wears several hats and they pitch in wherever needed. That's the beauty of indie film.

Securing Locations

Here's one of my pet peeves because this is where many indie filmmakers fall short. Too many times, filmmakers don't spend the time to find locations that will enhance the story they are telling. Not only can great locations add to the cinematic experience but a good location will help take our actor to that world that we need to create to tell our story. It makes that world real for the actor and enhances the performance they give. Below is a shot from the film *Love Wine*. We secured the use of Pelee Island on Lake Eerie (Ontario Canada side). The island was very lush and cinematic.

Figure 9-Pelee Island in Ontario (Love Wine film)

Many locations can be secured for little or no money. It's one of those things that independent filmmakers can take advantage of to add production value to their film for very little cost. Most locations that I approach are eager to be involved with a feature film. Be honest with them about the type of movie you are making, how long you will need the location, and be sensitive to scheduling the use of the location at their convenience. Also be sure to have a location contract on hand and the assurance that you will show proof of liability insurance prior to the shoot. You do not want to shoot on location without securing liability insurance. If someone gets hurt or you damage the premises, without insurance you're up a creek. We'll talk more about liability insurance later.

Of course you want certain concessions as well, such as being able to control customer traffic during the shoot and the ability to shut off noisy motors that may be running as well. Always leave the premises just as you found them. Sound blankets should be used when moving equipment on hard floors to avoid scratching them. The film crew should also be cautioned at each location to be careful moving equipment in and out of the locations as to avoid dinging up doorways and walls.

The director and producer should always do a walk-through of the location after the shoot has been completed to verify that no equipment or any mess or trash has not been left behind. Always respect the premises because you may need to come back for pickup shots. Never burn bridges. Some locations will ask you for before and after photos to assure them that no damage has occurred. The location contract also gives you the right to show images of the location in your film in all media worldwide.

When on location, sometimes you'll find that people aren't aware that a film is being shot and may be doing activities that are impacting the shoot (like blasting their stereo). The producer or a representative of the production should visit the location and very pleasantly ask that they hold off with their activities until the shoot is completed. Most people are nice enough to comply. You will, however, find the few who don't care and will not comply. Look at the good side, there's always automated dialogue replacement (ADR). We'll talk about ADR and how it's used to fix dialogue later in the book.

Closing Streets

Streets can be a real problem for filmmakers unless proper methods are used to control traffic and pedestrians. Filmmakers will need to contact the city (for city streets) or county (for county roads) government offices to request a street or road closing permit. There are forms to fill out and associated fees (like $25) to get a street or road closed. If you need barricades, I believe there's an additional fee for those as well. However, it's worth the costs. I've known guerilla filmmakers who have just strolled onto a street location and just started shooting without getting a street closing. They had pedestrians wandering into the set and the noise from traffic was horrible. Do it right. You'll appreciate having control of your location. Of course, it isn't perfect because you can't control everything (dogs barking, kids playing, horns honking, etc.), but it's better than no control of the immediate environment.

When closing streets, it's always smart to post a couple of available crew members at each end. Sometimes, you may trap local home or business owners in or out of their home or business. The crew member posted at the end should have a two-way radio so they can notify the production crew that a car is coming through so the director can halt production until they get an all-clear signal.

Generally when closing streets, the department of roads will drop off the barricades at the points where the streets are being closed off. It's the job of the film crew to put them up and take them down according to the period in the permit.

Shooting in Small Towns

Whatever you are considering shooting, seriously consider shooting it in a small town in your area. Shooting in small towns is great! I say this for numerous reasons. First, a lot of these towns have older buildings with character, which is of course great fodder for the cinematographer. They will love shooting against these rich backdrops. When you consider locations, drive through some small towns in your local area and take photos. You'll begin to see what I mean. Find ones with older rustic downtown areas and older homes. That's just the first advantage. The second advantage is that the people are friendlier and more willing to help. The bigger the city, the more difficult it is to get anything done. I've produced movies in both small towns and larger cities. Hands down, the small towns are the winner.

In small towns you can close down just about any street and shoot in any place. At one point in our last movie, we had several streets shutdown at the same time in the downtown area. They didn't have an issue at all. The police department even allowed us free reign of the building to shoot numerous scenes. The only time they pulled the reigns back in was when they received 911 calls. Then we had to back off. The Chief of Police even offered to let us use his new helicopter. We declined, but now that I think of it, we could have gotten some pretty awesome aerial shots with it. Oops. Maybe next time. When I was shooting my first film (a short), the Police Chief offered to loan us a shotgun. Again, I declined. The police departments in these small towns are just amazing to work with. We met with the police department to discuss the staging of a crime scene and how it would be handled in real life. They even provided us with a police car with lights whirling, an officer, and crime scene markers for free. By meeting with the local top officials and professionally presenting the film project to them, you'll be surprised how much assistance they will give you. Anything that police professionals help you with adds production value to your film.

By meeting with local real-estate owners and developers in these small towns, you can discover vacant buildings that can be used as a remote headquarters or as location sets. We actually got three buildings for free (with power and water) from a local real-estate owner just by asking. Two of the buildings were used for a headquarters and wardrobe/equipment area and the third was made-over (set decoration) and used as a mystic shop. It worked out perfectly.

While headquartered in the small town, make friends with locals and pull them into the film production. They can be invaluable. One of our actors was from the small town where we were shooting quite a few of our scenes and knew practically every restaurant owner in the area. She approached them and they ended up providing free food every night we shot in the local area. Naturally, you provide them a thanks in the closing credits as a small way of paying back. We also held a premier of the film at their only theater downtown when the film was completed to show our appreciation. We also gave half the profits from that premier to the downtown development organization to sponsor summer events for kids. So, you will find that small towns will give you tons of support, just remember to find ways to show your appreciation.

Developing A Shooting Schedule

If someone tells you that they have figured out the breakdown of the script into the number of shooting days, they're yanking your chain. There are so many elements that can go wrong while shooting a film that can impact your schedule. It's almost impossible to figure out which one is going to happen to you on the set. Let's see if I can name a couple… *"The DP overslept and someone needs to pick him up…"* or *"Oh, you know those batteries that we were supposed to have been charging, well so and so forgot and well guess what?"*

It goes on and on and on. Welcome to indie film. The great thing about making indie movies is that you actually got it made. The problem with indie film is that you have very limited funds and a limited time to get it shot. Our last film was a hundred page script and I wrote a shooting schedule to get it shot in seventeen days. Didn't happen, but we took a hell of a swing at it and got most. We ended up shooting a lot of pickup scenes on several weekends to get the shots we needed to finally glue it together and get it to run. Indie filmmakers are crazy. They're up at dawn and shooting until midnight. Then they have meetings and review footage. Then they have a few beers and go to bed. That's they're insane schedule and they love it.

Apart from the script, the shooting schedule is the single most important document on the set Everything on the set runs from it. It is the bible to the production manager. The production manager must know how to read the shooting schedule and how to use it to keep the shoot on track. We did the shooting schedule in a couple of different ways so that it made more sense to the Production Manager and crew. We initially did a master shooting schedule that showed every scene in the script and every location. See Figures 11 to 18, *The Darkening Shooting* schedule pages 1 through 8. We also did breakdowns for each location. There turned out to be 27 locations when you counted street locations. I've only included a couple of them so you get the general idea (See Figures 19 to 21).

What's important here is that you understand what we've included, where it came from, and the different things that it means to everyone on the crew. The shooting schedule is best managed as an Excel spreadsheet. In the old days, film sets used a production board that had strips of paper which contained the scene information. We initially purchased one of these but quickly found that it was easier to manage in Excel.

You'll notice that on the upper left hand side of the page, we have legends for the rows that identify what information appears across the page. Such as:

- Breakdown Page
- Day or Night (D or N), Evening (E)
- Scene #
- Extras (E), Volunteer Police (VP)
- No. of Pages
- Vehicles

The Script Breakdown Page

The breakdown page is assigned a number that is the same as the scene number in the shooting script. The two are linked. The shooting schedule points to the breakdown page which contains pertinent notes about each scene such as:

- Cast Members
- Extras
- Wardrobe
- Volunteer Police
- Stunts
- Props
- Makeup
- Music
- Vehicles
- Special Effects
- Green screen
- Sound

Producers can create their own categories and choose not to use ones on the form. Producers should tailor these for their own use. We added volunteer police because we knew that we had an agreement with the sheriff's office to use a few on the film and needed a place to indicate in which scene they were required. The prop master would also be notified by the PM of any special props noted in the "prop" section. Any resource needed for shooting a scene can be documented on this form and helps as a reminder to the PM and producer.

Day or Night (D or N), Evening (E) – This single letter abbreviation designates at what time the scene takes place. Typically, you just want either day or night. We had scenes designated as evening as well.

Scene # - This is the scene number in the shooting script.

Extras (E), Volunteer Police (VP) – This tells us if we need extras or any volunteer police for   the scene. You'll just want to use extras.

No. of Pages – This tells us the length of the scene in 1/8ths. Each scene in the screenplay, for breakdown purposes, is separated into 1/8ths. Imagine that you fold a page of the script in half. Now fold it in half again. Now fold in half a last time. Unfold it. Where the creases are, represents an eighth of a page (See Figure 10).

Vehicles - This lets us know if vehicles are needed for the scenes.

For our film some of these additional abbreviations such as extras (E) and volunteer police (VP) were added. The producer and PM can create a similar spreadsheet and track whatever resources that works for their film. As a producer, plan on spending a solid week developing this shooting schedule (that's what it took me). Then plan on your PM rewriting it (another week). The production team will then meet to discuss how this creates the actual shooting schedule for the complete shoot.

Indie filmmakers shoot films by location. Budgets don't allow for shooting the film sequentially from beginning to end. All scenes that are to be filmed at one location will be grouped together to be shot at that location. Once all of the scenes that take place at that location have been shot, it's on to the next one. I always write it into my location agreements that I have an extra sixty days for pickup shots. That is, I may be back if my editor discovers that I didn't get a shot that's needed and I need to "pick it up." It happens.

Tally up the eighths at each location. Remember that for each scene, there may have to be wardrobe changes, lights moved, lenses changed, makeup touchups, etc., so discuss this with the director and DP there so that the estimates are more accurate. Figure at least an additional half hour to an hour for scenes that require wardrobe or lens changes between scenes. Calculate in at least three takes on a scene since even indie filmmakers like choices and feel comfortable with their takes.

Try to push the schedule for at least four to five pages a day. So let's say that you have a scene that's two pages long. That's sixteen eighths (16/8). You also have another four scenes that are half pages long. That's another sixteen eighths (4 x ½ (4/8s) = 16/8s). And you have another scene that is one page long (8/8s). Add all of the eighths together and you have forty eighths (40/8s) which equals five pages of script. Schedule that for one day of shooting. So for a 90 minute film, plan for an 18 or 19 day shoot. If you can only get the crew and actors for 14 days, plan on picking up the rest of the film on additional weekend shoots.

Figure 10 shows a page from a screenplay divided into eighths (1/8). Note that the page begins with the remainder of a previous scene and is one eighth of a page long. The next scene (starting with INT. YOUNG'S CAR – DAY) is five eighths long (5/8). The last two scenes are each one eighth (1/8) of a page long.

3

1/8th

JACK
It's a long story.

Nick gently places the plastic case down on the counter.
Everyone stares at it waiting for an explanation. Jack
takes a deep breath and begins...

INT. YOUNG'S CAR - DAY

CLOSE UP: On a younger Jack, 12 years old, his hair curly-
q'd in the front and his shirt buttoned to the top as the
car he's riding in moves along. The skyline of Chicago is
visible against the morning rising sun through the car's
rear window.

JACK (V.O.)
It was the summer of 1964. Grandma
invited me and my brother Tom...

5/8ths

As we pull back we see that he's sitting next to his
brother TOM, 13 years old, wearing black rimmed glasses,
his hair curly-q'd in the front and his shirt buttoned to
the top. Tom pushes up his glasses with his finger.

JACK (V.O.) Continues
...to stay with her over the summer.
My dad said that we'd been down south
before but we were very little. All I
knew is what Dad told us...they lived
way down south where there was nothing
but cotton and mud.

In young Jack's lap is a shoebox beaming with green Army
men and toy cars.

JACK (V.O.) Continues
I brought my Army men just
in case it got too boring.
(Beat)
It wouldn't be.

2/8ths

EXT. YOUNG'S CAR-GRAVEL ROAD - LATE AFTERNOON

In southern Missouri, a cloud of dust follows the lone car
as it moves down a gravel road. Cotton fields and rusty
tin-roofed shacks adorn both sides of the road.

INT. YOUNG'S CAR-GRAVEL ROAD - LATE AFTERNOON

Jack watches as the rundown shacks pass by. One of the
shacks has several black children playing in the yard.

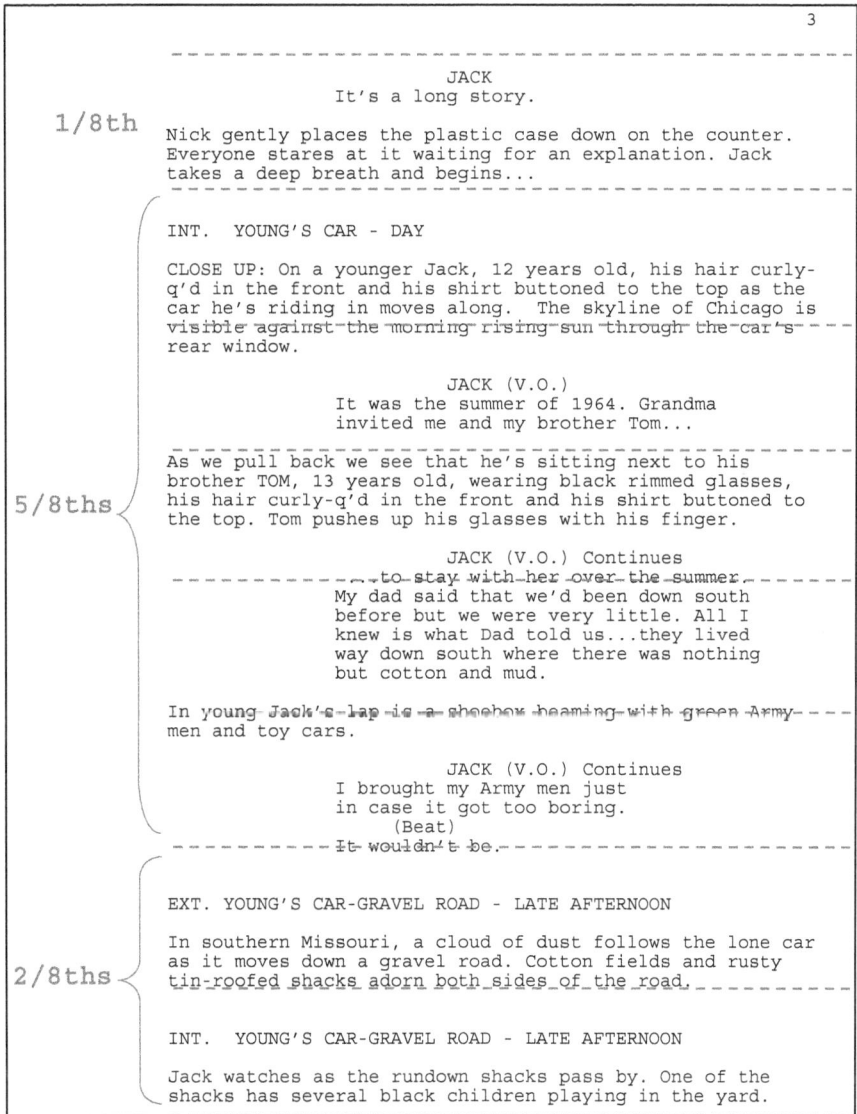

Figure 10-Screenplay Page Breakdown into Eighths

Title: The Darkening
Director: Jackie Young
Producer: Dan/Jackie Young
Production Manager: Brenda
Asst. Dir.: Patricia Young
Cinematographer: Tim Stotz
Script Dated: 2-06-2011

Scene No.	Breakdown Page	Day/Night	Extras/VP	Pages	Vehicle	Description	Characters (present)
1	1	E		1/8th	V	EXT Country Rd	James, Boys in truck, Old Woman #1
2	2	E		8/8th		INT Truck	James, Dead Body, Boys in truck
3	3	E		8/8th	V	EXT Country Rd - CU on beer can	James
4	4	E		6/8th	V	EXT Country Rd - Kyle finds body	Kyle, Dead Body
5	5	E		1/8th	V	EXT Street - Kyle watches harrison House	Kyle
6	6	E		1/8th	V	EXT Old Harrison House - Dad leaves	Robin, James' Dad
7	7	E		1/8th	V	EXT Street - Kyle's black eyes	Kyle, Young James, Young Brad
8	8	E		1/8th	V	EXT Old Harrison House - Kyle moves in	Kyle, Robin, Young James, Young Brad
9	9	E		2/8th		INT Old Harrison House	Kyle, Robin
10	10	E		1/8th		INT Harrison House - Old	Kyle
11	11	E		3/8th		INT Harrison House - Old	Kyle, Robin
12	12	E		1/8th		INT Harrison House - CLOSEUP	Kyle, Robin
13	13	E		1/8th		INT Neighbor's House - Calls police	Old Woman #1
14	14	E		1/8th		INT Harrison House - Old	Kyle, Robin
15	15	E		1/8th	V	EXT Harrison House - Old - James returns	Kate Harrison
16	16	E		2/8th		INT Harrison House - Old	Kyle, Robin, Kate Harrison
17	17	E		1/8th		INT Harrison House - Old - CLOSEUP	Kyle, Robin, Kate Harrison
18	18	E		2/8th		INT Harrison House - Old - James Cut	Kyle, Robin, Kate Harrison
19	19	E		1/8th		INT Harrison House - Old - Kyle watches	Kyle, Robin, Kate Harrison
20	20	E	VP	1/8th	V	INT Harrison House - Old - Kyle in doorway	Kyle
(—)	N/a		VP		V		
21	21	D		1/8th		INT Harrison House - Old	Kyle, Kate Harrison
22	22	D	VP	1/8th	V	INT Harrison House - Old	Robin
23	23	D		1/8th		INT Harrison House - Old	Kyle
24	24	D	VP	3/8th	V	INT Harrison House - Old - COPS Arrive	Chief, Kyle, Kate Harrison
25	25	D	VP	1/8th	V	INT Harrison House - Old - CLOSEUP Jam	Kyle, Kate Harrison
26	26	D		1/2th		INT James & Kristy's Apartment - Bedroom	James, Kristy, Kate Harrison
27	27	D		1/8th		INT James & Kristy Apartment-Bathroom	James, Kristy
28	28	D		7/8th		INT James & Kristy's Apartment - Bedroom	James, Kristy, Kate Harrison
29	29	D		1/8th	V	INT Chief's Car - Arrives at Café	Chief, Robin
30	30	D		3/8th		EXT Café - Robin not impressed	Chief, Robin
31	31	E	E	10/8th		INT Café - Gives her checkbook	Chief, Robin
32	32	D		1/2th	V	EXT Harrison House - Present	James, Kristy
33	33	D		3/8th		INT Harrison House - Present	James, Kristy, Kate Harrison

Figure 11-The Darkening Shooting Schedule, Page 1of 8 (all locations)

Title: The Darkening
Director: Jackie Young
Producer: Dan/Jackie Young
Production Manager: Brenda Your
Asst. Dir.: Patricia Young
Cinematographer: Tim Stotz
Script Dated: 2-06-2011

Brkd. Page	D/N/E	Scene No.	No. of Pages	Scene	James (1)	Kristy (2)	Dr. Phillips (3)	Chief (4)	Brad (5)	Kyle (7)	Liz (8)	Robin (9)	Sandy (10)	Karen (11)	Kate Harrison (12)	Brad's Mother (13)	Robin's Girlfriend (15)	Hostess (17)
66	N	66	1/2t	INT Brad's House - Memory of his mother					X							X		
65	N	65	1/8t	INT Brad's House - Memory of his mother				X							X	X		
64	N	64	5/8t	INT Brad's House - Memory of his mother			X	X							X	X		
63	D	63	7/8t	INT Doctor Phillips Office - Brad scene			X	X							X	X		
62	D	62	6/8t	INT Doctor Phillips Office - Brad scene			X					X						
61	D	61	1/2t	INT Doctor Phillips Office - Brad scene			X	X				X						
60	D	60	1/8t	EXT Mystic Shop	X	X												
59	D	59	14/8t	INT Mystic Shop - Back Room	X	X	X											
58	D	58	3/8t	INT Mystic Shop	X	X	X											
57	E	57	6/8t	EXT Street - Front of Mystic shop	X	X												
56	N	56	1/2t	INT HARDWARE STORE - They meet Robin	X	X						X						
55	D	55	1/8t	INT Harrison House - Old - FLASHBACK												X		
54	E	54	1	INT HARDWARE STORE - They meet Robin	X	X						X					X	
53 N/a	D	53		DELETED														
52	D	52	13/8t	INT Prison - Doc & Karen see Kyle			X			X				X				
51	D	51		DELETED														
50	E	50	2	INT Fine Restaurant			X		X									X
49	D	49	3/8t	INT Doctor Phillips Car			X		X									
48	D	48	2/8t	EXT DOCTOR PHILLIPS CAR			X		X									
47	E	47	1/8t	EXT Doctor Phillips Office - Brad sees Jame	X		X	X	X									
46	E	46	13/8t	INT Doctor Phillips Office - CLOSEUP on sc	X	X	X											
45	E	45	5/8t	INT Doctor Phillips' Office	X	X	X											
44	D	44	8/8t	INT Harrison House - Present	X	X												
43	D	43	1/8t	INT Hardware Store	X	X												
42	D	42	3/8t	INT Harrison House - Present - Bathroom	X	X												
41	D	41	7/8t	INT Harrison House - Present - Kristy on phon		X												
40	D	40	1/8t	INT Harrison House - Present	X	X												
39	N	39	2/8t	INT Harrison House - Old - CLOSEUP of drug														
38	N	38	1/8t	INT Harrison House - Old - Dad dies														
37	N	37	5/8t	INT Harrison House - Present	X	X												
36	D	36	1/8t	EXT Harrison House - Present - Kristy & Aud		X												
35	D	35	1/8t	INT Harrison House - Present - James Freaks	X													
34	D	34	3/8t	INT Harrison House - Present		X												

Figure 12 - The Darkening Shooting Schedule, Page 2 of 8

Title: The Darkening
Director: Jackie Young
Producer: Dan/Jackie Young
Production Manager: Brenda Your
Asst. Dir.: Patricia Young
Cinematographer: Tim Stotz
Script Dated: 2-06-2011

Breakdown Page	Artist	No.	34	35	36	37	38	39	40	41	42	43	44	45	46	47	48	49
Day or Night (D or N), Evening (E)			D	D	D	D	N	N	D	D	D	D	D	E	E	E	D	D
Scene No.			34	35	36	37	38	39	40	41	42	43	44	45	46	47	48	49
Extras (E), Volunteer Police (VP)																		
No. of Pages			3/8t	1/8t	1/8t	5/8t	1/8t	2/8t	1/8t	7/8t	3/8t	1/8t	8/8t	5/8t	13/8t	1/8t	2/8t	3/8t
Vehicles (V)			V		V											V	V	V
			INT Harrison House - Present	INT Harrison House-Prsent- James Freaks	EXT Harrison House - Present - Kristy &Judy	INT Harrison House- Present	INT Harrison House- Old- Dad dies	INT Harrison House-Old - CLOSEUP of drug	INT Harrison House-Present	INT Harrison House-Present -Kristy on phon	INT Harrison House - Present - Bathroom	INT Hardware Store	INT Harrison House-Present	INT Doctor Phillips' Office	INT Doctor Phillips Office - CLOSEUP on sc	EXT Doctor Phillips Office - Brad sees Jame	EXT DOCTOR PHILLIPS CAR	INT Doctor Phillips Car
Character	Artist	No.																
Waiter		18																
Doctor's Daughter		19														X	X	X
Mystic		20																
Mystic's Daughter		21																
Guard # 1	Bill Daer	23																
Guard # 2		24																
Real Estate Lady		27	X		X													
Young James		30					X	X										
Young Brad		31																
James' Dad		32					X	X										
Old Woman # 2	Mom	42										X						
Dr Michaels (V.O.)	Brenda	43								X								

Breakdown Page	Artist	No.	50	51	52	53	N/a	54	55	56	57	58	59	60	61	62	63	64	65	66
Day or Night (D or N), Evening (E)			D	D	D	D		D	D	N	D	D	D	D	D	D	D	N	N	N
Scene No.			50	51	52	53		54	55	56	57	58	59	60	61	62	63	64	65	66
Extras (E), Volunteer Police (VP)			E					E		E	E									
No. of Pages			2		13/8t			1	1/8t	1/2t	6/8t	3/8t	14/8	1/8t	1/2t	6/8t	7/8t	5/8t	1/8t	1/2t
Vehicles (V)																				
			INT Fine Restaurant	DELETED	INT Prison - Doc & Karen see Kyle	DELETED		INT HARDWARE STORE-They meet Robin	INT Harrison House - Old - FLASHBACK	INT HARDWARE STORE-They meet Robin	EXT Street - Front of Mystic shop	INT Mystic Shop	INT Mystic Shop - Back Room	EXT Mystic Shop	INT Doctor Phillips Office - Brad scene	INT Doctor Phillips Office - Brad scene	INT Doctor Phillips Office - Brad scene	INT Brad's House- Memory of his mother	INT Brad's House- Memory of his mother	INT Brad's House- Memory of his mother
Character	Artist	No.																		
Waiter		18	X																	
Doctor's Daughter		19	X																	
Mystic		20											X	X						
Mystic's Daughter		21										X								
Guard # 1	Bill Daer	23			X															
Guard # 2		24			X															
Real Estate Lady		27																		
Young James		30							X											
Young Brad		31																X		
James' Dad		32																		
Old Woman # 2	Mom	42																		
Dr Michaels (V.O.)	Brenda	43																		

Figure 13-The Darkening Shooting Schedule, Page 3 of 8

Title: The Darkening
Director: Jackie Young
Producer: Dan/Jackie Young
Production Manager: Brenda Your...
Asst. Dir.: Patricia Young
Cinematographer: Tim Stotz
Script Dated: 2-06-2011

Scene No.	Breakdown Page	Day/Night (D/N), Evening (E)	No. of Pages	Extras (E), Volunteer Police (VP), Vehicles (V)	Scene Description	Characters Present
67	67	D	2/8t		INT Brad's Garage - Dead cat scene	James; Young Brad
68	68	N/A	4/8t		SFX Shot -Brad Fakking in darkness	Liz
69	69	D	3/8t		INT Doctor Phillips Office - Brad returns	Dr. Phillips; Liz
70	70	D	1/8t		INT Doctor Phillips Office - Outer office	Liz; Docor's Daughter
71	71	D	3/8t	V	INT Mansion - Wife on phone with Doc	Dr. Phillips; Liz; Matte Collins
72	72	D	1/8t		INT Doctor Phillips Office - Doc hangs up	Dr. Phillips
73	73	D	1/8t		EXT Doctor Phillips Office - Brad see Jam...	James; Liz
74	74	D	15/8t		INT Doctor Phillips Office - His office	James; Dr. Phillips; Docor's Daughter
75	75	N/A	1/8t		SFX - James falling into black	James
76	76	D	5/8t		INT Doctor Phillips Office - later	James; Dr. Phillips
77	77	N	1/8t		INT Doctor's Phillips Office - Breakin	Liz
78	78	N	1/3t		INT Doctor's Phillips Office - Breakin	Liz
79	79	N	1/8t	V	EXT Club - Killer stalks Robin	Frank
80	80	N	4/8t	E	INT Club	Robin; Sandy; Robin's Girlfriend
81	81	N	3/8t	E	INT Club	Robin; Sandy
82	82	N	1/8t	E	EXT Club	Robin
83	83	N	1/8t	V	INT KILLER'S CAR	Robin; Frank
84	84	N	1/8t	V	EXT KILLER'S CAR	Robin; Frank
85	85	N	2/8t	V	EXT Robin's Car	Robin; Frank
86	86	N	1/8t	E	INT Club- Band scene	Bartender
86a	86a	N	4/8t		EXT ROBIN MURDER SCENE	Robin; Young Brad
87	87	N	2/8t		INT Harrison House -Present - Bedroom	James
88	88	D	21/8t	VP	EXT Robin Murder Scene	Chief; Brac; Deputy; Frank
89	89	D	2/8t		EXT Chief's Brother's House	Chief; Brac; Neds Brother
90	90	D	2/8t	V	EXT Cemetary	Chief; Reporter
91	91	D	8/8t	E	INT Harrison House - Present	James; Kristy; Reporter; Neds Brother
92	92	N	2/8t		Flashback - Robin's Murder Scene	James; Robin; Young Brad
93	93	N	1/8t		EXT Murder Scene	Robin; Young Brad
94	94	D	2/8t		INT Harrison House - Present	James; Kristy
95	95	D	1/8t		EXT Harrison House - Present	James
96	96	D	5/8t		INT Doctor Phillips Office	James; Dr. Phillips
97	97	D	1/8t	E	INT James' Car	James; Robin
98	98	N	1/8t	V	Flashback - Robin's Murder - Use cut fron...	Young Brad

Notes: "Use extra with Robin" (Sc. 97); "Need to use some of the older..." (Sc. 90); "91a- Footage of funeral is shot"; "Murder scenes a..." (Sc. 86a)

Figure 14-The Darkening Shooting Schedule, Page 4 of 8

Title: The Darkening
Director: Jackie Young
Producer: Dan/Jackie Young
Production Manager: Brenda Young
Asst. Dir.: Patricia Young
Cinematographer: Tim Stotz
Script Dated: 2-06-2011

Scene No.	Breakdown Page	Day/Night/Eve	No. of Pages	Vehicles	Scene Description
99	99	E	1/8t	V	EXT City Street -
100	100	E	2/8t		INT Alley
101	101	D	9/8t 1/8t	VP/E	INT Karen's Apartment/House
102	102	D	1/8t		INT Brad's Apartment
103	103	N	5/8t 3/8t	V	INT Doctor Phillip's office - Brad shows
104	104	N	3/8t 4/8t	V	INT Killer's car
105	105	N	1/8t	V	INT Doctor Phillip's office
106	106	N	1/8t	V	EXT Doctor's Office
107	107	N	1/8t	V	INT Killer's Car
108	108	N	3/8t		INT Karen's Car
109	109	N	1/8t		INT Karen's Apartment Hallway
110	110	N	1/8t		INT Karen's Apartment - Bedroom
111	111	N	1/8t		INT Karen's Apartment Building Hallway
112	112	N	3/8t		INT Karen's Apartment - Bedroom
113	113	N	1/8t	V	EXT City Street - at Light
114	114	N	2/8t	V/V	INT James' Car
115	115	N	3/8t	V/V	INT James' Car
116	116	N	3/8t		INT Harrison House- Present
117	117	D	10/8t		INT Karens' Apartment
118	118	D	1/8t		INT Harrison House - Present - Kitchen
119	119	D	7/8t		CLOSEUP- Headlines Karens' Murder
120	120	D	3/8t		INT Chief's Office
121	121	D	2/8t	V	INT Doctor Phillips Office
122	122	D	24/8t		INT Doctor Phillip's Office
123	123	D	1/8t		EXT Airport
124	124	D	7/8t	V	INT Doctor Phillip's Car -at airport
125	125	D	2/8t		INT Brad's Apartment
126	126	D	6/8t		INT Brad's Apartment - Building Hallway
127	127	D	17/8t		INT Brad's Apartment
128	128	D	3/8t		INT Brad's Apartment - Bedroom
129	129	D			Deleted
130	130	D	2/8t		INT Police Station -Chief's Office?
131	131	D	21/8 8/8t		INT Police Station Briefing room

No.	Artist	Character
1		James
2		Kristy
3		Dr. Phillips
4		Chief
5		Brad
6		Deputy
7		Kyle
8		Liz
11		Karen
14		Cab Driver
25		Desk Sergeant
28		Matte Collins
29		Frank
34		Baggage Boy 1
35		Baggage Boy 2
36		Newscaster
37		Reporter
38		Previous Chief

Notes within grid: "Green=screen" (Scene 129); "Voiceover by Deputy or" (Scene 108/107); "Brad sees a portion of the same b" (Scene 102); "101a-Shoot footage" (Scene 101).

Figure 15-The Darkening Shooting Schedule, Page 5 of 8

Scene No.	Breakdown Page	Day/Night (D/N/E)	No. of Pages	Veh (V)	Scene Description	James (1)	Kristy (2)	D. Phillips (3)	Chief (4)	Brad (5)	Deputy (6)	Deputy Brown (22)	Desk Sergeant (25)	Lawyer (26)	Frank (29)	Young James (30)	Notes
132	132	D	1/8t		EXT Harrison House - Present					X	X						
133	133	D	7/8t		INT Harrison House - Present		X			X	X						
134	134	D	14/8t, 16/8t		INT Harrison House - Present	X				X	X						
135	135	D	16/8t		INT Briefing Room	X	X			X	X						
136	136		1/8t		INT Brad's Apartment					X							
137	137		15/8t	3/8t	INT Briefing room	X	X			X			X				
138	138	N	3/8t		INT Police Station - Hallway	X				X				X	X		
139	139	N	1/8t		INT Darkness	X											Greenscreen shot - James
140	140	N	8/8t		INT Police Station - Command center	X				X	X	Bra... X					
141	141	N	2/8t		EXT Police Station	X											
142	142	N	5/8t	V	INT Doctor's car	X	X	X									
143	143				Deleted												
144	144	N	1/8t	V	EXT Hospital - At Chief's Car				X								Chief is walking towa...
145	145	N	10/8,3/8t		INT Doctor Phillips office	X		X									
146	146	N			INT Harrison House - Present	X											
147	147	N	3/8t		INT Police Station - Hallway					X			X	X			
148	148	N	1/8t	V	INT James/Kristy's Car - At Brad's Apart		X										
149	149	N	9/8t		INT Doctor Phillips Office	X		X									
150	150	N	3/8t		INT Brad's Apartment Building - Hallway					X			X				
151	151	N	11/8t		Int Brad's Apartment					X			X				
152	152	N	1/8t		Int Brad's Apartment						X						
153	153	N	1/8t	V	EXT Harrison House - present						X						
154	154	N	1/8t		INT Blackness	X											Greenscreen shot - James fallir...
155	155	N	4/8t		EXT Harrison House - Old - on Street	X		X									
156	156	N	4/8t		INT Harrison House - Old	X		X									Can we change the
157	157	N	20/8t		EXT Harrison House - Old	X		X							X		
158	158	N	2/8t		EXT Doctor's Office			X							X		
159	159	N	2/8t	V	INT James/Kristy's car		X			X							
160	160	N	1/8t	VV	EXT downtown street		X	X		X					X		
161	161	N	3/8t	V	INT Doctor Phillip's car	X		X									
162	162	N	1/8t	VV	EXT Downtown street - dark alley	X		X		X					X		
163	163	N	1/8t		INT Doctor's Office	X				X							
164	164	N	3/8t		EXT Brad's Apartment Building					X							
165	165	N	26/8		INT Doctor's Office		X	X		X					X		Need recorde...

Figure 16- The Darkening Shooting Schedule, Page 6 of 8

Title: The Darkening
Director: Jackie Young
Producer: Dan/Jackie Young
Production Manager: Brenda Young
Asst. Dir.: Patricia Young
Cinematographer: Tim Stotz
Script Dated: 2-06-2011

Title: The Darkening
Director: Jackie Young · **Producer: Dan/Jackie Young** · **Production Manager: Brenda Young** · **Asst. Dir.: Patricia Young** · **Cinematographer: Tim Stotz** · **Script Dated: 2-06-2011**

Character legend (Artist No.): 1 James · 2 Kristy · 3 Dr. Phillips · 4 Chief · 5 Brad · 7 Kyle · 8 Liz · 12 Kate Harrison · 28 Matte Collins · 29 Frank · 30 Young James · 31 Young Brad · 32 James' Dad

Scene / Breakdown Pg	D/N	Pages	Veh	Scene Description	1	2	3	4	5	7	8	12	28	29	30	31	32
199	N	1/8t	V	EXT Street-Harrison House													X
198	N	1/8t	VN	EXT Harrison House - Old								X				X	X
197	N	2/8t		INT Harrison House -Old												X	X
196	N	1/8t		EXT Backyard - Near Harrison House									X				
195	N	2/8t		EXT Backyard - Near Harrison House — *This is a field or wee[ds]*	X								X				
194	N	3/8t		EXT Harrison House - Old	X								X				X
193	N	2/8t		EXT Miller's Crossing -James Closeup - Pa[n]	X												
192	N	1/8t		EXT Miller's Crossing -Overhead shot	X	X	X	X					X				
191	N	1/8t		EXT Miller's Crossing -Closeup of Matte's e[ye]									X				
190	N	1/8t		EXT Miller's Crossing -POV of Darkening									X				
189	N	1/8t		EXT Miller's Crossing -CLOSEUP - Of Matt[e]									X				
188	N	1/8t		CLOSEUP - Of Darkening coming out of jar	X												
187	N	8/8t		EXT Miller's Crossing - Bridge	X	X	X	X					X				
186	N	9/8t		EXT Miller's Crossing - Bridge	X	X	X	X					X				
185	N	1/8t	V	EXT Miller's Crossing - Road to Bridge									X				
184	N	6/8t		EXT Miller's Crossing - Bridge	X	X	X	X	X				X				
183	N	1/8t	V	EXT Miller's Crossing - Road to bridge			X										
182	N	3/8t		EXT Miller's Crossing - Bridge	X	X	X		X								
181	N/A	1/8t		INT Blackness — *Greenscreen shot - Find a way to show*	X												
180	N	3/8t		EXT Miller's Crossing - Bridge		X	X		X				X				
179	N	1/8t	V	EXT Highway			X										
178	N	1/8t		EXT Miller's Crossing - Bridge		X	X		X				X				
177	N/A	1/8t		INT Blackness — *Greenscreen shot - Figure a way to s[how]*	X												
176	N	2/8&9/8t	V	Ext Miller's Lookout Bridge		X	X		X				X				
175	N	2/8&9/8t	V	EXT Doctor Phillip's Office — *Show "Closeup" of phone a[...]*										X			
174	N	2/8t		INT Doctor Phillip's office										X			
173	N	1/8t		INT Doctor's Car		X											
172	N	1/8t	V	Ext Miller's Lookout Bridge — *Need "Mil[...]"*		X	X		X				X				
171	N	3/8t	V	INT Doctor's Car		X	X		X				X				
170	N	1/8t	V	INT Doctor Phillips Office - Outer Lobby										X			
169	N	25/8t		INT Mansion		X			X	X			X				
168	N	3/8t	V	EXT Mansion		X	X		X				X				
167	N	1/8t	VN	EXT Downtown street- dark alley										X			
166	N	1/8t	V	INT Doctor's car		X	X		X				X				

Figure 17-The Darkening Schedule, Page 7 of 8

Title: The Darkening
Director: Jackie Young
Producer: Dan/Jackie Young
Production Manager: Brenda Young
Asst. Dir.: Patricia Young
Cinematographer: Tim Stotz
Script Dated: 2-06-2011

Breakdown Page	Day or Night (D or N), Evening (E)	Scene No.	Extras (E), Volunteer Police (VP)	No. of Pages	Vehicles (V)	Set / Description	Notes
200	N	200		1/8t	V/V	INT Harrison Truck	
201	N	201		1/8t		EXT Yard/Field - Kyle's body	Special effects s...
202	N	202		1/8t	V	EXT Yard/Field - POV of Darkening	
203	N	203		2/8t	V	INT Harrison Truck	
2C4	N	2C4		2/8t	V	EXT Street - Near Harrison House	
205	N	205		2/8t	V	EXT Street - Near Harrison House - Closeup o	
206	N	206		3/8t	V	EXT Harrison House - Old - Across street	
207	N	207		1/8t	V	EXT Harrison House - Old - Across street	This is the same shot as w
208	N	208		1/8t		EXT Harrison House - Old	Again, sa
209	N	209		2/8t		INT Harrison House - Old - Kitchen	
210	N	210		1/8t		INT Harrison House - Old - Living room	
211	N	211		4/8t		INT Harrison House - Old - Kitchen	
212	N	212		1/8t		INT Harrison House - Old - Kitchen	Closeup
213	N	213		1/8t		INT Harrison House - Old - Kitchen	Ka
214	N	214		2/8t	V	EXT Harrison House - Old	
215	N	215		1/8t		EXT Harrison House - Old - Closeup on door	
216	N	216		3/8t		INT Harrison House - Old - Living room	
217	N	217	VP	3/8t		INT Harrison House - Old - Living room	Sirens in background / Closeup
218	N	218		3/8t		INT Harrison House - Old - Living room	
219	N	219		15/8		INT Prison visiting room	Alex a
220	N	220		5/8t		INT Prison hallway	Melissa is playing C

Cast:

Character	Artist	No.
Kristy		2
Dr. Phillips		3
Chief		4
Brad		5
Deputy		6
Kyle		7
Kate Harrison		12
Frank		29
Young James		30
Young Brad		31
James' Dad		32

Figure 18-The Darkening Schedule, Page 8 of 8

(3-day shoot) HARRISON HOUSE - OLD (20 Yrs Earlier)

Title: The Darkening
Director: Jackie Young
Producer: Jackie Young
Production Manager: Brenda Young
Asst. Dir.: Patricia Young
Cinematographer: Tim Stotz
Script Dated: 2-06-2011

Breakdown Page	Day or Night (D/N/E)	Scene No.	Extras (E), Volunteer Police (VP)	No. of Pages	Vehicles (V)	Scene Description	James (1)	Dr. Phillips (3)	Kyle (7)	Kate Harrison (12)	Frank (29)	Young James (30)	Young Brad (31)	James' Dad (32)	Old Woman #1 (41)
6	E	6		2/8t	V	EXT Old Harrison House - Dad leaves								X	
7	E	7		1/8t	V	EXT Street - Kyle's black eyes		X		X			X		
8	E	8		1/8t	V	EXT Old Harrison House - Kyle moves in		X	X				X		
9	E	9		2/8t		INT Old Harrison House		X	X						
10	E	10		1/8t 3/8t		INT Harrison House - Old		X							
11	E	11		1/8t		INT Harrison House - Old		X	X						
12	E	12		1/8t		INT Harrison House - CLOSEUP		X	X						
13	E	13		1/8t		INT Neighbor's House - Calls police									X
14	E	14		1/8t		INT Harrison House - Old		X	X						
15	E	15		2/8t		EXT Harrison House - Old - James returns	X								
16	E	16		2/8t		INT Harrison House - Old		X	X	X					
17	E	17		1/8t		INT Harrison House - Old - CLOSEUP		X	X	X					
18	E	18		2/8t		INT Harrison House - Old - James Cut		X	X	X					
19	E	19		1/8t		INT Harrison House - Old - Kyle watches		X	X	X					
20	E	20	VP	1/8t	V	INT Harrison House - Old - Kyle in doorway		X							
N/a															
21	D	21		1/8t		INT Harrison House - Old		X		X					
22	D	22	VP	1/8t	V	INT Harrison House - Old		X							
23	D	23		1/8t		INT Harrison House - Old			X						
24	D	24	VP	3/8t	V	INT Harrison House - Old - COPS Arrive		X	X		X				
25	D	25	VP	1/8t	V	INT Harrison House - Old - CLOSEUP James				X	X	X			
38	N	38		1/8t		INT Harrison House - Old - Dad dies					X	X		X	
39	N	39		2/8t		INT Harrison House - Old - CLOSEUP of dad					X	X		X	
55	D	55		1/8t		INT Harrison House - Old - FLASHBACK				X		X			
155	N	155		4/8t		EXT Harrison House - Old - on Street	X	X							
156	N	156		4/8t		INT Harrison House - Old (Can w)	X	X			X			X	

Figure 19 - The Darkening Shooting Schedule, Harrison House (old)

HARRISON HOUSE - PRESENT

Title: The Darkening
Director: Jackie Young
Producer: Jackie Young
Production Manager: Brenda Young
Asst. Dir.: Patricia Young
Cinematographer: Tim Stotz
Script Dated: 2-06-2011

Breakdown Page	Day/Night	Scene No.	No. of Pages	Vehicles	Description	James	Kristy	Chief	Brad	Deputy	Real Estate Lady	Ned's Brother	Reporter	Dr Michaels (V.O.)
No.						1	2	4	5	6	27	33	37	43
Artist														Brenda
32	D	32	1/2t	V	EXT Harrison House- Present	X	X							
33	D	33	3/8t		INT Harrison House - Present	X	X		X					
34	D	34	3/8t	V	INT Harrison House - Present	X			X					
35	D	35	1/8t		INT Harrison House-Present- James Freaks	X								
36	D	36	1/8t	V	EXT Harrison House - Present - Kristy &Judy		X		X					
37	D	37	5/8t		INT Harrison House- Present	X	X							
40	D	40	1/8t		INT Harrison House-Present	X	X							
41	D	41	7/8t		INT Harrison House-Present -Kristy on phone		X							X
42	D	42	3/8t		INT Harrison House - Present - Bathroom	X	X							
44	D	44	8/8t		INT Harrison House-Present	X	X							
87	N	87	2/8t		INT Harrison House- Present - Bedroom	X								
91	D	91	8/8t (E)	V	INT Harrison House - Present	X	X			X	X	X		
94	D	94	2/8t		INT Harrison House - Present	X	X							
95	D	95	1/8t		EXT Harrison House - Present	X								
116	N	116	3/8t		INT Harrison House- Present	X	X							
118	D	118	1/8t		INT Harrison House - Present - Kitchen	X	X							
119	D	119	7/8t		CLOSEUP- Headlines Karens' Murder	X	X							
132	D	132	1/8t		EXT Harrison House- Present			X	X					
133	D	133	7/8t		INT Harrison House- Present		X	X	X					
134	D	134	14/8t		INT Harrison House- Present	X		X	X					
146	N	146			INT Harrison House- Present		X							
153	N	153	1/8t		EXT Harrison House - present			X						

Extras (E), Volunteer Police (VP)

Figure 20-The Darkening Shooting Schedule, Harrison House (present)

DOCTOR PHILLIP'S OFFICE

Title: The Darkening
Director: Jackie Young
Producer: Jackie Young
Production Manager: Brenda Young
Asst. Dir.: Patricia Young
Cinematographer: Tim Stotz
Script Dated: 2-06-2011

Scene Description	Breakdown Page	Day/Night	Scene No.	No. of Pages	Vehicles	James	Kristy	Dr. Phillips	Chief	Brad	Deputy	Kyle	Liz	Robin	Sandy	Karen
INT Doctor Phillips' Office	45	E	45	5/8t		X		X								
INT Doctor Phillips Office - CLOSEUP on	46	E	46	13/8t		X		X								
EXT Doctor Phillips Office - Brad sees Jar	47	E	47	1/8t	V	X		X		X			X			
EXT DOCTOR PHILLIPS CAR	48	D	48	2/8t	V			X				X	X			
INT Doctor Phillips Car	49	D	49	3/8t				X				X				
INT Doctor Phillips Office - Brad scene	61	D	61	1/2t				X		X				X		
INT Doctor Phillips Office - Brad scene	62	D	62	6/8t				X		X						
INT Doctor Phillips Office - Brad scene	63	D	63	7/8t				X		X						
INT Doctor Phillips Office - Brad returns	69	D	69	3/8t				X		X				X		
INT Doctor Phillips Office - Outer office	70	D	70	1/8t				X						X		
INT Doctor Phillips Office - Doc hangs up	72	D	72	1/8t				X								
EXT Doctor Phillips Office - Brad see Jame	73	D	73	1/8t	V	X		X		X						
INT Doctor Phillips Office - His office	74	D	74	15/8t	V	X		X						X		
INT Doctor Phillips Office - later	76	D	76	5/8t		X		X								
INT Doctor's Phillips Office - Breakin	77	N	77	1/8t						X						
INT Doctor's Phillips Office - Breakin	78	N	78	1/8t						X						
INT Doctor Phillips Office	96	D	96	5/8t		X		X		X						
INT Doctor Phillips's office - Brad shows up	103	N	103	5/8t				X		X						
INT Doctor Phillip's office	105	N	105	4/8t				X								X
EXT Doctor's Office	106	N	106	1/8t	V											X
INT Killer's Car	107	N	107	1/8t	V											
INT Doctor Phillips Office	121	D	121	2/8t	V			X	X	X						
INT Doctor Phillip's Office	122	D	122	24/8t				X	X	X						

Character / Artist list:
1. James
2. Kristy
3. Dr. Phillips
4. Chief
5. Brad
6. Deputy
7. Kyle
8. Liz
9. Robin
10. Sandy
11. Karen

Figure 21- The Darkening Shooting Schedule, Doctor's Office

Scene #	**THE DARKENING**	Date: _____
Script Page: _____	BREAKDOWN SHEET	Sheet:_____
Page Count: _____		Int/Ext: _____
		Day/Night_____

Scene Description: _____ Page # ____
Setting: _____
Location: _____
Sequence: _____Script Day: _____

Cast Members	Stunts	Vehicles
Extras	Props	Special Effects
Wardrobe	Makeup	Green-screen
Volunteer Police	Music	Sound

Figure 22-The Darkening Breakdown Page

From the shooting schedule the PM will also create actor **call sheets**. These are sheets handed out to actors to let them know when they are required on the set, where to report, what to bring, etc. See Figure 23. You usually want to hand these out in advance and not wait until the day of the shoot. They're not helpful at that point.

Films			Jack Young		402-630-3962
Drexel Street		HQ: address here, city	Dan Young		815-690-7851
, Nebraska			Brenda Young		??????
(402) 731 7037					

I/E	D/N	Set / Scene Description	Length	Cast	Location
E	N				
E	N	Old Harrison House - Evening	1/8	Kyle, James Dad, Kate, Young James	319 S. 3rd St Rockford
E	N	Old Harrison House- Evening	2/8	Kate, Young James, James Dad	319 S. 3rd St Rockford
E	N	Old Harrison House- Evening	1/8	Kyle, Young James, James Dad, Kate	319 S. 3rd St Rockford
E	N	Old Harrison House- Evening	1/8	Kate, Kyle, James Dad	319 S. 3rd St Rockford
I	N	Old Harrison House (Day)	1/8	Kate, Kyle, James Dad	319 S. 3rd St Rockford
I	N	Old Harrison House (Day)	2/8	Kate, Kyle, James Dad	319 S. 3rd St Rockford
I	N	Old Harrison House (Day)	3/8	Kate, Kyle, James Dad	319 S. 3rd St Rockford
I	N	Old Harrison House (Day)	1/8	Kate, Kyle, James Dad	319 S. 3rd St Rockford
E	N	Old Harrison House – Neighbor's house (Night)	1/8	Neighbor (calls police)	Confirm with neighbor (S. 3rd street, Rockford
I	N	Old Harrison House (Day)	1/8	Kate, Kyle, James Dad	319 S. 3rd St Rockford
I	N	Old Harrison House (Day)	1/8	Young James	319 S. 3rd St Rockford
I	N	Old Harrison House (Day)	3/8	Kate, Kyle, James Dad, Young James	319 S. 3rd St Rockford
I	N	Old Harrison House (Day)	1/8	Kate, Kyle, James Dad, Young James	319 S. 3rd St Rockford
I	N	Old Harrison House (Day)	2/8	Kate, Kyle, James Dad, Young James	319 S. 3rd St Rockford
I	N	Old Harrison House (Day)	1/8	Kate, Kyle, James Dad, Young James	319 S. 3rd St Rockford
I	N	Old Harrison House (Night)	2/8	Kyle, Chief (Young Alex) Sheriff (Jack), James Dad, Extra Cops	319 S. 3rd St Rockford
I	N	Old Harrison House (Day)	1/8	Kate, Young James	319 S. 3rd St Rockford
I	N	Old Harrison House (Day)	1/8	Kyle, James Dad	319 S. 3rd St Rockford

23	I	N	Old Harrison House (Day)	1/8	Kate	319 S. 3rd St Rockford
24	I	N	Old Harrison House (Day)	2/8	Kyle, Kate, Young James, James Dad, Cops 1,2,3	319 S. 3rd St Rockford
25	I	N	Old Harrison House (Day)	1/8	Kate, Young James	319 S. 3rd St Rockford
			total	3 6/8		
206	E	N	Old Harrison House (Evening)	3/8	Kate, Young James, James	319 S. 3rd St Rockford
207	E	N	Old Harrison House (Evening)	1/8	James Dad	319 S. 3rd St Rockford
208	E	N	Old Harrison House (Evening)	2/8	James Dad, Kate, Young James	319 S. 3rd St Rockford
209	I	N	Old Harrison House (Day)	3/8	James, Young James, Kyle, James Dad	319 S. 3rd St Rockford
210	I	N	Old Harrison House (Day)	1/8	James, Kyle	319 S. 3rd St Rockford
211	I	N	Old Harrison House (Day)	4/8	Young James, James Dad, Kate (take twice)	319 S. 3rd St Rockford
212	I	N	Old Harrison House (Day)	1/8	Kate, Young James, James Dad	319 S. 3rd St Rockford
213	I	N	Old Harrison House (Day)	1/8	James Dad	319 S. 3rd St Rockford
214	E	N	Old Harrison House (Day)	2/8	Young James	319 S. 3rd St Rockford
215	E	N	Old Harrison House (Day)	1/8	Young James	319 S. 3rd St Rockford
216	I	N	Old Harrison House (Day)	3/8	James Dad, Young James, Kate	319 S. 3rd St Rockford
217	I	N	Old Harrison House (Day)	3/8	James Dad, Young James, Kate	319 S. 3rd St Rockford
218	I	N	Old Harrison House (Day)	3/8	James Dad	319 S. 3rd St Rockford
			total	5 6/8		

NOTE: The scenes from the "Old Harrison" house occur twenty years earlier. Make sure tl
props and vehicles that appear in shots are AT LEAST twenty years old.
Scenes 205 thru 217 are picked up at the same time as scenes 7 thru 20 with James' fath
replacing Kyle for the scene.

*Figure 23-**Example of a Call Sheet***

You'll have one of these for each day of shooting. You can see that it's a very aggressive work schedule with over five pages to shoot. Note that I have removed addresses and phone numbers from our example for reasons of privacy. You will want to include these in case actors or crew need to contact you. Also note that we developed a wardrobe system with assigned numbers so it was easier to figure out which wardrobe the actor was supposed to be wearing for each scene. My sisters took pictures of each actor's wardrobe and had a large board with the pictures posted and the assigned numbers (1,2,3, etc.). These numbers show up in the call sheet under "wardrobe." Be sure to add any special instructions for actors like early reporting and info for those requiring SFX makeup.

Developing Shot Lists

Since we are looking at the shooting schedule and breaking down the script, let's discuss data extracted from the shooting script that the director and DP or cinematographer will use. It's called a **shot list**. I'll assume that most likely since we're talking indie film, the producer and director may be one in the same. If not, that's fine. Why are shot lists important? On our last film not only did I have the role of director, but I also edited the film. What you find once you start editing a film is that you are missing specific shots that would make it flow much better, but someone forgot to get the shot. A lot of times on indie film sets, things are very hectic because you have a compressed schedule, smaller crews, and don't want to have a location locked down for too long, especially if it's a business you are getting for free. The point is that the director and DP are focused on getting that scene shot and moving on to the next. Sometimes you don't get full coverage on the scene because of these things. Maybe you forgot to get a wide shot of the couple sitting outside the café or didn't get close-ups of the couple that approaches and are arguing. You get it, right?

A shot list is a list of all the coverage (shots) that makeup the scene – master, wide, medium, and close-ups. With a shot list, you are less likely to forget that overhead shot or **jib shot** (jib is a long arm that raises the camera into an overhead position, see page 85) that would have made it a really cool scene. Like the jib shot of the husband driving up to the driveway in his new sports car.

Anyway, if you rely on your memory, you may forget that shot you needed and the editor will be looking for it. These are some of the pickup shots that you may have to go back to the location to get. These are dangerous because if you wait too long, things can change - the actor cuts his hair or the owner paints the room a different color. If you have a shot list, you can also delegate some of them to the B-camera operator. If shots at the location are needed and there are no actors involved, or they are just walking up to the house or business, the B-operator can pick these up. The shot list should include information such as frame size, angle, and movement. Frame size refers to the frame in relation to the subject matter (actors and locations). Following are typical frame sizes used in film production:

- Master shot (location establishing shot)
- Wide shot - shows the full body of a person from head to toe
- Medium wide - goes from head to knees
- Medium shot - goes down to the waist
- Medium close up - goes from the chest up
- Close up - just the face
- Extreme close up - shows only details such as eyes or a hand

Angles for shots can consist of:

- Straight or from the front
- Over the shoulder
- Side shots
- Looking down on the character from a high angle
- Looking up from a low angle
- Ground level shots
- Overhead shots (crane or jib arm shot)
- Steady cam shots (requires steady cam rig)

Movement for shots can consist of:

- Zoom
- Pan
- Dolly
- Tracking
- Jib arm
- Dolly zoom (vertigo shot)

Shot Degree Rules

There are a couple of rules for using these shots. If you don't adhere to them, the editor will not be happy and some scenes may need to be re-shot. These are the **180 Degree Rule** and the **30 Degree Rule**.

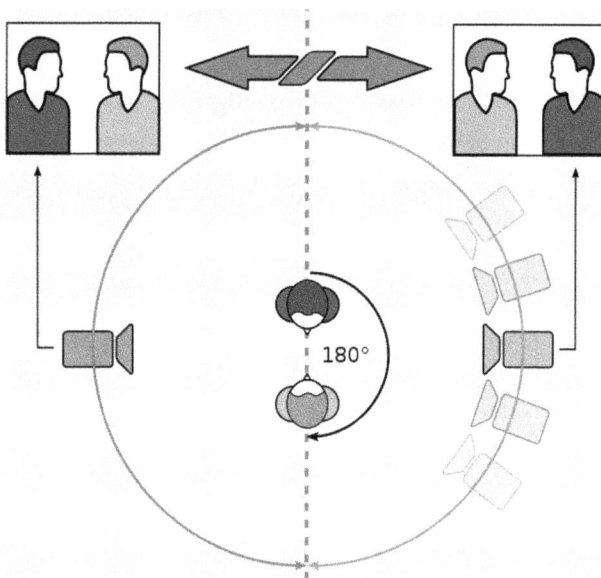

*Figure 24-**180 Degree Rule (Wikipedia Commons)*** *

180 Degree Rule - When shooting dialogue between two or more actors and their dialogue close-ups, the 180 Degree Rule must be observed. If not, when the film cuts from close-up on actor A to close-up on Actor

B, it will appear that the actor is looking in the wrong direction. Figure 24 shows the camera placement during filming. The camera should never be placed in the red area while used to shoot the close-ups. It should be positioned on one side or the other and remain within the 180 degrees. Imagine a round table with the two actors at the table. If shooting the conversation, the camera should not cross the imaginary dotted line.

30 Degree Rule – This rule is relative to what is called **jump cuts**. Jump cuts are improper transitions between cuts from one cut to the next when there isn't enough change in the angle of the shot (by at least 30 degrees). So if the camera doesn't move at least 30 degrees between shots of the same subject in succession, our brain doesn't detect that anything significant has changed from our perspective. This creates an effect that will be noted by the audience and pull them away from the story. In essence, the perspective of an edit looks too much like the previous edit. If the perspective change (or angle of the shot) is not drastic enough, it isn't justified and can be disturbing to the audience. The figure below shows a 30 degree stereoscopic perspective from a viewer. If changes in perspective fall within the 30 percent field, we will question the camera change.

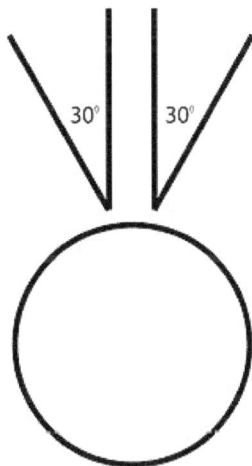

*Figure 25-**30 Degree Rule (Wikipedia Commons)***

Camera, Sound, & Lighting

Okay, first of all, I'm a screenwriter, producer, director and although I have a technical background, I am in no way a subject matter expert on cameras, lenses, or sound equipment. I have done research enough to be able to make purchases in what I thought we needed. I wasn't always right and yes, ended up selling equipment because it wasn't right for our needs. There's a learning curve to filmmaking. You're not going to be right the first time. Get used to it. Do your research, try things, and most of all try to bring in others who are the subject matter experts to help guide you through what you don't understand. For every decision on equipment, you will find ten people who will argue for it and ten people who will argue against it. Just make the decision. If it's wrong, fix it and move on. That's what producers do.

If you're old enough, you may remember some of the best cinematic films shot with 35mm film that captured beautiful vista shots such as John Ford's *She Wore a Yellow Ribbon*. These great films that were cinematic masterpieces are yet to be rivaled by digital cinema. However, not many of us indie filmmakers can afford to rent Panavision cameras much less purchase the amount of 35mm stock to shoot our next cinematic masterpiece.

Without the digital revolution, many of us filmmakers could not afford to get into the game. The aesthetics of real film is hard to capture with digital cameras and I'm not sure we'll ever get there, but we can sure get close. Digital though, does provide benefits not found when shooting with film. The cost is of course number one. It makes filmmaking affordable. It also makes instant dailies available. With film, dailies have to be developed in a lab, and this is another expense that filmmakers must consider. Film also must be processed in a lab and converted to digital for post production.

For filmmakers, film doesn't appear to be a viable choice unless you have a budget in the millions. Even then, digital may be a better choice since theaters are converting to digital screens and accepting digital prints rather than 35mm dupes as the print media. Many theaters today wouldn't know what to do with a 35mm print. It would sit on the shelf. Since 35mm prints must be converted to digital for editing, the real 35mm product doesn't ever actually get to most theaters. Even if a 35mm print were delivered to a theater, it would be converted from digital format into an analog media (35mm print) anyway, using a transcoding technique such as laser to imprint the 35mm print.

Indie filmmakers of today owe a lot to recent developments in digital technology. Without it, we would still be using black bags to load 16mm and 35mm film cassettes. My first film, a short shot in 1997, was done using a Super 16mm film camera. If you've never shot on film, you quickly realize that film is not only expensive, but so are costs of making the film and converting it to digital for editing. Besides that, 16mm is grainy when blown up on the big screen. It doesn't compare to digital HD.

On my first full feature as executive producer/producer we used the same model 24p digital camera that George Lucas had used on *Attack of the Clones*, the Sony HDW-F900 camera (CCD technology). The camera allowed the use of interchangeable lenses and had a beautiful image as well as excellent depth of field. Everyone on the set was stunned with the high definition images that it captured. This was in 2001 and was the first time I had seen HD. Today, over a decade later, with the flood of companies trying to establish a foothold in the HD camera market, the price has come down from the over $150K price tag on the F900 to less than $5K for many name brand HD cameras now available.

Not only did the camera technology change but also the software editing tools required for HD. Back then, there was only a handful of editing houses around the nation that could edit in full HD. The cost of having an editing house edit your film was in excess of $25K. Today, that same (or better) HD editing power is on the desktop. The hardware platform required for rendering HD movies has leaped from single CPU machines since then to multiple CPU workstations that can easily render a complete film in a single day. My editing workstation is a Quad Processor with 3 GByte speed processors with over 3 Tarabytes of disk storage and 12 GByte RAM. We'll talk more about editing in the post production section of this book.

The film camera is the filmmaker's essential tool. The camera and lens choices will make a big difference in how the final product looks. Below are examples of the camera and one of the major lenses used on our last film, *The Darkening*.

*Figure 26-**Panasonic AF100 and Angeneux 20-120mm Cinema Lens***

Camera Formats

As a producer, you should hire talent such as experienced camera people and sound engineers who can examine camera and sound equipment specifications and requirements and give you good solid advice on making these decisions. However, in indie films many times the producer is the same person directing and the same person running the camera. Try to avoid this since we shouldn't try to do everything ourselves. But keeping that in mind, I will make an effort to cover some of the equipment you will need. I will try to not get too deep and keep the producer perspective on the subjects. Do your own research and reading on the subject and consult those who are experts when possible.

You will find a wealth of cameras available to filmmakers from just about every major camera manufacturer out there. It helps to begin identifying your camera needs by identifying your requirements. There are a set of questions you must ask yourself to narrow in on a camera that will work for you.

What is your budget? – Budgets dictate how much we have to spend towards equipment rentals or purchases. If you are shooting a no-budget film or low-budget film, you may want to look at what's called **prosumer** HD cameras. These are higher end consumer cameras but are moderately priced. If you have a larger budget, you may be able to rent a Red One camera, a professional level camera.

Short or feature film? – If shooting a short film, you have the option of shooting with a **DLSR camera**. These types of cameras are basically photo cameras capable of shooting short segments of video. Their quality is excellent, but they will lack the features associated with a video or digital film camera such as XLR inputs for sound and larger media storage capability. Some filmmakers have shot entire features with this these cameras as well.

Theatrical, TV, DVD, VOD, cable? – If you know that you are going to these markets, you'll need a camera that provides depth of field and allows the use of higher quality lenses. If shooting for DVD or video on demand markets, you can get away with lower resolution products such as 720x480 lines of resolution. For theatrical, you'll want a minimum of 1920x1080 lines of resolution. TV and cable markets will want products in 1920x1080 as well.

Drama or documentary? – If shooting a documentary, you can choose to shoot with lower end prosumer HD cameras that have a zoom lens mounted on the camera. These types of cameras do not provide any real depth of field but for documentaries, that is acceptable.

Lens Requirements? – Larger quality cinema lenses make a big difference in the final product. Larger quality lenses (like cinema lenses) will only work on larger format cameras. Some cheaper prosumer cameras do not allow interchangeable lenses and come with the lens attached to the camera. These typically do not provide very good depth of field and are more useful for shooting documentaries. Make sure you understand the size of the frame (i.e., 1/3, 2/3, 4/3. etc.), the type of lens mount, and what lenses will work on that particular type of camera. Adapters can be used for adapting the lens mount (i.e., a PL mount adapter allows the use of PL mount lenses).

Editing format requirements? – If you have an existing editing platform such as Premiere Pro or Final Cut Pro (FCP) and have a preference for the type of data format that you want, this may influence the camera that you select. Many distributors may ask for a final film product in **Pro Res** format (a high end HD resolution Apple Codec). Premier Pro doesn't support the Pro Res format, but FCP does. However, data formats can be reformatted for final products. We chose AVCHD (AF100) because our editing platform was Premier Pro. Many editing platforms support a variety of data formats. Just keep in mind that there are some data formats not supported by these.

Camera frame rate requirements? - Many of the prosumer and higher end cameras support multiple frame rates for **under-cranking** and **over-cranking**. Over-cranking is shooting the sequence at a higher rate so that when played back, the footage is slowed down (slowmo). Under-cranking is selecting a slower frame rate so that when the sequence is played at the regular rate it speeds up the scene.

For our film, we looked at several cameras and lens combinations. We even configured an HVX200 with the Letus Adapter for a depth of field that allowed interchangeable lenses. What we discovered was that there was way too much glass and the F-stop ended up being around F-5 or greater. The F-stop drives lighting requirements so the higher the F-stop, the more lighting that is required. Look for cameras and lenses that work with low light and will have minimal lighting requirements.

Film cameras operate by exposing the image onto a film or digital plane or area of film used to record the image. Depending upon the film size (8mm, 16mm, Super 16mm, and 35mm) the area that the image is recorded will vary in size. Since we are looking at the best fit for our film needs, we are looking for a sensor size that corresponds to the best fit for our film looking as close to 35mm film product as possible. Figure 27 shows frame sizes from an actual 35mm down through smaller frame sized sensors. It also shows the different sizes of these image areas for film and digital.

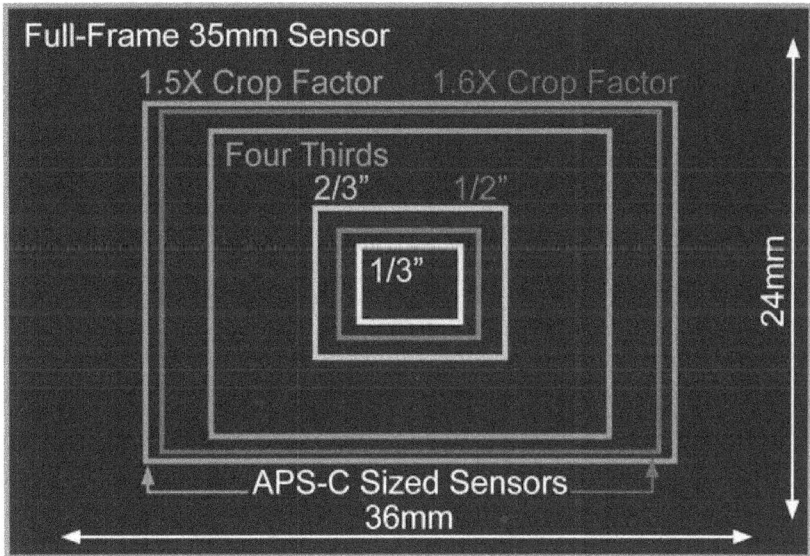

Figure 27-Sensor Sizes

What's important about these sizes is that indie filmmakers are looking to recreate the look of 35mm film. We are looking for the largest format closest to 35mm that provides a minimal 2K resolution. Resolution for feature film presentation is between 2K and 4K of resolution. Currently, the standard resolution is 2K (moving towards 4K). The image must contain enough resolution so that when the image is expanded on the screen, the resolution doesn't break down and become pixilated. There are a variety of cameras on the market, new and used, which vary in frame size and resolution and use either older CCD or CMOS sensor technology. The frame size will also dictate what lenses can be used with the camera. Some of the best quality lenses made for filmmakers are full frame cinema lenses and PL mounted. So how do you decide what format and what camera to choose?

I always look at what's being used in the industry to start with. Many films on the Internet Movie Database (IMDB) provide production details such as what format the film was shot in and sometimes the camera used. Research films that have that look that you'd like for your film and find out what they shot it with. Following is a list of the available digital movie cameras on the market. You'll note that photo cameras are listed as well. These cameras are able to shoot video as well as take photos. Most do not have features that are found on the video cameras. However, the video imagery captured on the photo cameras rivals or is even better in quality as some of the video cameras since many of them use the same type of CMOS technology for capturing images. Filmmakers who are making narrative dramas should choose cameras that allow the interchanging of lenses.

Below is a listing of many of the cameras suitable for filmmakers. By the time that you read this book, the listing will be out of date since new cameras hit the market about every six months or so. In fact, as I write this, Bolex is attempting to raise money on a group funding site to bring back a retro camera that looks similar to it's 1960s version of it's 16mm film camera. The hand-held camera would shoot in 2K and have similar features to many of the cameras listed in the table and have a retail price around $ 3,000.

So even though this seems like a fairly complete list, search out the web for brand-name vendors releasing new models for their specifications and pricing.

Brand	Camera	Model form	Sensor size	Lens Mount	Maximum video resolution	Frame rate(s⁻¹)	Codec	Maximum bitrate
ARRI	ALEXA[1]	Video	23.76 x 13.37 mm	Arri PL	2880 x 1620	0,75 - 120	ARRIRAW, ProRes	?
Blackmagic	Blackmagic Production Camera 4K[2]	Video	21.12 x 11.88 mm	Canon EF or MFT	3840 x 2160	23.98, 24, 25, 29.97, 30	ProRes, CinemaDNG RAW	880 Mbit/s
Canon	1D Mark IV[3]	Photo	27.9 x 18.6 mm	Canon EF	1920 x 1080	23.976, 25, 29.97 (50, 59.94)	H.264	?
Canon	1D X[3]	Photo	36 x 24 mm	Canon EF	1920 x 1080	24, 25, 30 (50, 60)	MPEG4	?
Canon	5D Mark II[3]	Photo	36 x 24 mm	Canon EF	1920 x 1080	24, 25, 30	H.264	?
Canon	5D Mark III[4]	Photo	36 x 24 mm	Canon EF	1920 x 1080	24, 25, 30	H.264	90 Mbit/s
Canon	7D[3]	Photo	22.3 x 14.9 mm	Canon EF/EF-S	1920 x 1080	24, 25, 30 (50,60)	H.264	?
Canon	60D[3]	Photo	22.3 x 14.9 mm	Canon EF/EF-S	1920 x 1080	24, 25, 30	H.264	?
Canon	550D[3]	Photo	22.3 x 14.9 mm	Canon EF/EF-S	1920 x 1080	24, 25, 30	H.264	?
Canon	600D[3]	Photo	22.3 x 14.9 mm	Canon EF/EF-S	1920 x 1080	24, 25, 30	H.264	?
Canon	650D[3]	Photo	22.3 x 14.9 mm	Canon EF/EF-S	1920 x 1080	24, 25, 30	H.264	?
Canon	C300, C300 PL[5]	Video	24.6 x	Canon EF,	1920 x 1080	1-30 (1-60)	MPEG2	50 Mbit/s

Brand	Camera	Model form	Sensor size	Lens Mount	Maximum video resolution	Maximum Frame rate(s⁻¹)	Codec	Maximum bitrate
Dalsa	Origin II[5]	Video	13.8 mm, 34 x 17.2 mm	Arri PL	1920 x 1080	30	?	?
Nikon	D3100[3][6]	Photo	23.1 x 15.4 mm	Nikon F	1920 x 1080	24 (24, 25, 30)	MPEG4	?
Nikon	D3200[3][7]	Photo	23.2 x 15.4 mm	Nikon F	1920 x 1080	24, 25, 30	MPEG4	?
Nikon	D4[8]	Photo	36.0 x 23.9 mm	Nikon F	1920 x 1080	24, 25, 30 (50, 60)	H.264/MPEG4	24 Mbit/s
Nikon	D5100[3]	Photo	23.6 x 15.7 mm	Nikon F	1920 x 1080	24, 25, 30	MPEG4	?
Nikon	D7000[3]	Photo	23.6 x 15.7 mm	Nikon F	1920 x 1080	24 (24, 25, 30)	MPEG4	?
Nikon	D800[9]	Photo	35.9 x 24 mm	Nikon F	1920 x 1080	24, 25, 30 (50, 60)	H.264/MPEG4	24 Mbit/s
Panasonic	AF-100, AF-101[10]	Video	17.8 x 10 mm	Micro Four Thirds	1920 x 1080	12-60	AVCHD	21 Mbit/s
Panasonic	DMC-G3[3]	Photo	17.3 x 13 mm	Micro Four Thirds	1920 x 1080	60 (60, 30)	AVCHD	?
Panasonic	DMC-GF2[3]	Photo	17.3 x 13 mm	Micro Four Thirds	1920 x 1080	60 (60, 30)	AVCHD	?
Panasonic	DMC-GF3[3]	Photo	17.3 x 13 mm	Micro Four Thirds	1920 x 1080	60 (60, 30)	AVCHD	?

Brand	Camera	Model form	Sensor size	Lens Mount	Maximum video resolution	Frame rate(s⁻¹)	Codec	Maximum bitrate
Panasonic	DMC-GH1[3]	Photo	18.89 x 14.48 mm	Micro Four Thirds	1920 x 1080	30	AVCHD	?
Panasonic	DMC-GH2[3]	Photo	18.89 x 14.48 mm	Micro Four Thirds	1920 x 1080	24, 60 (30)	AVCHD	22 Mbit/s
Panasonic	AJ-HPX3700[11]	Video	2/3" CCD x 3	2/3 inch bayonet mount[12]	1920 x 1080	24, 1-60	H.264, AVC-Intra 100	?
Panasonic	AJ-HPX2000[13]	Video	2/3" CCD x 3	2/3 inch bayonet mount	1920 x 1080	60 (interlaced)	DVCPRO HD	137 Mbit/s
Panasonic	AJ-HPX3100GJ[14]	Video	2/3" CCD x 3	2/3 inch bayonet mount	1920 x 1080	30 (60)	AVC-Intra 100, DVCPRO HD/	68 Mbit/s
Panavision	GENESIS[15]	Video	24.89 x 16.86mm	?	1920 x 1080	30 (1-60)	?	?
Panavision	HD900[16]	Video	2/3" CCD	Panavision HD mount	1920 x 1080	30 (24)	HDCAM	?
Pentax	K-01[17]	Photo	23.4 x 15.6 mm	Pentax K	1920 x 1080	30p, 25p	M-JPEG	95 Mbit/s
Pentax	K-30[18]	Photo	23.7 x 15.7 mm	Pentax K	1920 x 1080	30p (25p, 24p)	H264	?
Pentax	K-5[19]	Photo	23.4 x 15.6 mm	Pentax K	1920 x 1080	30p, 25p	M-JPEG	95 Mbit/s
P+S Technik	PS-CAM x35[20]	Video	21.1 x 11.9 mm	PS-IMS	1920 x 1080	60p, (24-450p)	CineForm RAW	?

Brand	Camera	Model form	Sensor size	Lens Mount	Maximum video resolution	Frame rate(s⁻¹)	Codec	Maximum bitrate
P+S Technik	SI-2K[21]	Video	10.24 x 5.76 mm	PS-IMS	2048 x 1152	24p (1080p12-25), 24p (1080p12-85)	CineForm RAW	?
P+S Technik	WEISSCAM HS-1[22]	Video	15 x 12 mm	Arri PL, Panavision, Nikon, Canon EF, BNC-R	1280 x 1024	25p (1024p24-650), 25p (576p24-1150)	CineForm RAW	?
P+S Technik	WEISSCAM HS-2 MKII[23]	Video	22.18 x 22.18 mm	PS-IMS	1980 x 1080	25p (1080p24-2000)	CineForm RAW	?
RED	Epic Dragon[5]	Video	30.7 x 15.8 mm	PL, EF, F-mount	6144 x 3160 (2k)	?	REDCODE	?
RED	Epic Mysterium-X[5]	Video	27.7 x 14.6 mm	PL, EF, F-mount	5120 x 2700 (2K)	1-120 (300)	REDCODE	?
RED	One[5]	Video	24.4 x 13.7 mm	PL, EF, F-mount	4096 x 2304 (2K)	1-30 (120)	REDCODE	?
RED	One Mysterium-X[5]	Video	24.2 x 12.5 mm	PL, EF, F-mount	4480 x 2304 (3K)	1-30 (120)	REDCODE	?
RED	Scarlet	Video	27.7 x 14.6 mm	PL, EF, F-mount	5120 x 2700 (1K)	1-12 (1-120)	REDCODE	440 Mbit/s
Samsung	NX20	Photo	23.5 x 15.7 mm	Samsung NX	1920 x 1080	30	H.264	?
Sony	DSLR-A560[3]	Photo	23.5 x 15.6 mm	Sony A-mount	1920 x 1080	60, 29.97 (30)	MPEG4	?

Brand	Camera	Model form	Sensor size	Lens Mount	Maximum video resolution	Frame rate(s⁻¹)	Codec	Maximum bitrate
Sony	DLSR-A580[3]	Photo	23.5 x 15.6 mm	Sony A-mount	1920 x 1080	60, 29.97 (30)	MPEG4	?
Sony	F35[24]	Video	21.6 x 13.3 mm	Arr. PL	1920 x 1080	1-60	?	?
Sony	NEX-5[3]	Photo	23.4 x 15.6 mm	E-mount	1920 x 1080	60 (30)	AVCHD	?
Sony	NEX-5N[3]	Photo	23.4 x 15.6 mm	E-mount	1920 x 1080	60 (30)	AVCHD	?
Sony	NEX-7[3]	Photo	23.4 x 15.6 mm	E-mount	1920 x 1080	60 (30)	MPEG4	?
Sony	NEX-FS100[25]	Video	21.6 x 13.3 mm	E-mount	1920 x 1080	1, 2, 4, 8, 15, 30, 60	MPEG4 AVCHD	28 Mbit/s
Sony	NEX-VG10[26]	Video	23.4 x 15.6 mm	E-mount	1920 x 1080	60i, 30	AVCHD	24 Mbit/s
Sony	NEX-VG20[27]	Video	23.4 x 15.6 mm	E-mount	1920 x 1080	60, 30, 24	AVCHD 2.0	24 Mbit/s
Sony	NEX-VG30	Video	23.4 x 15.6 mm	E-mount	1920 x 1080	60, 30, 24	AVCHD 2.0	24 Mbit/s
Sony	NEX-VG900[28]	Video with still capable with feature identical as Sony Alpha	35.8 x 23.9 mm (Full Frame)	A-mount	1920 x 1080	60, 24	AVCHD 2.0	28 Mbit/s

Brand	Camera	Model form	Sensor size	Lens Mount	Maximum video resolution	Frame rate(s⁻¹)	Codec	Maximum bitrate
		A99 (RAW, etc)						
Sony	PMW-F3K, PMW-F3L[29]	Video	21.6 x 13.3 mm	E-mount, L-mount	1920 x 1080	1, 2, 4, 8, 15, 30, 60	MPEG2	35 Mbit/s
Sony	SLT-A33[3]	Photo	23.5 x 15.6 mm	Sony A-mount	1920 x 1080	60, 29.97 (30)	MPEG4	?
Sony	SLT-A35[3]	Photo	23.5 x 15.6 mm	Sony A-mount	1920 x 1080	60, 29.97 (30)	MPEG4	?
Sony	SLT-A37[3]	Photo	23.5 x 15.6 mm	Sony A-mount	1920 x 1080	60, 29.97 (30)	AVCHD	?
Sony	SLT-A55[3]	Photo	23.5 x 15.6 mm	Sony A-mount	1920 x 1080	60, 29.97 (30)	MPEG4	?
Sony	SLT-A57[3]	Photo	23.5 x 15.6 mm	Sony A-mount	1920 x 1080	60, 29.97 (30) (NTSC countries) 50, 25 (PAL countries)	AVCHD/MPEG4	?
Sony	SLT-A65[3]	Photo	23.5 x 15.6 mm	Sony A-mount	1920 x 1080	60, 29.97 (30)	MPEG4	?
Sony	SLT-A77[3]	Photo	23.5 x 15.6 mm	Sony A-mount	1920 x 1080	60, 29.97 (30) (NTSC countries) 50, 25 (PAL	AVCHD	?

Brand	Camera	Model form	Sensor size	Lens Mount	Maximum video resolution	Frame rate(s⁻¹) (countries)	Codec	Maximum bitrate
Sony	SLT-A99[3]	Photo	35.8 x 23.8 mm	Sony A-mount	1920 x 1080	60, 29.97 (30)	AVCHD	?
Vision Research	Phantom 65[30]	Video	52.1 x 30.5 mm	Arri PL (standard), Nikon F / Mamiya 645 (optional)	4096 x 2440	141, (1080p320)	Cine RAW	2341 Mbit/s
Vision Research	Phantom Flex[31]	Video	52.1 x 30.5 mm	Arri PL (standard), Nikon F / Mamiya 645 (optional)	2560 x 1600	1455 (1080p2570)	Cine RAW	3181 Mbit/s

Figure 28-Sensor Size Listing (Courtesy of Wikipedia Commons)

THE NUTS & BOLTS OF INDIE FILM PRODUCTION

Producers need to bring a director of photography (cinematographer) on as early as possible to discuss the type of camera and lenses that are needed for production. You can start by searching out local cinematographers or videographers in your local area. You can also talk with local colleges that have film or video classes to search for one. Sit down with them and discuss the type of movie, your distribution plans, and most of all, the budget that you have available for film equipment.

You can also Google for the latest HD cameras being used for shooting film. You'll soon see that new cameras are hitting the market about every six months or so. Look for a camera that will have a work flow that is manageable. On our first feature, the Sony F900 camera we were using recorded on very large tapes. We had to rent a special setup to even view the dailies. Today, many of the cameras out will record on small digital media cards or to portable drives. The data can flow straight from this media directly into a laptop in order to review dailies while on the set. Look for this type of work flow.

Having budgeted for equipment on my last two films, I can tell you that even with low budget filmmaking, if you're not borrowing film equipment from a local college (which will have limited and out dated equipment anyway) figure to spend at least $10K to $20K for equipment rentals or purchase for the minimal equipment. If you're thinking long term (more than one film), you may want to consider purchasing a used camera, lenses, good tripod head, tripod, and lighting on eBay. Sometimes, filmmakers can find good deals. Try to find a deal where the seller transfers the warranty to you.

Look for cameras that don't use motors, such as earlier versions that recorded to tape. The drum and motors have a limited life. They also have inherent noise (all motors do), and if you record audio with the camera, the audio tracks will be noisy. Cameras with motors also deplete your battery very quickly. Look for cameras that are motorless and record to digital media. They don't have the noise issues and will run much longer on the battery. Remember, when you're on the set, your camera relies on battery power, so make sure when you find a camera to get a of couple spare batteries and chargers. So are we beginning to narrow down the type of camera that will meet an indie filmmaker's requirements? Let's review some of the basic requirements we know that we need.

- Camera records minimum 1920x1080 (or greater)
- Camera has large enough sensor that allows use of large format quality lenses. This allows the use of large glass such as cinema lenses
- Camera has capability for interchanging lenses. Make sure that the brand has adapters available on the market to allow adapting to different styles of mounts such as PL. You'll need this to get that depth of field that you need.
- Camera has XLR inputs for audio. Recording audio on the camera provides a backup sync method for editing.
- Records to inexpensive digital media. Be careful because some media cards that some cameras use may be proprietary type and expensive (like P2 cards). Find ones that uses inexpensive media cards.
- Camera has multiple frame rates (most do) that allows for under and over cranking
- Does white balancing (WB) (some also do black balancing). Basically, you can automatically white balance the image.
- Recording Format- most editing platforms can handle a variety of formats. Talk with your editor (if you have one) to discuss getting the best data format for the film. Some cameras even allow recording in different data formats.

Extra Camera Items

When looking at cameras, here are some extra items that help take filmmaking to a higher level.

Lenses

Great lenses will add so much to your film. They are worth

begging, borrowing and well…renting. Over the hundred years or so of movies, there have been some incredible pieces of glass made for cinema. Ten years ago, indie filmmakers could only dream of using these lenses in their arsenal of filmmaking. Today, some of these older lenses manage to pop up occasionally with a fairly decent price tag. We were able to find a company in Ohio (Visual Products) that refurbishes cinema lenses and did a beautiful job of reconditioning an Angeneux 20-120mm Cinema Zoom lens for us at a reasonable cost. When looking for cinema lenses that will add to that look for your film and that are just amazing pieces of glass, look for Angeneux, Zeiss, Cooke, Cannon, Red, and Lomo (Russian lens). If you can't afford to purchase one (they run from several thousand to around $30K) there are plenty of film equipment rental places.

Depending on your DP or camera person, they may prefer to use prime lenses. Prime lenses have a single focal point (i.e., 15mm, 28mm, 50mm, 100mm) where the lens is best focused. Some DPs prefer a set of primes that range from lenses for close-ups to master shots of a location. These lenses vary in costs and quality like any other products. For an indie filmmaker, I'd suggest finding the camera first that meets requirements (see above) and then accruing a set of Nikon or Cannon primes that cover the range for shooting close-ups, medium shots, wide shots, etc. For our film, we used the Angeneux for almost everything because its range was from 20mm to 120mm. However, it can't focus on anything closer than around 3½ feet, so we had additional Nikon prime lenses available for tight shots such as car interior shots.

Try to find lenses that are fast, and what I mean by that is that they have a very low F-stop such as 1.2, 1.4 or 1.8. The lower the F-stop, the less light needed for the lens to capture the image. Indie filmmakers may want to shop around for older Lomo (Russian) cinema lenses in PL mount. Typically, you can pick them up for around $ 450 to $ 800 a lens. Zeiss makes some of the top of the line prime cinema lenses, but they are extremely pricey. If you plan on using a focus puller on the lenses, make sure that the lenses come with a focus gear and that the gear teeth count (like 32) matches your focus puller gear. Modified older lenses are popular with filmmakers today. There are several companies that specialize in modding older lenses by "declicking (removing the stops in the F-Stop ring so it's smooth) and adding focus gears (Duclos Brothers is one that comes to mind).

On our film, we used a Nikon 50mm F1.4 prime lens for shooting at night and we almost didn't need to light the scene (I said almost). Standard telephoto or camera zoom lenses (non-cinema lenses) do not work very well for shooting films. If you zoom, the image will bloom or expand as you do. Cinema lenses are designed mechanically so that they do not bloom the image up when you zoom in. That's why they are more expensive than regular camera zoom lenses. So stay with using zoom lenses made for film cameras or go with an extensive set of primes or do a combination of both in your filmmaking arsenal.

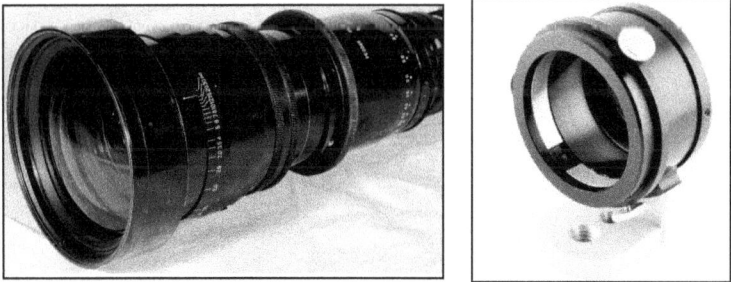

*Figure 29-**Lomo 20-120mm Cinema Lens & Lomo Adapter***

*Figure 30-**PL to 4/3 Lens Adapter***

Focus Follow

A **focus follow** is an attachment (basically a gear) that aligns with a gear ring around the lens allowing for lens focusing by a person other than the camera operator. Since the person operating the camera may have their hands full with framing the subject while they are moving on the set, it is extremely helpful to have another person pulling the focus (via the focus follow) to keep the scene in focus. If your film is destined for the big screen, a word of caution…make sure your shots are in focus. If shots aren't clear, you may not be able to tell from viewing on the camera's viewfinder or even that laptop that you view dailies on. It will, however, become very obvious on the big screen, very obvious. Be smart and view dailies on the biggest screen you can find (at least a five foot screen) so that if you aren't getting shots in focus you know early enough to do something about it. Finding out in post is too late. And finding out at the theater can be embarrassing. Gee, how do I know that?

Mattebox

A **mattebox** is a shade box that attaches to the end of a lens to block the sun or other light source in order to prevent glare and lens flare. It also holds glass or plastic filters in place in front of the lens. They come in a variety of sizes and brands with some being fixed and others that swing out to allow you to change lenses. Most come with flaps or barn-doors that can be adjusted to block additional glare. It is not a critical piece of production hardware but does come in useful on sunny days.

Lens Cleaning Kit

If you don't receive one of these with the camera, lens cleaning kits can be bought at most camera stores. Always have a kit available on the set. However, the DP (if also running the camera), the camera person, or the camera assistant should be the only ones touching the camera.

You don't want any other crew members handling or cleaning the camera lens...bad idea. Improper handling of the lens could scratch it permanently.

Tripods and Heads

Here's another area that filmmakers need to pay attention to. When we began acquiring film equipment, we bought several tripods and heads. We quickly found that with cheaper tripods and heads it was hard to get clean and smooth panning shots. If you are serious about films, you MUST borrow, rent, or acquire a good head and tripod. We finally settled on a top-of-the-line Miller head. Look for fluid tripod heads that are built for larger cinema cameras and have level indicators. They're built solid and have ultra smooth movement. Higher quality tripod heads will have a 100mm or 150mm bowl on the bottom of the tripod head. Make sure that when you look for a tripod, that the bowl size of the tripod matches the bowl size of the tripod head. Remember, that once you capture the audience in your film, you don't want a jerky camera movement yanking them out of the experience.

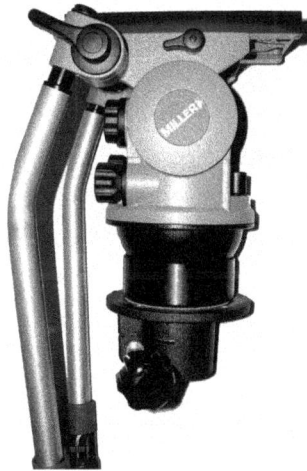

*Figure 31-**Miller Fluid Tripod Head***

Baby Tripod

Baby tripods are very short tripods that are used for shots near the floor or when shooting upwards. Something low, like a pillow or bean bag can be used as a substitute. Our DP on our last film used a bat pillow (yes an ugly yellow pillow with a bat insignia on it) for low floor shots.

Spreader and Portable Tripod Dolly

A spreader is just that, it spreads apart your tripod at the bottom and secures it into position. Some spreaders have wheels to allow moving the tripod around, others will have pointed feet for exterior use. Most collapse when you are ready to move the tripod. A portable tripod dolly is a base that the tripod sits on that allows it to be mobile. My brother, Dan, who works at a plastics manufacturing plant, made one by hand (see Appendix D to make your own). He basically cut a tri-base shape and added wheels that rotate 360 degrees. Have a small pedal brake for locking into position. We attached a spreader to the top to lock the tripod legs into place. It worked like a charm.

Rails

Rails are circular metal or aluminum rods that have metal plates holding them together that allow the mounting of cameras, lenses, focus follower and other accessories into one solid unit. It's like a base to build your ideal camera. If you plan on using large cinema lenses (which can weigh as much as 18lbs) this will put a lot of pressure on the digital camera lens mount. The rail system provides support for the lens and camera. It is also what the focus follower and matte box are mounted to. There are also shoulder rigs that connect to the rail system to make it more shoulder friendly. The rail system mounts directly to the tripod head via a quick-disconnect plate.

Dollies

A **dolly** is a rail system with two tracks that can be straight or circular where a vehicle is pushed or pulled along the track. The track should be absolutely free of any bumps or unevenness. A good track system is made of steel and is leveled with wooden wedges. Indie filmmakers can substitute a cheaper version or make one that is composed of PVC pipe. Small wheels angle-mounted to the bottom of the dolly cart wrap around the PVC tubing and keep the dolly cart from sliding off the rails. There are plenty of homemade designs available on the web. Be sure to make the dolly cart big enough and solid enough to support the camera, tripod, and the cameraman. It takes practice to start off the dolly evenly and to get a smooth dolly across the tracks.

There's nothing as beautiful as a well orchestrated dolly or tracking shot in a film. Used sparingly, they can add just that right touch to a scene. In our last film when our killer is stalking a victim and he's standing at the end of a hallway silhouetted by the light, pulling backwards down the hallway with a dolly shot was a natural fit. One of the most famous dolly shots is in the Alfred Hitchcock film *Vertigo*. The camera moves in at the same time that the cameraman pulls the zoom and the **vertigo shot** was born, also called the **dolly zoom** shot. The background of the actor appears to enlarge behind the actor. If you want to find out how good your DP is, ask him to do a vertigo shot. A panning shot is just that, it pans across, but a dolly shot can move towards the subject or away from the subject in a straightforward action or can track with the subject. This is called a **tracking shot**.

Figure 32-Dolly and Tracks on set of The Darkening

Jib Arms and Cranes

You've seen those dramatic scenes where we start high up in the shot and then gracefully swoop down to meet our main character as they enter the scene. Starting high up is the key. You have two choices. If you have considerable budget, you can rent a crane that will lift your camera higher than you've ever wanted to. If you have less budget, like most of us, you can rent or buy something smaller called a **jib arm**. Jib arms are mounted on sturdy tripods and it acts like a fulcrum or see-saw. A weight on one end balances your camera which sits on the other end. By pulling the weighted end down, it lifts the camera into the air. There are also extra gadgets you can buy or rent that allows a more automated control of your camera once it's in the air. You can buy controls for the axis movement or even the control of the iris and focus. There are lots of these remote control devices for the digital camera. Keep in mind that if you mount a manual lens (non-electronic control) and mount it on an electronic film camera, you will not be able to control the focus or zoom features of your lens with the camera. The camera must be able to communicate with your lens or you must make changes to the lens manually. This is one disadvantage of manual lenses used with the latest digital film cameras. However, a GOOD cameraman can get that jib shot without all that fuss. They know how to set the focus to get the shot. I've seen it done.

Be aware that there are a lot of useful products for digital film cameras if you have the funds and the time to spend on setting them up correctly. Cranes can easily handle any camera you throw at it but not so when working with jib arms. Most are built for light video cameras and may not support a heavier camera or heavy lens. Know the weight of your camera when it is fully loaded and then you can determine which jib arm will support it. Also make sure that when using jib arm setups that you make sure to secure the tripod carefully using sandbags. Also assign a couple of crew members to the tripod to ensure it remains stable during shooting.

Batteries and Chargers

As we discussed earlier, a shooting day can be very long and could be as long as twelve hours. Even the best heavy duty battery for digital cameras is most likely not going to make it that long. I've seen heavy duty camera batteries last up to eight hours. You don't want to get caught with a dead battery on the set so make sure to bring a of couple backup batteries. Most modern batteries don't need to be completely discharged to be recharged due to built in memory and can be thrown back into the charger without completely depleting it. ALWAYS make sure that all of the batteries being used for production hit the charger every night for a fresh charging. There are multiple chargers on the market that can handle several batteries at once. Assign someone on the crew the task of making sure all batteries are charged every night and thrown back into the charger when run down. A good emergency practice is to always have the AC adapter plug-in for the digital camera handy so if for some unknown reason all the batteries go dead, you can always resort to an AC adapter. Just make sure that AC power is available.

White Card for White Balancing

A white card (roughly 2ft x 2ft) for white balancing on the set is mandatory for digital filmmaking. Most digital film cameras will have a White Balance (WB) function. This allows the camera to be calibrated to white, which in effect calibrates the other colors automatically. The camera operator will have a crew member hold up the white card where the scene is being blocked, focus the camera on the white card and hit the WB function button on the camera. We had a scene on our last film that was shot during sunset. During sunset, natural light from the sun can have an orange hue associated with it. We forgot to white balance the shot and the actors' faces had an orange tone. This creates a problem for the editor in post. Now they have the task of trying to remove the orange from the scene when it could have been solved by white balancing on the set. Always white balance when in doubt.

Sound Slate (Clapper)

Everybody knows what this is. It's the black and white sound slate that is clapped in front of the camera that has the scene and take number on it. The arm swings down and gives the editor a mark to sync the picture and sound to. It's simple but works. However, if not done properly, it can create a lot of problems in post (editing). The slate must be held in front of the camera at the focus point of the camera. In other words, it MUST be in focus! If it isn't in focus, the editor cannot read what scene or take number it is. If you have six takes and none of the slates were in focus, you have a lot more work than you need in order to sync things up. This is why members of the crew must be trained on how to properly slate a shot. A backup is to leave the camera audio on (one channel is fine). This attaches the audio to the video files. In post, this audio file can be used as a backup sync method. Cheaper sound slates section off info for the film into director, DP, and producer. It also includes an area to chalk-in the scene number and take number. There are also electronic versions of the sound slate available on the market.

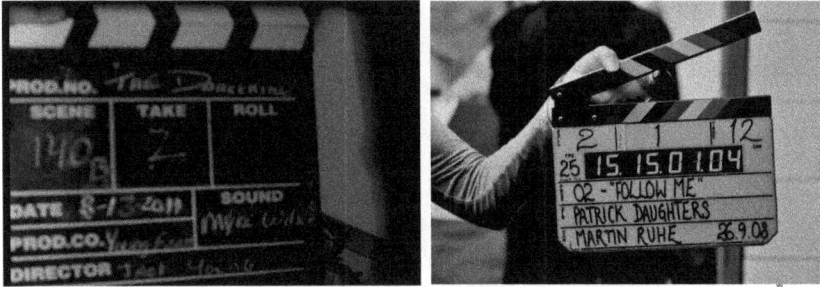

Figure 33-Wooden/Slate Clapper (Wikimedia Commons)
Electronic Version (Wikimedia Commons)

Field Sound Recorder

Sound is half the battle for filmmakers. Sure your DP has a plan to capture your film cinematically, but find a good sound engineer for the set who will capture the best audio you can get. If you don't, your editor will not be happy. Seems we do a lot to try to keep our editor happy. We should. He's the guy that's going to make your film look and sound great. So what do you need to capture some good if not great sound on the set?

Field recorders come large or small, tape or digital. They require good microphones, so the type of microphone will somewhat drive the recorder you choose. Most high quality microphones use XLR type connections so this is a consideration when choosing a recorder. It should have XLR inputs. It should also have adjustments for the inputs and have indicators that tell you when you are overdriving and clipping your audio. Usually an indicator for audio will tell you when are driving the amplifiers in a safe region. This is indicated usually when your signals are within a green area of an indicator. When driving the signal in the yellow area, this indicates that you are going into distortion. Red indicates that not only are you distorting the signal but overdriving and most likely clipping off the top portions of your audio signals. Simply put, record your audio in the mid range of your recorder so that you don't get distortion or damage your audio beyond repair.

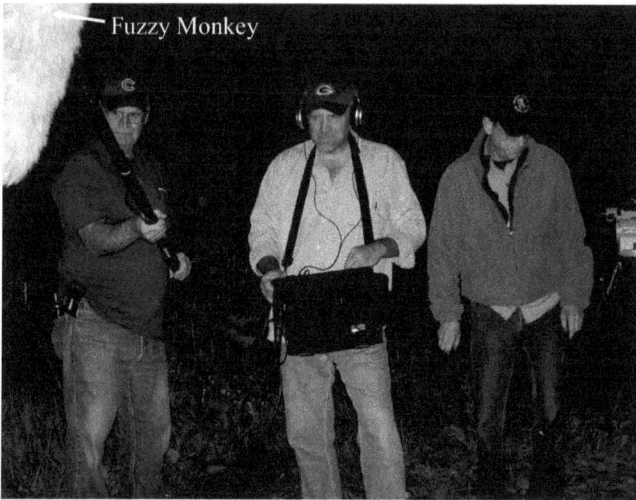

*Figure 34-**Bill, Dan, with Tom Young on the Set Recording Audio***

*Figure 35-**Brenda and Dan Young Recording Club Audio***

Sound recorders record in a variety of formats WAV, FLAC, MP2, and MP3 formats. The WAV format usually works well for film. They usually record to media cards or have an external interface for streaming the data out. Recorders provide sampling rates that vary from recorder to recorder and can vary between 32kHz to 192kHz. Typically, most select a 48Khz sampling rate which is more than fine for film. Bit depth rates also are typically 16 or 24 bit. Choose 24 bit for higher quality. Recorders should have gain controls, headphone jacks, and have an easily accessible rechargeable battery. For our film, we chose the Sound Devices 702. It's a little pricier but provides excellent quality for film and has a great workflow. Filmmakers should shop around and consider borrowing, renting, or purchasing a good recorder for their film production.

*Figure 36-**Sound Devices 702 Field Recorder***

What's nice about digital recorders like the one above is that they don't use motors to drive tape transports (like older DAT recorders) which, as we know, generates noise and consumes battery power. Recorders like the 702 will run forever on a heavy duty fully charged battery. Look for a recorder that has XLR inputs, does 48Khz, and 24 bit sampling, gives you WAV files, allows gain adjustments, tells you when you're overdriving the amps, and has an easy work flow (i.e., from media card to editing workstation).

A recorder is no good without some good microphones. There are numerous microphones on the market that filmmakers can use on the set (interior and exterior) in all price ranges that include among a few:

- Audio-Technica
- Azden
- Sennheiser

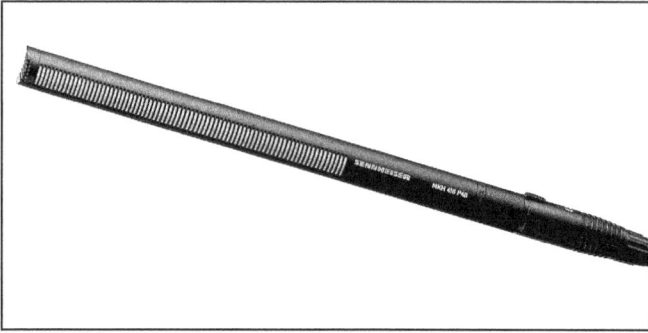

*Figure 37-***Sennheiser MKH 418 P48 Shotgun Microphone**

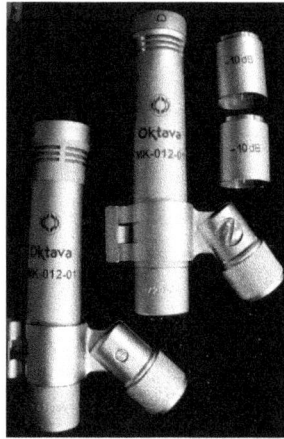

*Figure 38-***Russian Made Oktava MK-012 Microphones (pair)**

They can vary from a couple hundred for an Azden or Audio-Technica microphone to around $1,500 for the Sennheiser MKH-418. Be careful buying older Sennheiser shotgun microphones that require additional external power supplies. We initially purchased a used Sennheiser MKH 816 P48U that was used on a Clint Eastwood action film. It was a beautiful mic but required an external power supply for its 48Volts supply. We eventually sold the microphone and went to a smaller Sennheiser (MKH 418) that didn't require the external power supply. Microphones like the Sennheiser 418 can be used for interiors and exteriors. Short boom microphones work great for interiors and exteriors. Try to find enough funds in your budget to either rent a top end microphone such as the Sennheiser 418. You'll appreciate the sound of a better mic on the set. Make sure the microphone has the type of interface that matches the requirements of your field recorder (i.e., XLR).

The Azdec microphone turned out to be a fair microphone, but if the batteries (enclosed in the body) die, without warning, you lose sound without being aware. Make sure that you acquire a microphone that gets its power from the field recorder rather than depending upon a couple of AA batteries.

Another microphone that is popular among indie filmmakers is the Russian made Oktava microphone. The Oktava is a cardioid, omni, hypercardioid microphone all rolled into one. The kit has a variety of capsules that can be screwed onto the end of the microphone to make it change the way it gathers sound. We included a set of these in our film production arsenal and they deliver very good sound for the price. Most of the time, however, we stayed with the Sennheiser microphones. They deliver.

Naturally, if you are using a boom microphone, you'll need a boom pole. You can find all kinds of discussions on the web just about boom poles. They can also vary in price from $39 to hundreds of dollars. Buy a boom pole that is sturdy and rubber coated because boom poles are sensitive to movement by the boom operator. With a boom pole, you'll also need a microphone housing for the boom microphone. Boom mounts for microphones are basically a suspension mount that isolates the microphone to reduce induced noise. Make sure that you get the right boom pole for the mount when pairing up the pole and your microphone mount.

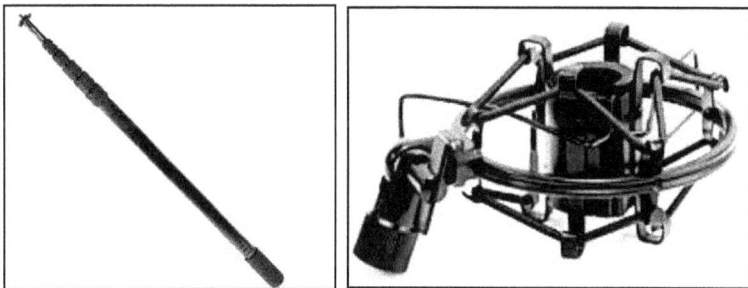

*Figure 39-**Microphone Boom Pole and Boom Microphone Mount***

*Figure 40-**Blimp for Microphone***

You'll need one last piece of sound equipment, besides a good set of headphones. If you are shooting exterior shots, most likely you will encounter wind from time to time. Wind can play havoc on microphones. A **blimp** is a cover for the microphone that blocks the wind but at the same time allows the sound to get to the microphone. The microphone, centered inside the blimp, is protected from wind by the outer layer and foam in the interior. A handle is mounted to the bottom of the blimp that allows it to attach to the boom pole. A shaggy cover (we call a "fuzzy monkey") can also be wrapped around the exterior of the blimp for added protection from the wind. And believe me, it works extremely well. We did a lot of exterior shooting on our last film and it worked perfectly.

Lighting

Although I've heard of films being shot with nothing but natural lighting, good lighting on the set will give you control of every shot. The director of photography or cinematographer will use the lighting to set the look of the film. If it's film noir, the lighting will create that shadowy film noir look. For most indie filmmakers, the best choice (if it isn't film noir) is to light the set for the best image possible. A different film look can be created in post (editing). Just get the best image possible on the set. There are a variety of light sources that can be used for film. Some of the most popular are practical lighting, Fresnel's, LEDS, fluorescent, and HMIs.

Practical Lighting

Practical lighting utilizes part of the scene for lighting such as lamps, street lights, etc. During the filming of our last movie we had a dilemma. The area where we were staging a murder scene on a deserted country road was pitch-black. It would be very obvious if we threw up a light to light the scene. We had a couple of LED lights that looked like work lights. We staged them to look like the police were using them to light the crime scene. We shot the scene with the lights in the frame as if they belonged there and at the same time got our scene lit. As long as it looks natural, find creative ways to incorporate the lighting into your shots.

Fresnel Lighting

This is the most popular type of film lighting among indie filmmakers and the most affordable. Get yourself a 150 watt, a 350 and a of couple 650s you're ready to go. However, be aware that Fresnels use tungsten bulbs and can get somewhat hot. When you strike the set, you'll need to give them some time to cool down. They are still a great bang for the buck. They come with barn-doors for more control of the light and with most, the light bulb can be moved forward or backward with a knob that controls the width of the stream of light. A **scrim** (a wire screen) can also be placed in front of the lens to reduce the light's intensity.

*Figure 41-**Arri Fresnel Light***

A note of caution when handling Fresnel bulbs. Don't handle the bulbs with your bare hands. You can leave oil residue on them and ruin the bulb. Always use a cloth glove or tissue. And ALWAYS have at least a couple of spare bulbs on hand for your lights.

Soft Box Lighting Lit

Arri packages a soft box lighting kit that works great for softening the light. A soft box light kit can also be bought separately from a variety of vendors and is basically a wire box with a white shroud that fits around your light. See the photo in the section on dollies. It's at the top right of the photo.

Figure 42-Soft Box Light

LED Lighting

LED lighting is a lot cooler than tungsten lighting such a Fresnels. We used a couple of small LED lights on our last film and did note that you have to be careful because in some cases we saw some strobing effects. The prices are starting to come down on these.

Fluorescent Lighting

The Kino Flo fluorescents are very popular among filmmakers.

They are a little pricey for indie filmmakers but do run cooler than the fresnels. We used a small hand held fluorescent light for the car interiors. It put out about the perfect level of light for that purpose.

HMI Lighting

Some of the most expensive lights out there are the HMI lighting. HMI lighting uses a ballast system, generates more light than other methods, and runs cooler than tungsten lights (Fresnels).

1,000 to 10,000 Watt Lighting

Sometimes you'll need to bring in the bad boys. These lights can generate more than 10,000 watts of light when needed. Using several of these lights, you can recreate daylight if you have to. Now, most of the time you may not need it, but there may be an occasion where lights below 1,000 watts just don't cut it. There are companies who specialize in lighting for film like "Lights On" who can rent you what you need, even the bad boys. You can also find these for sale occasionally at very low prices. I picked up an old 1,000 watt built-like-a-tank Mole Richardson for a couple of hundred dollars from a film equipment warehouse and found myself in real need of it in our last film. We had a scene on a bridge late at night and believe me it was pure black out where we were shooting. It was essential that we had the 1000 watt light for that scene. You should have at least one of these available for night time shoots or know where you can get one. Stands for older and larger lights are hard to find.

Gels

Gels can be used for artistic reasons or for color correction reasons. I've seen them used both ways on sets. On our short film *Manimals* (1997) we used gels in a scene to add colors to the background to make it look more sci-fi. The scene involved a mad scientist and his assistant. Most of the time I've seen it used on Fresnels for color correction. The Color Temperature Blue (CTB) gel was used for indoor lighting for our last films. The Color Temperature Orange (CTO) gel is used for color correcting exterior lighting. The gels correct the color temperature of a light to more closely match the white balance of a digital imager. Tungsten lights (Fresnels) typically have a color temperature in the range of 3,200 kelvins to 5,700 kelvins. The CTB corrects the color temperature to around 5,400 kelvins (nominal daylight). CTO corrects a "daylight" temperature to 3,200 kelvins. Most lighting kits include a set of gels. If not, these can be purchased from a camera shop or online.

Portable Generators

If you don't have exterior nighttime or isolated location shooting in your film, you probably won't require a generator. If you do, you can rent or borrow a generator to fit your needs. If you're lighting up a huge area with some big lights (2K or 10K watt) make sure you get a generator that will support it. Also note that generators are very loud and will impact your sound recording on that set. For our last film, we lit for the master shots of the scene with the big light and had the generator running. For close-ups in that location where we had dialogue, we shut down the generator and used LED lights that ran off AC adapters that plugged into the cigarette lighter.

Electrical

On the set, you will be tapping into the location's electrical service and most likely you will be hooking up quite a few lights and miscellaneous equipment. At some locations this raised some eyebrows so I gave the location owner a twenty dollar bill to cover their electric bill. But you'll need to bring enough heavy duty extension cords to get everything wired. Some film companies that use 220 VAC lighting (like HMI lighting) will have an actual **gaffer**, chief lighting electrician, on the set that will bring not only the cabling but also breakout boxes that the equipment connects to. They are savvy enough to get you electrical resources in any situation. If you don't have someone skilled in electricity, then make sure your equipment all runs on 110 VAC. Even with 110 VAC, make sure you buy heavy duty extension cords and heavy duty power strips or breakout boxes. In areas where the electrical cable is stretched across open areas, make sure that you secure the cable down with a gaffer tape so that nobody trips over the cabling.

Equipment Truck

Consider borrowing or renting a van or truck, otherwise you will be stuck filling several cars and vans with equipment. We rented a long cargo van for our last film and it worked fine. If you have to rent, shop around for a bargain.

Miscellaneous Equipment

The following is a list of things that you may want to throw into your filmmaking toolbox or budget. At some point during production, you will say "I wish we had a_____(fill in the blank).

External HD Monitor

Most digital film cameras will have a LCD viewer on the camera. However, most are very small and are really only good for getting a feel for the framing and possible color/lighting issues. If you plan on shooting a film for theatrical release, you really should consider adding an external monitor to your camera rig. It can either be mounted on the camera (like a 9 inch HD) or cabled to another location to a larger HD monitor. The main purpose is to ensure that scenes are in focus. It is difficult to tell on a small LCD monitor whether you have pulled focus ALL THE WAY. If you have not pulled focus correctly, it becomes very obvious on the theater screen. This should also be checked during dailies as well on a big screen.

Gaffers Tape

Okay, this is the fix all on the set product. It tapes up loose cables or wires, fixes things that break or come loose. It's like duct tape for filmmakers but without the residue that duct tape leaves.

Silicon Lubricant Spray/Clean Rags

If you plan on using dolly tracks (metal or plastic) pickup some silicon spray. A little on the tracks will make it glide like glass. If you are using these tracks on carpeted areas, make sure to wipe access away with rags so the fluid doesn't drip on the carpets and ruin them.

Quarter, Half and Full Apple Crates

These come in extremely handy when things need a little lift up in the air. You can pick these up in different heights. They're especially handy when shooting exteriors and there are uneven surface.

Sun/Wind Screen

You can rent these or make your own. It's basically a tarp stretched across a frame that is used for exterior shots. It blocks the wind and sun and helps control the outdoor environment. They come in a variety of sizes but usually are around 8'x8'. Using PVC pipe, some cheap tarp (neutral color), and some rope, you can make your own. See Appendix G for how to make one.

*Figure 43-**Sun/Wind Screen***

Sandbags

Much of the equipment on a film set requires some form of stand such as C-Stands, light stands, tripods, etc., which have a high center of balance and are prone to being knocked over or blown over by winds. Sand bags are a simple way of securing stands and tripods on the set. Most of the equipment on the set is expensive to replace and may be rented, so take measures to ensure that tripods with expensive cameras and lighting don't fall over for any reason by securing their legs with sandbags. They come in the shape of small saddle bags and fold over the legs. Plan on having a least a dozen or more available on the set.

Sound Blankets

These have multi-purposes on the set and look like quilts or packing blankets. They can be used to block unwanted noise on the set, used on the floor under equipment to prevent scratching of floors at locations, or for around sensitive equipment in the equipment truck to prevent damage.

Chalk for Sound Slate

You'll need to remember to pack a box of standard white chalk for the sound slate (wooden clapper type with slate writing area) if that's the type you're using on the set.

Field Recorder Bag

Called a variety of things such as **broadcaster utility bag**, these bags are used to carry the sound recorder while recording. About the only requirement for these is that it fits comfortably (because you'll be carrying hours at a time), allows you to access the controls of the field recorder unit, and has access to the cables coming in from the microphones. Extra cavities or pockets for accessories such as backup microphones and batteries are nice to have.

*Figure 44-**Broadcaster Utility Bag***

Grip Gloves

These resemble golf gloves, and are usually made of stretch nylon. They help to protect the grip from burning their hands on hot lights and are also used by the book operator to reduce noise while handling the sound boom.

Portable 35mm Digital Still Camera

A portable 35mm digital still camera comes in handy for the continuity person. They will need photos of actors' clothes and makeup and props on the set to assist in tracking items that may create continuity problems.

Collapsible Circular Reflectors

These are used by grips on the set to change the lighting conditions around the actor. They are held by a grip or can be secured in a C-stand. They come in a variety of colors such as translucent, gold, silver, white, or black. Collapsible reflectors can expand up to over three feet in diameter and collapse for easy storage. Some have one color on one side and another on the back side. These come in handy when you need just a little kick of light on a person's face. They are also essential in reflecting natural light when using only existing light for a scene.

Grease Pen

The focus puller (if you have one) will need one of these to write their marks on the focus follow disk.

Clothespins or C47s

Clothespins or C47s (film technical term) are used to clip on gels to light barn-doors.

Wardrobe Rack

If you have an extensive wardrobe on the set, a wardrobe rack can help to organize your wardrobe and keep them nice and neat for each use.

Folding Tables and Chairs

If you have food catered you will want a place to lay out the food and chairs for your actors to relax in.

Smoke Machine/Lightning Machine

Okay, here are a couple of cool toys for filmmakers. Some filmmakers like to smoke up the set with a smoke machine. It is a pretty cool effect if done right. It creates a smoky haze on the set. This is great for horror, sci-fi, or dark films. It's an oil-based smoke machine and you can pick them up anywhere. Remember to fan out the smoke so it's even otherwise it'll look like the room is on fire.

Lightning machines are just that, they create convincing lighting effects using your existing lighting. We used one on our last film and they are effective when using the right lights and timing.

Laptops on the Set

If your workflow includes being able to dump data on a regular basis, you should make sure to include a laptop in your budget to have on the set. Later we'll talk more about workflow on the set. If your media card doesn't fit into the media slot on the laptop, you'll need a media reader for all of your video and audio media cards. Plan on having up to 300

Gbytes of data at a minimum if you are shooting with a 2K camera. If you are using a 4K camera, plan on assigning a crew member (Unless you have a DIT) a full time position of managing all of the data and having at least 3 or 10 terabytes available for storage on the set. Use USB 3.0 or Firewire portable terabyte drives for this.

On the Set Editing Suite

If you have an aggressive editor and want to get a jump on post production, your editor can be editing footage on a daily basis. This also helps identify shots that you've missed and need to pickup.

Food, Motels, and Gas

Okay, here's the rule. If you're making an indie film, you have to feed people. There's nothing scarier than a hungry actor. Look, you're making a low budget or maybe even a no-budget film, and most likely you are asking them to defer salaries until you can make a profit, so the very least you can do is feed them. I'm not asking that you put out a spread of lobster and prime rib, just an assortment of food that will keep them at bay. Just making the effort to feed them says a lot. We're not talking about throwing out a bag of Cheetos or chips either.

Recruit the help of companions or friends who have done this type of thing (feeding large groups of people) to help. It's also a good idea to solicit from the actors and crews what types of foods they prefer in order to develop menus. Knowing this, you can shop around for bargains prior to the shoot to gather the menu items. Try to have fresh fruits and vegetables available along with some bottled water.

On our last film, one of our actors knew a lot of the restaurant and fast food owners in the area and solicited food from them. For about half our shoot, we received free food (sandwiches, Italian dinners, fried chicken dinners, etc.) from local business owners. You can solicit the local food business owners in your local area for either free food or discounted prices in exchange for acknowledgement in the end credits of the film (the credits that read "special thanks to..."). However, in case you can't come up with free food, figure out a budget based on the size of your crew. Calculate a food budget based on putting together buffet style dinners.

Do not invite the actors and crew to restaurants and offer to pick up the check. This will blow your budget. Figure that you'll spend a couple thousand dollars for a two week shoot just to provide some basic dinners. With the help of the local community, you can bring the costs of feeding your cast and crew way down.

If you plan on shooting at a remote location (like an island or another state), you'll also need to plan on booking accommodations for the cast and crew. This can get expensive very quickly. On an indie film budget, you're not going to be able to afford five star hotels. On our first feature film, we ended up shooting at a remote location for an extended period of time. We found that renting large bungalows was more efficient and cheaper than renting rooms at a hotel. It also allowed the actors to get to know each other.

Another item that you need to consider in your budget is gas funds. Transportation for a film can consist of the equipment truck or van, actor transportation vehicles, or even recreational vehicles (RVs) used for actors and makeup (optional). Even at the minimum, you'll have to provide funds for the equipment truck for the length of the shoot. With the price of fuel on the rise, you have to calculate fuel costs into your budget. On most indie films that are shot local, most actors are comfortable with finding their own transportation to and from the set. However, on remote shoots where the actor may not have personal transportation, you'll need to add the costs associated with a vehicle to chauffer them around and its associated fuel costs.

Liability Insurance Costs

You must have liability insurance for shooting on locations. It's a must. The amount depends on the type of scene you are shooting (stunts, car chases, etc.) and how much damage or the type of injuries that could exist. If you're shooting a typical dramatic film that doesn't involve a lot of dangerous stunts, basic coverage of around $1,000,000 is fine. If you shop around, you can find this type of coverage for around $700. The cost will vary depending on whether the film involves stunts or animals and the length of the shoot. If you are firing weapons, plan on the rate climbing up another few hundred (around $900 for a quote). You'll be asking for a short term production quote. It's best to request quotes from a number of companies during preproduction. Many locations will ask for proof of insurance prior to signing a location agreement. You need location agreements signed early to make sure you have all of the locations locked down. People can get hurt and damage to property can happen on location. You don't want to be personally liable so make sure you read the section on company structures and liability. Note in Figure 45 that the special event permit (used to close a street for shooting) requires proof of insurance. Clause "C1" states *sponsor must submit evidence of public liability insurance , insuring the sponsor and naming the City as an additional insured in the following minimum coverage's: Bodily injury including death: $300,000/occurrence/aggregate and Property damage: $50,000/occurrence/aggregate.*" If you secure a $ 1 Million dollar liability insurance policy, it'll easily cover their requirements.

B. Conference requirement
 If requested by the City Clerk, the sponsor must attend a conference in order to clarify or offer suggestions concerning the proposed event.

C. Insurance requirement
 1. Insurance is not required for residential block events. For all other special events, however, the sponsor must submit evidence of public liability insurance, insuring the sponsor and naming the City as an additional insured in the following minimum coverage's:
  Bodily injury including death: $300,000/occurrence/aggregate
  Property damage: $50,000/occurrence/aggregate
 2. The insurance must be written by an admitted carrier licensed to do business in the State of Illinois and having at least a B+ First Division of Ratings and "VI" Second Division of Ratings as listed in Best Insurance Guide, latest edition.
 3. If location or route includes a State Highway*, the Illinois Department of Transportation shall also be named as an additional insured.

D. Permit issuance
 Once the application has been approved by the Department Heads of the City, and, provided that all required documents have been submitted, a permit will be issued by the City Clerk.

E. Use of City-owned equipment
 All required City equipment (barricades, cones, etc.) must be picked up at the City Yards (1001 N. Island) Monday through Friday (except holidays) between the hours of 7:30-11:30 a.m. or 1:30-3:00 p.m. All equipment must be signed out by the sponsor or sponsor's representative at the time it is picked up. All equipment shall be returned on the following City business day.

C:\Documents and Settings\jack\My Documents\Connie's Documents\Special Event Permit Application.doc

Figure 45-*Special Event Permit (portion)*

Some locations may require to be named as an additional insured in the location insurance. If you get requests like this, contact the company issuing the insurance and ask them how to handle the request. We did this on several location agreements and were able to resolve their request with the insurance company.

Wardrobe

Don't overlook wardrobe. It can add great production value if done correctly. I'm sure that you've seen awards being given for best wardrobe on the annual Academy Awards show before. Depending on the type of film you're making, it could play an important part. If you plan on a period piece (a film set decades or centuries ago) you will have your hands full with wardrobe and will need to bring in people who are experienced with this. There are also some wardrobe warehouses or costume warehouses that collect wardrobes and rent them out.

Stay away from outlets that cater to Halloween because these are usually not up to the quality that you need for film. Local community playhouses may also have a costume department that will have some wardrobe selection that is higher quality. Be careful with the type of film that you are making because there may be hidden wardrobe costs.

For modern day films there will still be wardrobe costs. Make sure you identify these wardrobes early on (such as police uniforms, doctor uniforms or smocks, prison inmate uniforms, zombie clothing, etc.) to be able to budget them correctly. Figure 46 shows a few of the actors from our last film. We wanted the costumes to look authentic, so we bought our uniforms from the same place as law enforcement purchases theirs and went to a badge company to have authentic police badges made. I didn't want to have to avoid closeups where the audience would see that the badges were faked. Of course, we never did a closeup on the badge, it was just comforting to know that we didn't have to avoid a closeup if one came along.

Figure 46-Actors' Wardrobe from "The Darkening"

Props and SFX

Good props can also add to your production value. Instead of using a toy gun for a scene, you can acquire a non-firing weapon that looks real. They're pricier than toys but are well worth it. They come in every make and model from small pistols to automatic weapons. Be aware that they must be controlled at all times on and off the set. Because they look so convincing, they will usually have an orange plug that should be kept in the barrel when not being used and especially when being transported. Some are capable of firing blank bullets. Extreme care should be exercised with these since they can be lethal if used incorrectly.

On our film, we met with local police to show them the guns and to demonstrate (shoot them). If you are using weapons and discharging them, you must let the local police know and must also include this piece of information in your location agreement. Believe me, you will cause a lot of undue drama if the police arrive with their guns drawn because a shooting was reported. Make sure that you, the crew, and the cast understand the procedures involved with handling a weapon (even if it only fires blanks) and the dangers involved. You should seek out a person in your area with a background in weapons use and safety training to be on the set during the use of a firearm.

Also, you will need to include this information in your liability insurance contract. Adding weapons and firing blanks will add several hundred dollars to your insurance quote. Remember that you can always add this in post (flash and sound) and it looks just as believable. In our film, we show several guns being fired and only one is real. The others were SFX and you can't tell which is which. See this book's section on editing and special effects on adding realistic gunshots.

As for other props like police cars, gun-belts, badges, etc., try to find real ones. It'll look more realistic and convincing. If you can't afford to rent it or buy it on eBay, contact local professionals about supporting the film by loaning you props. You'll be surprised what they can come up with. It never, ever hurts to ask. People love films and think it's cool to help on them. Make sure you give them appropriate credit during closing credits for helping out.

Makeup

Here's the trick with HD. I noticed early on with our first film in HD that it will show everything, I mean every blemish on your face. This is where makeup becomes important. Make sure you find some good makeup people in your area to get onboard. I know what you're going to say, "I can't afford makeup people." Well, you CAN'T afford NOT to have makeup people. You'd be surprised what you can find in your local area. First, search for makeup people that have worked on films. They're experienced. If you can't find them (or can't afford them), contact your local cosmetology school (most cities have one) and solicit help from them. It's a win-win situation for them and you.

Try to find a team which consists of one lead makeup person who is used to supervising others and have him/her bring three or four assistants to help out. With students, they may not be able to commit full time to the film so you'll need coverage for your shooting schedule. They can develop a schedule among them to provide support. That's what we did on our last film and it worked out great.

If you are shooting a horror film, you'll need to search out someone in your local area that can do special effects makeup. They should have experience working with latex, blood, prosthetics, etc. Look at samples of their work and films, if they've done them, and make a decision on the quality and fit for your film. Some of these SFX makeup people hang out and help with haunted house makeup. Perhaps that's a place to start. Usually, if you put the word out, they'll contact you. When you are auditioning and doing local advertising for actors, also add that you are looking for makeup and SFX makeup people (if doing that type of film) as well as soliciting for actors. Ask to look at a portfolio of their work (photos or films).

*Figure 47-**Scene from "The Darkening"***

Contracts

So we've talked about screenplays, locations, financing, plans, actors, and film equipment as a part of preproduction planning. Now, I'd like to talk about writing contracts before we move from preproduction to production. If you make sure that everyone, and I mean EVERYONE has signed a contract/agreement you will sleep a lot better at night. Again, I'm going to reference *Contracts for the Film & Television Industry* by Mark Litwak as a good basis to start with. And again, I'm going to remind you that it's always a good idea to have an entertainment lawyer review them. I know that most indie filmmakers don't have the funds to pay for lawyers to review contracts but at least ask around in your area or ask your friends. You may get lucky.

Contracts are required for actors, directors, DP (cinematographer), producers, locations, product placements, extras, basically anyone involved in the production. It protects their rights and your rights. Some require a transfer of rights, and for others a simple "work for hire" contract will do. Rights are required for all media world-wide so that you can pursue domestic and worldwide distribution of the film. Appendix C contains examples of contracts for cast & crew, locations, and producers.

If you think that you may need ADR (automated dialogue replacement) work or possible pickups (re-shoots of scenes), make sure to write this into the actor's contract/agreement. I always add six months to a year for pickup and ADR. Also remember to ask for rights for additional promotional products such as trailers, movie posters and anywhere their likeness might be used. Here is a list of contracts you should plan to set up before shooting:

- Screenwriter Contract
- Producer Contract
- Actors Contract
- Director Contract
- Director of Photography (Cinematographer) Contract
- PM Contract
- Crew Contracts
- Extra Contract (Master Contract List)
- Editor Contract

- Music Agreement/Contract
- Band/Musicians Agreement/Contract
- Scoring Licenses/Contract
- Product Release Agreement/Contract
- Locations Agreements

If you are deferring salaries, as most indie filmmakers do, you'll need to discuss the deferred rates. When deferring salaries, check the SAG site for the latest actor day rates for your budgeted film (i.e., budget bracket of film) and use this as the basis for the deferment. Following is a sample contract for the actor who played Deputy Brown.

PRODUCTION TITLE: The Darkening
DIRECTOR: Jack Young
PRODUCER: Young Films LLC

ACTOR RELEASE FORM

To Whom It May Concern:

I _____(the undersigned) hereby grant to ___Young Films LLC___ the right to photograph me and to record my voice, performances, poses, actions, plays and appearances, and use my picture, photograph, silhouette and other reproductions of my physical likeness in connection with the independent motion picture tentatively entitled "The Darkening" (the "Picture").

I hereby grant to ___Young Films LLC___, their successors, assigns and licensees the perpetual right to use, as you may desire, all still and motion pictures and sound track recordings and records which you may make of me or of my voice, and the right to use my name or likeness in or in connection with the exhibition, advertising, exploiting and/or publicizing of the picture. I further grant the right to reproduce in any manner whatsoever any recordings including all instrumental, musical, or other sound effects produced by me, in connection with the production and/or postproduction of the Picture.

I agree that I will not assert or maintain against ___Young Films LLC___, your successors, assigns and licensees, any claim, action, suit or demand of any kind or nature whatsoever, including but not limited to those grounded upon invasion of privacy, rights of publicity or other civil rights, or for any reason in connection with your authorized use of my physical likeness and sound in the Picture as herein provided.

By my signature here I understand that I will, to the best of my ability, adhere to the schedule agreed to prior to the beginning of my engagement. Additionally, I agree, to the best of my ability, to make myself available should it be necessary, to rerecord my voice and/or record voice-overs and otherwise perform any necessary sound work required after the end of filming. Should I not be able to perform such sound work, I understand that Young Films LLC may enter into agreement with another person to rerecord my dialogue and/or record voice-overs and use this sound work over my picture or however they deem appropriate.

I hereby certify and represent that I am over 18 years of age and have read the foregoing and fully understand the meaning and effect thereof.

---

*Figure 48-**Actor Release Form***

I've removed personal information, but of course yours will include it. Each contract should address the specific rights that you require for film production. As with actors, you need permission in all areas of media where their image may be shown. Others may contribute to the production in a different way but will have rights to those pieces they contribute. These rights are what the producer must secure in writing. For instance, a cinematographer or the cameraman creates the visual aesthetics by capturing motion "pictures." Just as a photographer may own rights to the pictures they take, so does the cinematographer own rights to the motion pictures that they create. Appendix C shows a sample contract for a cinematographer to acquire these rights for the film.

I cannot stress the importance of contracts. Making a quality film is no easy accomplishment and requires the investment of time and effort of hundreds of people in all areas. Our last film, although low budget, still involved the assistance of over 150 people. Document everyone's involvement and ensure whether or not any rights are required and that those rights are covered by an agreement or contract.

Preproduction Weekly Executive Producer Status/Budget Report - (recommended)

If you are lucky enough to have investors for your indie film, they will want some occasional reporting on how the funds are being spent. You'll need to negotiate what they want for reporting and how frequently. I'd suggest that once a week the producer submits a report to the executive producers on the status of the film and whether the film is on budget or over/under budget. If the film is under or over, an explanation is provided. If the film is behind schedule, a mitigation plan should be provided to put the film back on schedule. The budget analysis should be provided to the producer by the line producer (if staffed) for reporting to executive producers. Otherwise the producer will do this on lower budget films.

Preproduction End Executive Producer Status/Budget Report - (recommended)

At the end of preproduction the producer submits a final report to the executive producers on the status of preproduction and whether the film is on budget or over/under budget for the preproduction phase. If the film is under or over, an explanation is provided. The executive producers are informed whether the shooting date and principal photography of the film is a go. Again, the line producer should provide the funding analysis of completion of preproduction to the producer for reporting to executive producers.

PRODUCTION

Production is where **principal photography** of all scenes takes place. Principal photography is all of the visual images required for editing into a complete film. For indie film most of the principal photography comes from shooting on location. Indie filmmakers will also capture most of the sound required for the film at this time. For indie filmmakers, this is the cheapest and most practical way for gathering the film's audio track.

On the set, the Production Manager (PM) is in charge of all production activities and runs the production from the developed shooting schedule (see section on shooting schedules). The PM is assigned the responsibility to run production by the film's producer. The PM schedules and arranges for all resources needed for each scene. On a smaller scale indie film, the producer may also act as the film's PM.

Make sure that your production manager is a person that can handle multiple fires at a time because I guarantee that there will be problems. On our short film, our PM couldn't handle the pressure and ended up camped out in a bar at the VFW that we were using for a headquarters location. On our first feature film, our PM quit just before production started over a dispute with one of our producers so we entered production without a PM. Needless to say, production suffered because of it. We spent a good part of every morning trying to figure out what was being shot each day. It was a bloody mess.

If you can't find an experienced PM, you'll need to be able to spend some time with someone who has the right skill set for going over schedules and understanding how you want production to run. On our last feature my sister Brenda filled in as PM and did one hell-of-a-job at it. As the producer during preproduction, I spent time with her going over the shooting script and shooting schedule. Brenda had been involved from the beginning so she was familiar with the actors, locations, and script. Make sure to bring your PM in early so that they can get familiar with all of the elements of production and the required resources. After all, the PM's job is to manage all of the film's resources in support of production so it makes sense to bring them in as early as possible. A good PM will have a backup plan to the backup plan for resources needed on the film set. If a generator is needed for a shot, not only will the PM ensure that a generator has been arranged, but will have a second company with a generator ready to go should the first company not deliver.

Let's review what we need in-place to begin production.

Shooting Script

You should have the screenplay where you want it at this point. If not, why are we going into production? You should have already broken down the script into all of the elements that drive production (such as actors, locations, props, costumes, etc.). If you are the director on the indie film, you'll want to be involved with the shooting script. It's the place that you want to add notes about camera angles and special shots you'd like to come out of the scenes with. Since a lot of indie filmmakers wear several hats (screenwriter, producer, director, etc.) one can really take advantage of this and use the screenplay as the blueprint for the film. Many times as screenwriters we hear that studios don't want us to put camera angles and directions in because they don't want to tell the director how to do their jobs. On indie films, we have the luxury of building some of that into the shooting script so take advantage of it.

Shooting Schedule

You should have a shooting schedule developed that covers every day of shooting. If you can afford it, try not to be so aggressive in your schedule (five pages a day is aggressive). I know that most of us work for a living and taking more than a couple of weeks off is difficult but make an effort to get a minimum of three weeks to shoot your indie film. The other option is to do like most indie filmmakers and pack a two week schedule and pick up whatever gets missed on the weekends. This is what we did on our last film. Although a little riskier, this works as long as you don't wait too long to come back for those pick up shots.

Your shooting schedule can be in an Excel spreadsheet, on paper, or maintained on a white board. The PM will be using this to create daily call sheets for the actors that will tell them when and where they need to report each day. The PM should also generate a daily breakdown sheet that details any needed resources for each scene. These can be maintained on a laptop in Excel. Printed copies can also be maintained in a notebook. The call sheet should be e-mailed or sent to each of the actors earlier, prior to the day of the shoot.

Communications

Make sure you have cell phone numbers of EVERYONE involved with the production such as actors, crew members, director, PM, DP (cinematographer), location owners, transportation captains, makeup, etc. The PM should maintain this listing of phone numbers. The PM will make sure that all information pertinent to the production is passed on to all parties. What we found on our last film was that developing a cast Facebook page for posting notices for film and crew was very effective for communications during the production phases of the film.

Crew Considerations

By this time, the producer should have identified all members of the production team. If not and you are working with a low budget, volunteers from local film schools and colleges can be recruited to fill out the crew. Remember that you can't do everything yourself and soliciting help works both ways. Allowing students to intern on your set helps provide you with additional help and at the same time assists those interested in a film career with learning the craft.

Directing Notes (The Mechanics)

If this is your first film as a producer and you're also acting as the director (which I don't suggest because producer duties will interfere with directing) here's some tips on how to run the set. Work with the DP (cameraman) to block the actors for each scene. **Blocking** is basically walking the actors through entering and exiting locations and where they will deliver their lines. The DP will want to know where to set up the camera and lighting for each shot during the scene. The DP, if just blocking for lighting, can use stand-ins for the actors.

At each mark on the set, the DP will need to pull focus. Again, this is where an assistant to the DP comes in handy. If the camera has a focus follower, the DP may choose to train the assistant in the art of pulling the focus to ensure that each mark the actor hits is in focus. It also allows the actors to get familiar with the set. The grips will be directed by the DP as to where to place the lighting and any other lighting requirements (such as scribs, gels, bounce cards). It is also an opportunity for the sound engineer and boom operator to determine where the microphones on the set will be placed to avoid being visible in the frame and to avoid boom shadows.

Once the actors have been blocked, the director will ask his assistant to get silence on the set. To indicate that the director is ready to shoot a scene, the assistant will call out to the cast and crew: "Picture up. Quiet on the set!" Once silent, the director will call out "roll sound" to indicate that sound is being recorded. If ready, the sound engineer, who has the headphones on and is monitoring sound on the set, will respond back "rolling sound." The director will then ask the cameraman to record video by calling out "roll camera." The cameraman will let the director know that he is prepared to film by responding "camera rolling." The director will then ask the first camera assistant to slate the scene by calling out "slate." The assistant will step forward, putting the slate in front of the camera where it is in FOCUS.

You don't realize the importance of slating a picture correctly until you edit a film where the slate is not in the frame correctly nor in focus. The most important two pieces of information on the slate are the scene number and the take. Since sound is captured on the set independently of the camera recordings, it becomes increasingly difficult to sync the proper take to the sound recordings if the slate is not readable. During dailies, the director and producer should note whether or not the slate is being properly displayed in front of the camera.

The assistant calls out the scene number and take number out loud (i.e., "Scene 1. Take 1.") and claps the arm of the slate (clapper) together. After the assistant steps away from the set, the director calls to the actors to begin the scene with "action."

After each take is shot, the director calls out "cut" to signify the end of that take. The director should take care to not call out cut too early because during editing of the film, editors like to have some extra footage to play with. If a take ends directly after an actor does his/her line, then there becomes very little to edit and choices for the editor become limited. As each take of each scene is filmed, the director may also call out "print it" to signify the take that he/she likes best. On larger productions, a script girl may document this in the script that will become the director's cut of the film.

The Director's Vision

I like the word vision. In the filmmaking business, I think that everyone should have his or her own vision for the film. For instance, the screenwriter has a vision for the story that he/she is telling. In addition, the cinematographer has a vision for how the story should visually be told. The director and the editor should also have their own vision for the film. The cinematographer will tell his/her story by the way he or she cinematically paints the visuals while the director will tell his/her story by the way he/she directs the emotions of the actors to faithfully portray the characters.

The previous paragraph discussed the mechanics of directing on the set — how the actors say their lines in front of the camera lens and how that is captured in a set of shots that will eventually make up the scene. It is the director's job to find the heart of the scene and to capture that on film. Filmmakers should aspire to come away from the scene with more than just a series of necessary shots.

Workflow Considerations

As you recall, we mentioned how workflow should be a consideration when deciding upon the equipment for the film. Workflow is simply the methodology for the work that is done on the set, such as how the video and audio data is recorded and moved from the recording device (camera or field recorder) to an intermediate device, such as a media card and portable drive, for storage during production. Eventually all of the data will end up at the editing workstation of course for editing of the film. On the set, we need some methodology to track and store all video and audio data recorded.

Typically, modern digital film cameras record to a small intermediate media card, such as SDHC and SDXC. Once the card is full, it is copied onto a larger portable drive, such as a USB or Firewire drive, that is attached to a laptop. Most camera designs allow for duo cards so the cameraman can continue to film while the other media card is dumped. Once the card has been dumped to the drive, it can be returned to the cameraman for use after the secondary card becomes full.

This workflow, from media card to laptop disk storage allows for the data to be backed up (I recommend that the data be stored on two separate terabyte drives for redundancy) and made available for immediate review as a daily as well as made available to the film editor for possible early editing. Ron Howard likes to have editing stations available on his shoots so the editor can be editing at the same time the film is being shot. It's a great idea to get a jump on the film, considering that post production (editing) can take from three months to a year.

Sound Recording Considerations

For indie filmmakers, just about all of the sound for the film comes from recording on location. Later, we talk about doing Automated Dialogue Replacement (ADR) that will look and sound like what Hollywood does but on an indie budget. Just remember that to get good and usable sound on the set takes some effort and watching out for "gotchas."

When filming on location, it is critical that the sound engineer communicates to the director when there are background noises present that will ruin the sound recording. If you are shooting in a building and a motorcycle is approaching, the sound engineer should not be afraid to speak up and say "motorcycle." Of course, this requires another take after the sound engineer gives an all clear on the noise, but it's better than finding out in post that the shots were ruined and no one was notified.

Unless you are making a silent film, getting "room tone" is the next most important piece of audio that you need to capture on the set besides the dialogue. It's also another place where if not done right will cause your editor a big headache. Big studios have a lot more resources than indie filmmakers and if they could do automatic dialogue replacement (ADR) on all of the audio in a film, they could and not break into a sweat but not so for indie filmmakers. We must try to grab every bit of audio that we can on the set…and get it right. This is really a challenge that the producer must be up for. Getting clean sound on the set is not as easy as you may think. And I will tell you this. It will not always be clean and we'll talk more about cleaning up troubled sound takes in editing later.

There are three different and distinct sound tracks that you must try to capture while shooting on a set. If you can get these, you can deliver a motion picture with some amazing surround sound qualities. These are narrative, Foley, and room tone. Narrative is words that your actors speak. Foley are the sounds that your actors make when interacting with their environment such as walking, running, opening a door, slamming a door, setting a glass down, opening a beer. Foley is typically added in post for large productions but for indies, filmmakers should make attempts to capture this on the set.

Room tone is the sound that a location makes. It could be in a room of a house (interior) or outside (exterior). Whether or not you know it, there is a sound that envelops us, our environment. It's all those noises like the furnace or air conditioning on in the background or the birds chirping in the distance. Without this undercurrent of noise (most at a low level) we would be listening to a vacuum. Vacuums feel very strange on the ears because we are used to hearing these room tones wherever we go. It's everywhere. Now listen closely. You also must have this room tone recorded at the end of each scene for at least 60 seconds. Let me explain why in an example. Let's suppose that in one of our scenes we only did two takes but when you get to post production, you discover this horrible humming sound in the background. Both takes are ruined (audio wise). You find out that the building where you shot the scene has been demolished (little drama here) so you can't re-shoot the scene. Okay, take a deep breath. I'm going to help you fix it. So we only need dialogue and it's a fairly short scene. So we can ADR it.

ADR is basically an audio recording of your actors doing their dialogue for the scene while watching themselves on a big screen in order to get close to being in sync. Later in editing we'll talk more about how to tweak that. So you sit down with the actors and get their dialogue. You're in a clean room (sound wise) and you've got clean dialogue. That's a great start. You remove the old audio track and put in your new sound track or ADR. It sounds very strange. Your ears are telling you that something about what you're listening to is not right. When you ripped out the original sound track, you also removed the room tone.

Remember that room tone is underneath everything. Using the room tone that you captured from that scene, (or another if you can't clean it up) you now add it back. Now the scene has a room tone in the background and sounds correct. I'm simplifying it, but you get it. Room tone allows you to rebuild audio tracks in editing or when there is a lack of room tone, i.e., between narrative tracks that end and have a gap.

Room tone must also be as clean as you can get it. The sound engineer should be informed (or should know) to pickup room tone at each location. If shooting multiple scenes in the same room, he must pickup room tone before moving on to the next room or location. He doesn't need to get it at the end of each scene if the scenes are in the same room or location. However, any motors or devices that make noise must be turned off. Crew members and actors should leave or remain perfectly silent. Make the room tone as clean as possible. When ready to record room tone, just announce the cast and crew: "Sixty seconds for room tone. Quiet on the set!"

Foley, as I said earlier, is the insertion of sound effects into a film such as footsteps, doors shutting, car engines, guns firing, just about anything that makes a noise that isn't the actor's dialogue is usually replaced with Foley sounds. Since filmmakers don't have elaborate budgets and can't afford to hire Foley (most of us anyway) you must try to grab these sounds on location. What typically happens with noises on the set is that it gets stepped on by other noises. For instance, I may say my line as I put my glass down. Now the noise of the glass and my narrative are multiplexed in a single sound track. What if the noise of the glass being put down is extremely loud? Some people are talented enough to go into the sound track and fix this, others aren't. By knowing that these sounds can be separated on the set, the director can ask the actor to say the line then put their drink down. Now you have them separated and they can be pulled separately from the track.

Transportation Considerations

There are several transportation considerations. First, you'll remember that I recommended an equipment truck when discussing preproduction requirements. It may be an extended van, a small truck, or a large truck depending upon the extent of your film equipment. No less, for every location, you will need equipment and you'll need it there early so that the crew can setup the set.

On our film, our equipment truck driver was also the same person in charge of the props and equipment. If you can't find someone experienced, find someone organized and that is a good driver. Ensure that person has a complete listing of all equipment and is capable of supervising the **swing gang** (guys that will unload the truck). The swing gang will also assist in the striking of the set and the loading of the equipment back into the truck. Work with the driver/equipment person to help them develop an organizational approach for the truck and equipment.

Another consideration is transporting the actors and crew. Actors must get to the set early for makeup and may need transportation. An assigned transportation captain should work with the PM so that they are aware of any transportation needs for the cast and crew. Many times on location, there may be additional needs such as cables that go bad, extra props that were forgotten, and other small needs that will arise from nowhere. The transportation can also help run these errands to keep production moving.

Fixing in Post Gotcha's

Okay, you'll need to watch for this one. Indie filmmakers always have an unrealistic and brutal shooting schedule. They try to do the impossible because they don't usually have the budget to shoot more than a couple of weeks. I get it because I've been there. But on the set, you will hear this or may even say it, "oh, we can fix that in post." So listen up. Be careful believing that just about everything is fixable in post because it isn't. People on the set say this because it lets them off the hook for doing their job during the shoot. I know, because I had to edit our last film and the things that we believed were fixable in post were NOT! So don't make this mistake. If you had a $25 million budget and all the time in the world, perhaps it could be fixed, but on an indie budget it's not going to happen.

So think about what you're doing on the set. Don't let the crew convince you that shoddy work or filmmaking can be fixed in post. Sure, some things can be fixed in post, but why push work out you're not sure can get fixed when it can be shot correctly during the principal shooting schedule.

Filmmakers need to know the limitations of digital filmmaking and what can and can't be fixed in post. If the DP shoots an interior shot and overdrives the camera (blown out by hot spot) because he's trying to use the natural light streaming in through the windows, realize that it is most likely not fixable in post, even though they tell you so. Overdriving devices such as the digital camera or even the audio field recorder is never good, unless it is intended, and usually cannot be fixed in post. In the digital world, whenever a digital device is driven to operate outside of the device's normal operating range (over-lit, under-lit, overdriven, etc.) the video/audio product can be degraded. Your cameraman and sound engineer should both know the operating characteristics of their tools of the trade, like the camera and audio gear, and what happens when driven outside the normal operating range. Normally, data, as the result of being under or over driven, is difficult if not impossible to fix in post. Enough said.

Set Design Considerations

So you've secured your locations and you're ready to film, right? Sets are extremely important in creating that world where your film will exist. Too many times indie filmmakers are happy with just having a location and forget to put some effort into the set design. Even when there is no budget for real set decoration on an indie film, there are things that you can do to take the set design to a higher level.

In our last film, we needed a convincing mystic shop where a palm reader would tell our main characters of some foreboding forces that are at work. The set needed to be convincing so our audience could submerge themselves into this mystic world. We started with a vacant building on the town's main street and went from there. We searched out some existing mystic shops and took pictures of how the front of the location was designed. We took note of the mystic symbols and artwork painted on the storefront windows. We then re-created the design on our location using water-soluble window paints.

The interior design included a display case and shelves for mystic books and artifacts for sale. We solicited members of our crew and friends for anything mystic that might have to use as props for the shop. It turned out that several had more than enough to fill the shelves and display case. We then hung black and red alternating curtains, added a table draped in red and some chairs, and we had our mystic shop.

*Figure 49-**The Mystic Set (front office)***

Figure 50-The Mystic Set (back office)

At another two locations, we were confronted with the same issue, a lack of atmosphere. At one location, we needed office furniture to recreate a doctor's office. My sister had a professional relationship with an office company through her work so she had a contact we were able to work with for the office furniture. We added the furniture, a poster of Sigmund Freud we got on Amazon, some framed PHD degrees we Photoshopped, a desktop computer, and some flowers, and we had our psychiatrist's office. In indie filmmaking, it is important to tap into all of the local contacts where you are shooting your film and to get creative in how you can add details. With limited budgets, you'll need all the help you can get.

The point is that although the camera lens only ever sees a fraction of what we did, we approached the set from a holistic approach. If you are not familiar with set design or interior decoration, bring someone in that is and have them work with you to create convincing sets. When the set designs are more convincing, the actors are more convincing in their roles as characters in that make believe world that you have created.

Special Effects Considerations

Sometimes, special effects (SFX) shots don't pan out like you think or hope, especially in indie filmmaking. Our last film, *The Darkening*, had numerous special effects shots in it such as entities, vortexes, changing eyes, and gunshots. Not all turned out like we had hoped or planned. As a backup plan, you may want to shoot the scene with the SFX a couple of ways: one with the SFX setup (i.e., green screen) and another safety take without the SFX. This leaves you with an option to cutaway and to insert a scene if you need to. What's neat about doing SFX shots on the set that involve actor responses is that it allows the director to give the actor step-by-step directions.

For instance, let's say that an actor is reacting to a creature that is put into the scene later, for inexperienced actors it is helpful for the director to guide the actor through their emotions. Since many times we are just looking for a reaction shot from the actor, the director is free to verbally instruct the actor through the needed reactions. If we used an inexperienced actor and just said a monster just leaped from the bushes, go ahead and react, we may not be satisfied with the results. As the director you need to provide as much guidance as you feel is required by the actor.

Be aware that special effects by a professional SFX studio/house are very expensive and probably out of your budget range. What you can do is look for experienced SFX artists on film SFX sites (yes, they have their own sites) and post a want ad. They will most likely have some minimum that they expect you to pay artists on the site, but these are significantly lower than farming the work though a company. These artists are always looking for fun projects to work on in their spare time and make a little extra money. We will talk more about how to manage special effects for your film in the film editing (post) section of this book.

Production Headquarters

The center of the production machine is the production headquarters. This is the central hub from which everything comes from for the film production. You must have a location where the crew and actors can meet and the wardrobe, makeup, and the production management team can operate from. If you have multiple locations you'll need to setup a headquarters in each location. A headquarters can be a recreational vehicle or it can be a temporary office setup at a local Veteran of Foreign Wars (VFW) hall or in a vacant building that you requested the use of. Nevertheless, it's important to operations. Once you have a location, you'll need to arrange for power and water and ensure that you have bathroom facilities for the actors and crew. Divide the area into compartments such as production management (PM and assistants), wardrobe area, makeup area, equipment area, and an eating or dining area. The PM will need access to the Internet (remember that we setup a cast & crew film page for communicating) for email and other web resources, a computer or laptop for managing the shooting schedule, and a printer for printing out call sheets and contracts.

The producer, director, PM, DP, and crew should meet early before the actors arrive to go over the daily shooting schedule and what needs to get accomplished. At this meeting, everyone needs to get on the same page and understand the resources and issues associated with that day's shooting schedule. You do this each morning.

At the end of the day, a similar meeting is held to review the day's progress and to identify scenes that didn't get shot and problems that will need to be resolved for the next day of shooting. After the meeting, the producer and director should review the dailies to identify any technical issues or problems with the script or actors. They should pay particular attention to the quality of the film if the film is intended for theatrical release. Scenes that are slightly out of focus will not be presentable on a big screen. I'd recommend a five foot or larger HD screen to view for focus issues. Screens smaller than this may not be large enough to correctly identify focusing issues.

B-Roll/B-Camera

Every little bit is going to help with the shooting schedule. Consider bringing on a second camera operator (B-camera) to the film. The B-camera operator can be assigned to pick up a lot of shots that don't require the actors and besides it's good film training for them. Most films will have master establishing shots of the locations. These can be picked up by the B-camera operator and will take some load off of the A-camera operator. The producer should sit down with the director and A-camera operator to discuss this option. On one of our other films, the A-camera operator would get up extra early in the morning to shoot B-roll shots.

Locations & Street Shooting

In production you will be moving from location to location and filming all of the scenes associated with that location. It's important that you stay on schedule and arrive at the next site as you have defined in your location agreement. In your location agreement that we discussed earlier in the book, you should have defined what days you would be shooting there. If you fear that the date may slip, you need to speak to your point of contact at that location and let them know very early. Be aware that locations are tricky and if you cannot manage your shooting schedule and continue to slip, you may lose that site. This is where the PM and daily meetings come in handy. They can give you a heads up if the schedule is in danger of slipping. The producer needs to work closely with the director and PM to maintain the shooting schedule. If you load down the schedule as most indie filmmakers do, with a goal of shooting five or six pages a day, this is the risk that exists. If you extend your schedule to a three week or longer schedule, you can reduce the risk of the schedule slipping.

If you are closing streets for a location or shooting on a street location, you will have the same issue as previously mentioned — it will be on a specific date and you need to stay on that schedule. To change a street closing will be more difficult because this involves the city or county departments. If you miss your street closure date and can't get your permit through the system fast enough, you will be shooting at the location without a street closure permit. You'll end up dealing with traffic and other annoyances as you try to shoot.

Always take care of your locations. Set a policy for each site that crew members moving equipment should always treat the location like their own home and avoid any kind of damage to the premises. Ensure that you leave the location as you found it if not cleaner. If your scenes involve any liquids or blood, ensure that you use plenty of plastic to cover areas that could get splattered. In one of our films, the character gets her throat cut and is found on the floor in a pool of blood. The problem with the location was that the floor she was supposed to be found on was in the bedroom and it had a white carpet. To be able to shoot the scene, we added a circular throw rug that matched the décor. We taped plastic to the back of the rug with duct tape and then placed it on the white carpet. Now we were free to add the pool of blood without worrying about destroying it.

The trick to locations is being able to control the location whether it's a house, police station, or street location. Control is the key. In our last film we had a club scene where one of the murder victims goes just before she's murdered. We had heard of a local band from Chicago that was supposedly an upcoming and hot band and wanted to work them into the film. They were perfect for the club scene so we contracted them to play at the location for that night. We thought it would be perfect since they were working for us. We could ask them to start and stop their song as we needed. That part worked great, however, we didn't realize that the club actually had two halves and had scheduled another band to be playing that night in the other half. So although we could control our band, we had no control of the other band. So during shooting, someone would open the door between the two rooms and the other band's music would come blaring into our set. The shoot did not go smoothly at all, but we still managed to get what we needed. In these types of environments you need to make sure that you have control of everything going on.

Stunts and Weapons on the Set

As we discussed before, make sure that you identify stunts and firearms in your liability insurance contract. If this isn't disclosed and an accident happens involving weapons or stunts not identified in the coverage agreement, it may not be covered. Make sure that stunts and weapons are disclosed in the liability insurance contract. It's also a good idea to meet with local law enforcement officials (city and county) to discuss the use of weapons on the set. It's also wise to get advice from local weapons experts or professional stuntmen in your area. For our film, we met with local law enforcement officials to discuss the use of weapons on the set. Although we were using non-firing weapons (replicas) that fired blanks, we still wanted to get their buy-in with us using them in their jurisdiction. You also need to do this if you plan on firing blanks on the set. As I had mentioned earlier when securing locations, you'll need to disclose to them the involvement of weapons and stunts in your summation of how the location will be used.

You're thinking that this is doing nothing but creating more work for you and that you can "guerilla" shoot the scenes. DON'T think of it. Not only will someone call the police, but the replica guns today look so real that you could be shot. Also make sure that weapons are controlled by a designated weapon master, if you can find one, or the equipment master. The weapons should NOT be allowed to leave the set for any reason and should contain the orange plug in the barrel when being transported. Any blank shells should be controlled (the count) and when fired on the set, a policy should be enforced that includes clearing the set, providing earplugs for those remaining on the set, and instructions to the actors on the hazards and proper use of weapons and blanks on the set.

Cars – Shooting In and Out

You will most likely find yourself shooting a scene in a car. Both of our last two films had car scenes. If you have an equipment budget, there are cool mounts for cars that make shooting on them and in them a lot easier. Most use some form of suction cup to attach to the car without causing damage. There are front or side mount setups, or setups that attach to the side for those shots of the tires turning on the road (if you like those shots). If you're creative, you can search out the web for parts and suction cups (these can get pricey) and build your own rig. These can also be rented. If you can't afford to rent, don't panic, you can still shoot car scenes but in a limited fashion. You can also arrange for the dialogue to take place in the car before the car is driven away or after it parks.

Today's digital cameras are compact enough to allow shooting within the car. Just make sure that your set of lenses includes some with the right focal point for focusing in tight quarters. We used a 50mm f1.4 for interior car scenes. A fast lens and low light digital camera also helps if you have limited light within the car. We used a small hand-held fluorescent light as a **kicker** (a kicker is a light used as additional illumination to your main lighting) in the car to help with highlights and it worked very well. Of course if you want shots from the front of the vehicle, you can do what the DP on one of our last films did, he positioned himself on the hood of the car and shot through the front windshield while it was in motion. However, I wouldn't recommend it. The producer on the film was having a heart attack while we were filming.

In one of our films we needed the actress to appear to be held captive in the back of a SUV. She was coming around from being knocked out and we wanted a shot of her tussling around in the back. We did the old film cheat of having the car stationary and the crew gently rocking the vehicle about as we filmed her with the tailgate open. The shot was a close-up of the actress so the effect worked. If you don't have the budget, think of creative ways to get the shot.

Deep Thoughts About Acting

Every actor is unique in the way they approach their character. Some need time to prepare mentally for a scene while others are ready to blast into it at a moment's notice. In our last film, an actor playing the sheriff of a small town had one line in the scene: "Put on your gun, Steven." I wanted to get the right feeling behind it so I took him aside and explained how he had put the gun away years earlier, but now there was someone murdering people in his town. One of the victims had been his niece. If he put the gun on, someone was going to die. It had to be a powerful moment with sparse dialogue. The actor stepped away and stood alone away from the others thinking about what I had said so he could find the right emotion. I saw him do this on several occasions and it worked.

The same actor also liked to find his rhythm in the scene so if you asked him to pick up dialogue from a certain spot, it created problems for him. We tried on a couple of occasions to allow him to pick up dialogue like this and finally just had him start from the beginning. Each actor works differently and you have to find what works for each one.

Indie filmmakers shoot films by location and typically don't shoot the film in sequential order. It's not economical to shoot a scene then strike the set, go to the next location, shoot the next scene, strike the set and go to the next location, etc. However, when shooting by location, the scenes shot may come from the beginning or end of the screenplay. The director should pay attention to where the characters are in their arcs (if they have one). A **character arc** is how they change throughout the story. In our film, our doctor went from a caring psychiatrist to a cold-blooded murderer by the end of the film. We needed to gauge where his character was in every scene on his ride to madness. The actor would ask me, the director, on a madness scale of 1 to 10, where am I in this scene. He may have shot a scene from earlier in the script, then picked up a shot from later when he's an 8 on the crazy scale. Make sure that your characters bring the correct emotion and attitude for where they are in their character arc for that point in the story.

Directors and DPs

As we discussed earlier, both the director and DP (cinematographer) will both have a vision for the film. As a first time director on our last film, I did not realize the importance of the director's vision until later into the shoot. The director must convey to the DP his/her vision and what they feel they must come away with for the scene. In independent film, the cameraman and usually the cinematographer have a lot of control over the film, but the director MUST communicate his vision to the DP or you will end up with the DP's vision only.

Production Cadence

A production crew has to learn to work as a team. For indie filmmaking, there's a lot to do and usually a short time to do it. Following are some example times that you might use to begin establishing a schedule. For indie films, the full day is utilized for filming. Days can run from early morning to late at night. I've shot scenes near midnight on previous films. Typically, you want to try to get the actors freed up by 9:00 PM if possible. It still results in a ten or twelve hour workday for some actors. When working with SAG and union crew members, these hours will have to be negotiated or the shooting schedule extended to allow for shorter work days.

> **Morning production meeting** – (6:30 AM to 7:00 AM) The film crew meets early in the morning at headquarters or the location for a morning meeting. During the meeting the producer and PM go over the scheduled scenes to be shot. If any additional resources are needed for that day, these are discussed as well.

> **Equipment & crew to set** – (7:30 AM to 8:30 AM) The vehicles and equipment arrive at the set for setting up for the first scheduled scene to be shot. The DP may use crew members as stand-ins for rigging the lighting prior to the actors' arrival.

Actors arrive on set – (8:30 AM) The actors arrive on set and report to wardrobe and makeup. If the actor is wearing any special makeup they need to report an additional hour earlier minimum. Early reporting is dependent upon the complexity of the makeup. Producers should consult the SFX makeup person to get an estimate on the time for applying any SFX makeup and use this estimate for scheduling purposes.

Shooting scenes – (9:00 AM) Naturally, the length of scenes and the number of takes required to get it right will vary from scene to scene. Some scenes you'll get in one take while others may go through over six takes to find the one that works. Figure on an average of three takes per scene. Even if the actors hit it the first time, always shoot a safety take. There may be something in the first take that prevents you from using it and the editor will be searching for another take to use but not find it. Always get a safety. Editors like to have choices.

Try to get as much done before lunch but don't be a slave driver. If you start getting behind schedule, your PM or their assistant will remind you that you are slipping. Give the actors and crew an hour break to have lunch and relax. As I mentioned earlier, provide an area where they can sit down and relax during their breaks.

After lunch, work the crew and actors for another 2.5 to 3 hours and provide them a fifteen minute break in the afternoon. The next stretch of shooting should take you into the early evening. If the actors don't have any nighttime shooting to do, they can be cut loose around 6:00 PM. If actors have nighttime shooting, you'll need to provide a dinner break for an hour from 6:00 PM to 7:00 PM. After dinner, finish up the nighttime scenes by 9:00 or 10:00 PM.

Strike the set – After the actors have been released, the crew strikes the set. On many indie films some actors like to hang around and help with this. On indie films this is fine but on union films it may not be acceptable. The swing gang is supervised by the equipment master who has specific locations for each piece of equipment. The producer should have a sit-down with the equipment master to ensure that he has an acceptable plan for storing the equipment in the equipment truck that tracks and secures it. It's a good idea for the equipment master to have a master list of all equipment that is used to account for everything at the end of each shooting day.

Evening production meeting –After the actors have left and the equipment packed into the equipment truck, the producer, PM, DP, and director meet to discuss the day's accomplishments and any issues. This is followed by a brief review of the next day's shooting schedule by the PM.

Dailies – The producer and director review the day's footage. They note any issues that need resolving.

Executive producer weeklies (suggested) – Once a week the producer invites the executive producers to a review of footage to be displayed over a NetMeeting or similar type conference call meeting. The executive producers can see firsthand the result of the week of principal photography. If an editor is not working real-time editing on the set, the weekly dailies are in raw format only.

Production weekly executive producer status/Budget report (recommended) – Once a week the producer submits a report to the executive producers on the status of the film and whether the film is on budget or over/under budget. If the film is under or over, an explanation is provided. If the film is behind schedule, a mitigation plan should be provided to put the film back on schedule.

<u>Production end executive producer status/budget report</u>
(recommended) – At the end of production the producer submits
a final report to the executive producers on the final status of
production and whether the film is on budget or over/under
budget for the production phase. If the film is under or over, an
explanation is provided. The executive producers are informed
whether the film is ready to go into post production. If additional
pick-up shots are required to complete the film, this should be
disclosed along with the additional costs.

POST PRODUCTION

Okay, so you've finished principal photography and have the film "in the can" or for digital filmmakers, on your storage drives. You were able to review progress via dailies every day of shooting and have captured all of the shots that will make up your film. You also have captured your narrative on the set along with room tones for each location as well as capturing any Foley sounds that you could on the set.

In post production we're going to assemble all of these into a cohesive narrative film using an editing application (software) and editing platform (hardware). If you were lucky enough to have an editor on the set working the film on a daily or weekly basis (a suggestion I made earlier), then you are ahead of the game and the editor already has a rough edit of the film. If not, then you have some work ahead of you.

Editing a film is a very unique talent and it doesn't go unnoticed by the film industry as demonstrated during the Academy Awards every year. If you're lucky and have the budget, you can bring on an experienced film editor to edit your film. If you're including editing in your budget, make sure that you budget at least $20K for an experienced editor. If you intend on including special effects, scoring, or recognizable pop songs, you should have budgeted for those as well. To bring on a composer to write an original score will cost you from zero dollars for an unknown hungry composer to around $10K for an experienced film composer who has done feature films. If you're planning on having the composer's music conducted and performed by an orchestra (most large cities have an orchestra), then you'll need to budget even more funds for the score. An orchestra is composed of quite a few musicians and you'll need funds to cover them. Consider adding another $10K if you are considering this. However, today, composers can tap into music sample libraries and can create realistic sounding instruments from these libraries. ProScores is a music score library that is very reasonable and uses authentic musical instrument samples. I used this on our last film and was very impressed with the low price and extensive libraries. We'll talk more about using ProScores later in the editing and scoring sections of the book.

If you are thinking of including hit pop songs by known musicians, you'd better open your wallet wide because they will cost you. For one of our other films, I wanted to have "*I Heard it Through the Grapevine*" in the sound track. The total costs for sync and master rights were well over $80K. That's right, $80,000. Recognizable and popular songs are very expensive. If you don't have the budget, you can search out local or upcoming bands that are looking for exposure. Most of the time, they will provide sound tracks for free and just film end credit. Make sure that you have them sign a contract.

Editing

Okay, let's go back to our vision discussion. Here's where the editor will follow with his vision for the film. Of course, this is done with producer's approval and may actually be different from the director's vision of the film. Remember when we had the director on the set calling out "print it"? Those scenes, in the director's opinion, are the best takes and if HE were editing the film that would be his cut of the film. Well, that may not be what the editor chooses as a cut of the film. He now has the reigns. The sign of good editing is that it flows seamlessly and nothing about the edit pulls you out of the movie experience. Just as one bad scene with a bad actor will pull the audience out of the movie, editing, if not done right, can do the same.

The trick to getting a good product for editing is to not over drive or under drive your digital camera or digital sound recorder. To get good product, you must operate within the optimum operating characteristics of these devices. For video, if you have too much light or have "hot spots" of light, this will overdrive the CCD or CMOS chip in your video camera. If you do not have enough light, the image will be too dark or be under driven. Too much or not enough light will both affect the quality of the image. In either case, the editor will have to work to repair, if possible, under or over driven images. Sometimes these are beyond repair.

The same goes for the audio portion of editing. If you over drive the sound recorder amplifiers the sound will be clipped or flattened at the peaks. If the sound is too low, you will need to bring the dB (decibels) up in editing. However, when you amplify sound in post (bring dB level up), it not only amplifies the words of the actors (the narrative) it also amplifies the noise in the audio track. You, the editor, will then be stuck with the task of doing cleanup on the track by reducing the noise that will be amplified. Many of these problems with video and audio can be avoided by ensuring the DP lights scenes correctly and has the camera properly configured and that the sound engineer on the set is experienced and trained in setting the sound levels correctly. If the sound engineer hears noise spikes and sees that the levels have reached a distortion level they should inform the director so that another take of the scene can be shot with the sound recording levels adjusted for a proper recording.

Editing Platforms

Avid editing used to be the standard, but after film editing moved to the desktop, Final Cut (Mac based) and Premiere Pro (Windows & Mac based) have taken dominate positions for HD film editing. There are, however, numerous other applications in the market place, but these both offer the advanced tool sets to make your film look like a Hollywood feature. Avid editing systems, when they dominated the editing platforms, would cost anywhere from $250K to $500K for a complete system. This was of course in the day of Beta tapes and when the digital format was just taking a foothold in the film market. Again, I'm in no way a subject matter expert in the field of editing, but I can give you some perspective on editing since having edited our last film and experienced all of the gotchas that can happen in editing.

We picked Premiere Pro CS5 after doing research and having chosen the AF100 camera to shoot our last film. The AF100 generates data in the AVCHD format. As you will discover in the digital world of filmmaking, the less compression between the raw data that the camera captures and the final product, the better imagery that you will get. Although the AVHCD format is a compression format, it still delivers quality images suitable for indie filmmaking. The only drawback is that during the digital content packaging (DCP) of the film, we discovered that when blown up on a theatrical screen, we lost some of the color depth.

This may have been something that could have been corrected during the DCP process, but needs further investigation. I will talk more about DCP generation later in the book.

We chose the Premiere Pro CS5 Master Collection software because it included tools such as Adobe After Effects® CS5, (motion graphics and visual effects for film), Adobe Premiere® Pro CS5 (video and audio-editing), Adobe Audition® CS5 (audio editing), and Adobe Encore® CS5 (DVD and Blu-ray authoring). We also added Adobe Audition® for additional sound editing capability to the suite of tools. I know that you're thinking that you can't dish out the $2500 plus for these Adobe products, then do some shopping on eBay. You can find great deals on software. Just make sure that you get the license key and that it's for the correct platform (Mac or Windows) that you need. Stay away from OEM products out there since these usually don't include license keys and don't come with any support.

As for hardware, make sure that you have a workstation that has enough processing power, RAM, and terabytes of storage to support editing of the film. Although you might only have shot 350 gigabytes of footage, some products that you will need to generate will exceed that. If you have to generate a "Pro Res" (Apple HD HQ) version or digital content package (DCP) version of the film, both of these can easily exceed 500 gigabytes each or more. I'd plan on at least having two terabyte drives for editing purposes. If you're shooting with a 4K camera like the Red one, you'll need to plan on not only more drive space, you'll need to seriously consider your workflow on the set because a 4K camera can easily generate 1 to 7 Terabyte of data A DAY! That's correct. For 4K, you'll need very large and very fast drives on the set and in post.

If you're using external terabyte drives, make sure that you use a USB 3.0 interface for data transfer. The old USB 2.0 data transfer is quite a bit slower. You'll also need some serious CPU for rendering the film. In the old days, editing workstations had to be dedicated to rendering and could take days to render a complete film. Choose an editing workstation that has at least quad CPUs with at least 3 GHz speeds. You'll be able to render a complete film in one day. I had an engineer friend build our editing workstation from scratch. He was able to select one of the fastest

CPUs available for building it (Intel Core i5-2500K CPUs). You'll also need at least 12 GB of RAM and a good video card. We use an NVIDIA GeForce GTX 560 Ti card. There are a lot of good video cards developed for gaming applications that work great for film editing. I use two 19 inch monitors but that's probably the minimal size that you want for your editing workstation.

Figure 51 shows a screenshot from Premiere Pro CS5 of our last film. Note that the editing screen is divided into functional panels. Most of these panels serve multiple purposes by clicking on another tab. The panel at the bottom right that takes up most of the screen is where the work is done, the editing timeline. Here is where you edit the scenes and sound tracks together into a cohesive film. Without ever having touched a real editing platform, you can get spun up on basics in a few weeks. Of course, to master this kind of software can take years. I will go through some basics on editing but try to highlight problems or issues that result from production elements not being done correctly and some work-arounds for them, not that we screwed up anywhere in production (grin). For basics on setting up Adobe CS5 and other tutorials, see the Adobe site: http://tv.adobe.com/show/learn-premiere-pro-cs5

*Figure 51-**Adobe CS5 Premier Pro Editing Screen***

THE NUTS & BOLTS OF INDIE FILM PRODUCTION

Pick-Up Shots

The first thing that should happen is that the editor should put together a rough cut of the film to determine if any additional shots or scenes are needed. A rough cut is putting together all of the scenes in the timeline to get a feeling for the flow of the film. It's not a polished edit with transitions, special effects, colorization, etc., applied. It's important that the editor let the producer know as soon as possible if there needs to be scenes or shots picked up. If they are needed the production crew will need to return to a location to shoot the scene(s). This needs coordination as soon as possible because people and locations change and this could create continuity issues. The editor would also review all of the sound tracks to make sure he has all of the required sound tracks. Vocal tracks can be obtained through automatic dialogue replacement (ADR), but room tones will need to come from the locations. Determine if you need additional footage or location sound and get it as soon as possible.

Raw Film Data

I call this raw film data because it is the unedited data from the film shoot. Film experts will probably come after me explaining that raw data is the camera image before it's compressed, but for discussion, I'll call it raw data. The raw data will have been captured on some form of media, such as media cards or a portable drive. Anyway, that data if collected on location should have been stored in directories on portable drives connected to the laptop. Most laptop drives are too small for storing a complete film (300 to 500 GB of data) so most likely the data was dumped to these drives. A smart producer would have provided two separate drives with enough space to create an original and a backup.

  We begin by bringing in our raw film data into our editing workstation. First, let's review some requirements for our editing workstation.

- Computer (Mac or Windows based) that has minimal of 4 Cores (Quad Core) @ 3 GHz speed CPUs with duo monitor output capability.

- At least 12 Gb RAM (suggest 16 GB)
- Fast video graphics card with RAM (NVIDIA or better)
- 3-4 terabytes of storage (Internal SATA or SCSI, or external USB 3.0 or Firewire)
- Video editing software (Avid, Final Cut or Premiere Pro)
- Duo Hi-Res monitors (19 inch minimum-the bigger the better)
- Built-in or card capable of surround sound output (six channels)
- Speaker system (surround sound – six channels)
- Blu-ray/DVD writer and software
- Professional sound editing software (Audition, Soundbooth, ProTools, others) capable of editing and creating surround sound tracks.
- QuickTime Pro 7.0
- Media Player 9
- Uninterrupted Power Source (UPS) –Crucial for protecting your workstation from brown outs or power issues. Newer solid state drives are sensitive to this.

For our film project, I loaded all of the AVCHD (.mts) files into a directory on the editing system under the directory *movie_source_files*. The directories under the *movies_source_files* are labeled for each day of shooting. You may want to talk with your tech person and decide upon a directory structure to store your video and audio files during filming that makes sense to you and organizes the files. You'll quickly discover as you shoot, that a full feature generates tons of video files and assigns sequential numbering to them. The sequential numbers will not relate to scene numbers so you'll need to keep your files organized. If you remember, during preproduction, we developed a master schedule and schedules per location. The schedules and daily call sheets contain the scenes shot per location, which came from the latest shooting script. By using the location schedule or daily call sheets and matching this to your directories that contain each day's files, you can identify the scenes that you need to bring into your editing timeline with less searching through your directories. Figure 52 shows the directories containing the scenes from the film shoot.

*Figure 52-**Adobe Premiere Pro CS5 Media Browser***

In CS5, we simply select the media browser and look through the *movie_source_files* directories that contain the all of the video files. Drilling down into the video file directories, we then select the ".mts" files for import by either dragging into the media bin (shown outlined in red in Figure 52) or by double-clicking.

The video files are then selected from the file bin, and dragged to the timeline (see Figure 53) where they are edited together. Naturally in most editing applications like Adobe CS5, there are multiple video and audio tracks to allow for layering of the videos for such things as video special effects, lettering, etc. The media bin contains all video and audio files for all sequences within the project.

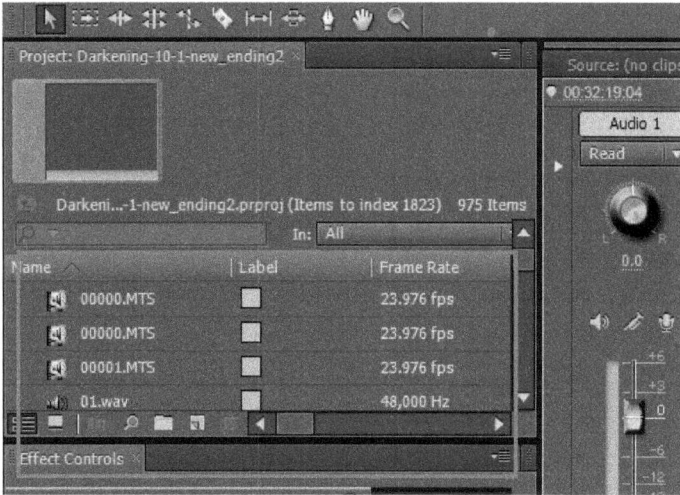

*Figure 53-**Adobe CS5 Media Bin***

You may however have multiple sequences in a single project. For instance, if you want to create a trailer, you can create a new sequence and import images and sound from your final film edit into your trailer sequence and not lose any of the video settings. It is also helpful when you want to import images from an existing sequence but want to retain all of the settings.

*Figure 54-**Moving Media Files to Timeline***

THE NUTS & BOLTS OF INDIE FILM PRODUCTION

The default background for most editing applications is black. This means if you took away the images on the editing timeline and rendered it, it would be black. So if your images on the timeline are perfectly aligned, and there is a gap between images, you will see black. If you're watching your film run and see a quick dropout to black, then your images are not properly aligned. If you want a black screen between scenes, then you can use this to your benefit.

The effects panel (see Figure 55) is selected by clicking on the effects tab. Adobe CS5 comes with a standard set of effects for video and audio but additional effects (such a Magic Bullet Colorista and Video Copilot Twitch, among many) may be added as plug-ins. The video effects panel is highlighted in red.

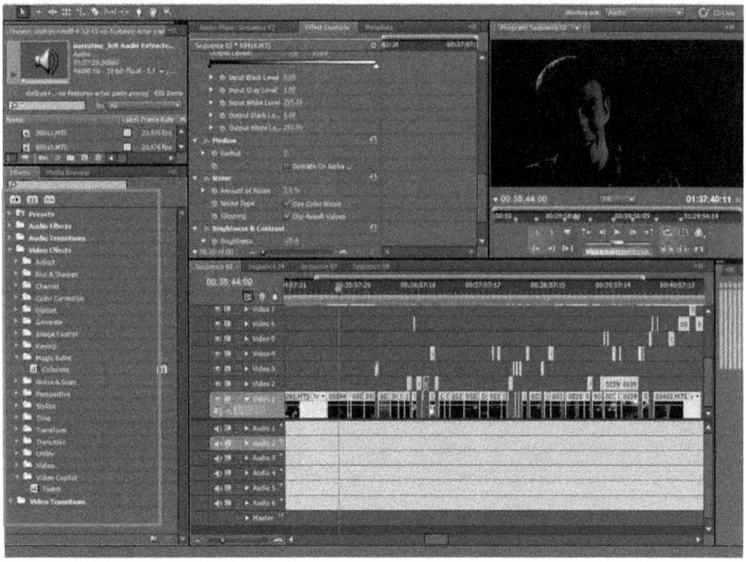

*Figure 55-**CS5 Video Effects Selection Panel***

Video effects are applied to scenes by selecting the effect and dragging to the scene in the editing timeline. Once the effect is applied, an effect panel window will open that allows changing of the parameters (see Figure 56).

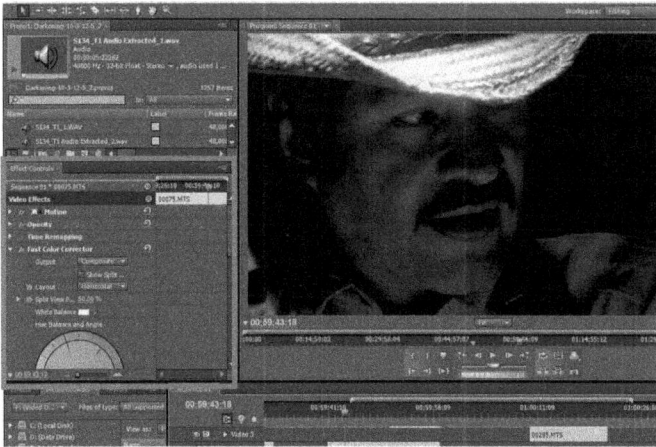

*Figure 56-**Effect Control Panel Display***

Making Video Look Like Film

The thing about video is that sometimes it looks too good – too clean. If you look at film, it does not have that distinct separation and crisp line. Lines and edges in film are more "blurred" and less crisp on the edges. When lines are too crisp and clean, we immediately think video. If we're trying to sell the illusion of film, then we do not want it to look like video. For images that look too sharp and crisp, there is a fix. If you are using one of the more advanced film editing platforms (like FCP or Premiere Pro) you can blur the edges of too-fine detailed images and apply some film grain with applications contained within the editing platform. Below, the image sharpness was reduced using tools under the Video Effects tab (Noise & Grain). Figure 57 is the image without the effect applied and Figure 58 is with the effect applied.

The idea is to remove the sharpness of lines that will make the film look too much like video. Adobe Premier Pro also has tools that allow the editor to add grain to the image. By blurring sharp lines and adding grain where needed, the final product will more resemble film. In Figure 57, note the detail in the broach that our actress is wearing. In Figure 58 after blurring some of the fine lines, notice how some of that sharp detail is now gone.

*Figure 57-**Before Un-sharpening Applied***

*Figure 58-**After Un-sharpening Applied***

Depth of Field

First of all, depth of field is a different concept from "Film Look", although depth of field in visual medium does give it a look more like film than video. Film Look has come to mean certain effects and coloring applied to films to give them a unique look. Many of the sci-fi and action films use an applied "Film look" to create brown, gray, or blue-tones to add a desolate or cold atmosphere to the look of the film. There are software products on the market like Magic Bullet that are used to apply a film look.

Depth of field is more related to focal planes. The Depth of field (DOF) is the distance between the nearest and farthest objects in a scene that emphasize objects in the frame. We've all seen those shots where the focus is pulled from one object to another in a shot to emphasize the object. When everything in the frame is in focus, they all compete for the viewer's attention. In some cases, this is fine. For instance, some director's feel that when shooting beautiful vistas in the background, they want the audience to get the full effect of the cinematic experience.

Some filmmakers feel that why spend the time and money for beautiful scenery and props when we're just going to blur them out of the scene. Generally though, depth of field allows us to guide our audience through what we want them to focus on in each scene. However, digital cameras with non-interchangeable lenses (lower end prosumer cameras) can only create that depth of field when the subject is a long distance from background objects. The figure below shows how objects in front and behind objects can be out of focus (not within the focal plane) while the object in the middle is in focus (within the focal plane).

Depth of Field

Editing Flow

If you're lucky enough, you will be able to find or hire, if you have the budget, an experienced editor for your film. On our first feature film production, we hired an editing house to do all of our post production work (editing, sound, scoring). Although we didn't have to worry about doing the post production work, it cost us $30K and we didn't have enough control of the final product. If you are turning your film over to a post production facility, then you can skip this section. If you are planning on doing your own post production (like most of us), then read on.

I did the editing, sound, and scoring of our last feature and although I learned a lot about it, I am in no way an expert editor. There are tons of videos on "YouTube" and on the web that provide instruction on editing. Whatever editing platform you are using, spend the time to read all you can about editing films and the platform you're using. Make sure that the tutorials and reading that you do cover both video and audio editing. Many of the film editing application vendors have helpful tutorials on their web sites (like Adobe) that you can access for free. Take advantage of these. Editing a film is a learned craft and is not as straightforward as you may think. You will find yourself facing may problems that will at times stump you but with the help of this book and Google, you can overcome them.

There are several areas of focus for an editor. The editor must put the video together with the recorded dialogue (from the set, location, or sound studio) and get them in sync along with any Foley sounds and sound effects and then layer on top of that the music score, required room tones, and special effects (SFX) that are required. On our film, we had to deal with all of these, and as a new editor, I found kinks with getting each one of these right.

The basic tracks that I started with was to build a working copy of all of the video shot and to get that matched up with the narrative audio from the actors captured on the set. Don't worry about the sound effects and music at this point. That will come later. For now, focus on telling the story in a naturally flowing timeline. As for flow, the director and producer should have worked out a shot list for each scene that tells the story in a cohesive way. For each location that is used in the film, we will open with a master establishing shot that introduces it. You don't need to do this each time your scene involves that location but rather for the first time that you introduce it in the film. We've all seen these establishing shots where we are introduced to the location. It may be a high crane shot that slowly sweeps down to show someone arriving at that location. This introduces the audience to the scene location.

After we are introduced to the location, we move on to the action of the scene. Many times editors prefer to trim down the beginning of the scene to move the audience right to the action. Remember earlier we discussed the length of the scene during the production phase and suggested starting the scene early and ending the scene late? We do this to give the editor something to edit. Whether the he or she chooses to edit this out is up to them.

Once established at the location, the editor will have choices of wide shots, medium shots, close-ups, or extreme close-ups to tell the story. Once dialogue from the actors start, the editor will make choices as to which actor will be focused on during the exchange. Many first time editors will use a simple technique of keeping the camera on the actor speaking during the exchange. It's a talking heads technique. When an actor speaks, we show them speaking. When another actor speaks, we show them speaking and so on.

Perhaps a better style is to review the footage of the exchange and to go with the actor who is giving the better performance visually. After all, film is a visual medium and if an actor is giving a better performance, whether the other actor is speaking or not, then we want our camera on them (use their footage). This, of course, needs some balancing. It's easy to get carried away and to get the scene unbalanced because you're keeping the camera on one actor all of the time (using only their footage or scenes). If you consider this technique, you'll find that you improve the film by focusing on performance rather than just following a talking heads technique.

Syncing of actor's dialogue is extremely important. Everyone hates to watch a film where the voice is out of sync with the actor's mouth. This ensures that sound on the set is carefully lined up using the sound slate for each scene. Another way that I mentioned earlier was recording an additional track (mono is fine) with the digital camera for a sync backup. Most digital cameras at the higher end record audio. Although you don't want to use it for the actual narrative sound track for the film, it's good enough for a backup sync track.

When you import your video files into the editing timeline, the video file will have an attached audio file if audio recording was turned on in the camera. This audio track can be used to sync the audio should you have issues with your regular sync methods. By aligning your sound recording file captured externally with your field sound recorder with the audio file captured from the camera, you can perfectly sync the audio. Typically though, you sync sound tracks to video tracks using the visual of the sound slate closing and the spike on the sound track that it makes when the sound slate arm comes in contact with the top of the slate. See Figure 59.

*Figure 59-***Slate Arm Closing at Beginning of Video File**

By syncing the arm closing with the spike in the audio track, you are assured that when the actors speak their dialogue, the words are aligned with the video. See Figure 60 for the sync spike in the audio track that you sync the movement of the sound slate to. Having the video and audio in sync is half the battle when editing.

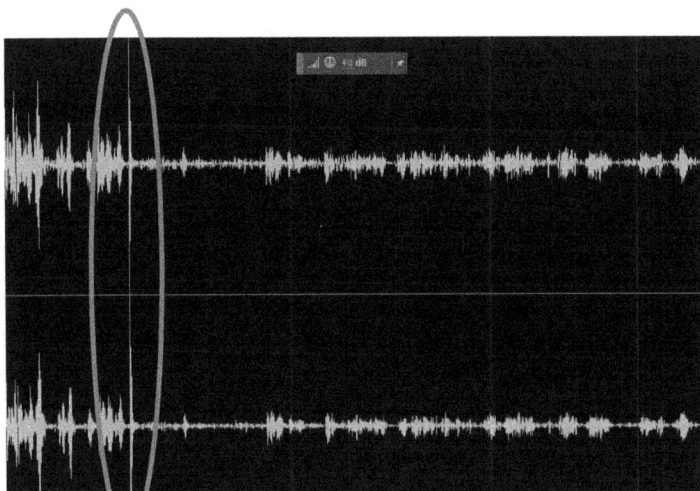

*Figure 60-**Sound Slate Spike in Audio Track***

The quality of the sound tracks is a different issue. As I mentioned earlier, during production you need to have control of locations. Part of the reasoning for this control involves sound. The more people and traffic that you have around your location, the more chance you have for introducing unwanted sounds into the audio that is captured. You also want to have the ability, or authorization, to shut down air conditioners, furnaces, and other devices that generate noise. If you don't and these can't be cleaned up in post, you will need to use ADR to replace the dialogue.

A lot of modern audio editing software today has embedded tools that allow you to clean up noise in the sound tracks. Audition and SoundBooth by Adobe both have very good tools for cleaning up noise and other artifacts that may show up in your audio captured on location. Figures 61 and 62 show how to select audio in your recorded soundtrack in Adobe Audition and selectively removing or reducing it.

Once you have decided on a sample to use for noise reduction, you may either select an area of the audio timeline or select the whole timeline by choosing "Edit" from the top menu, then "Select" and "Select All" for the entire audio timeline.

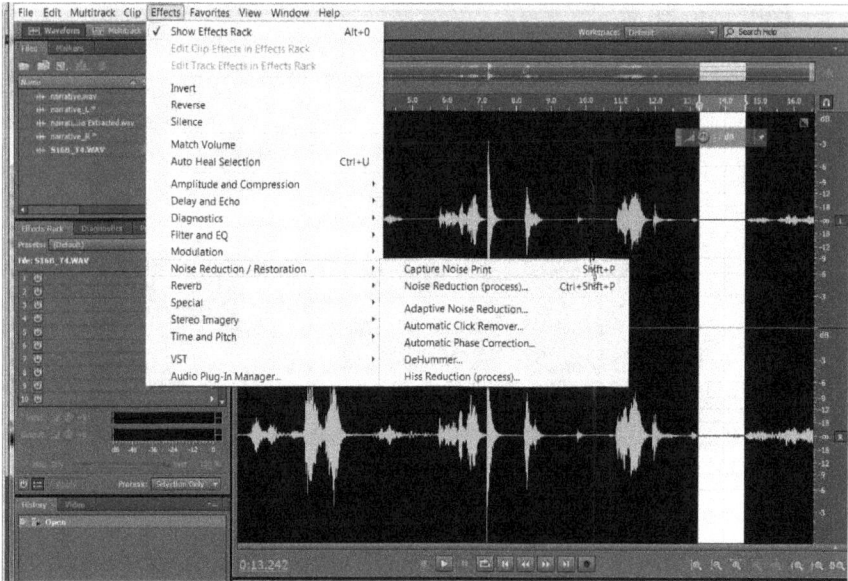

Figure 61-Sample Noise Selection in Abode Audition

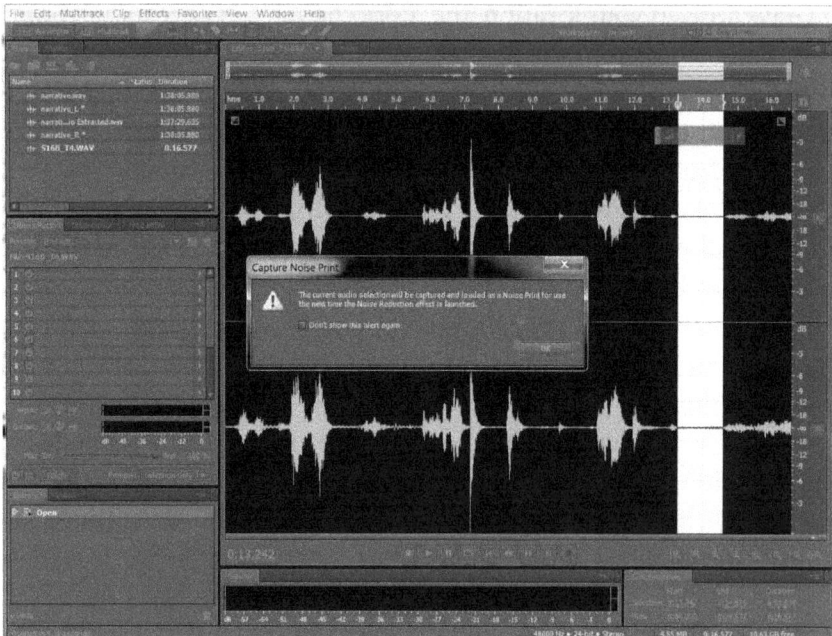

Figure 62-Sample Noise Selection in Abode Audition Response

Once you have decided on a sample to use for noise reduction, you may either select an area of the audio timeline or select the whole timeline by choosing "Edit" from the top menu, then "Select" and "Select All" for the entire audio timeline. This selects the part or whole timeline to reduce the noise based on the sample that you took earlier of the noise in the audio track.

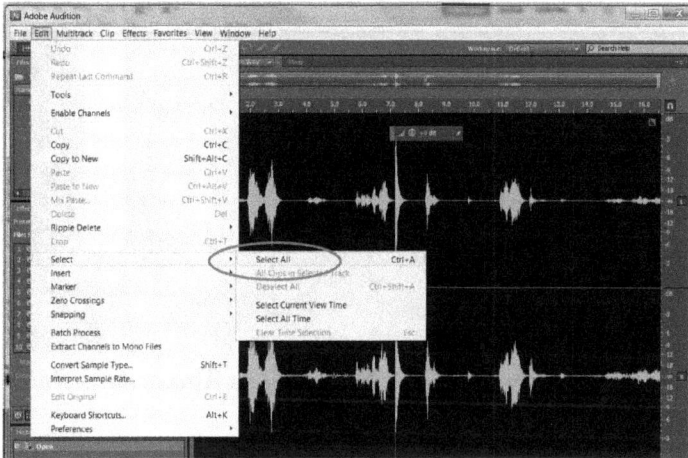

Figure 63-Selecting All of the Audio Timeline

Once the timeline has been selected, click on "Effect" from the top toolbar, then choose "Noise Reduction/Restoration" from the menu and then select "Noise Reduction (process)".

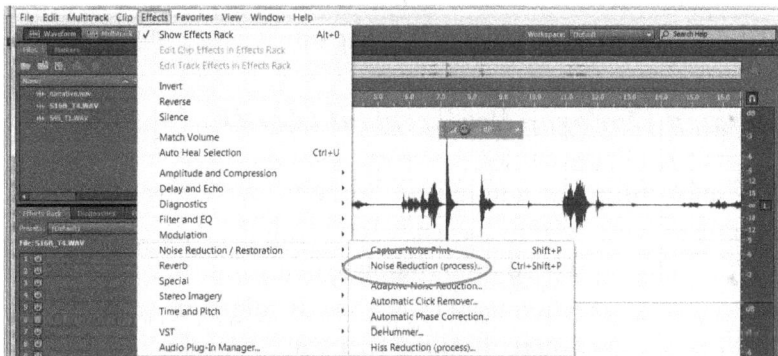

Figure 64-Selecting to Remove Noise

The screen in Figure 65 is displayed.

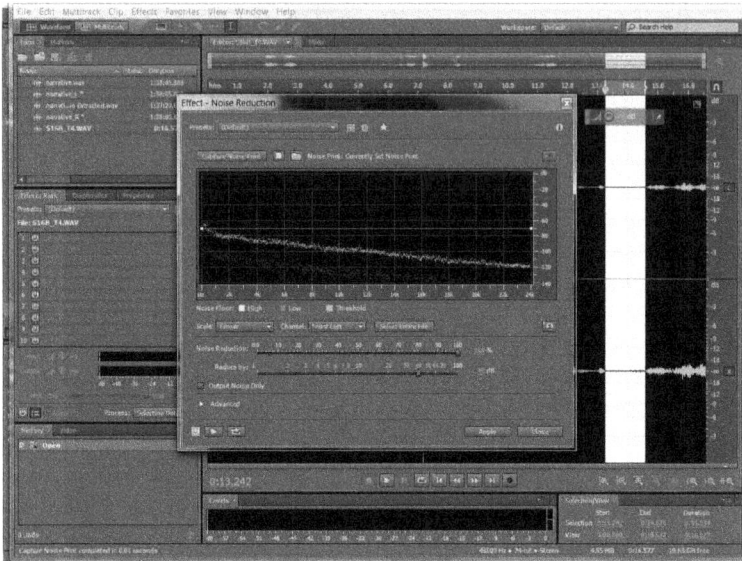

*Figure 65-**Sample Noise Selection in Abode Audition***

I'll caution you right away on using tools to extract noise from sound tracks. It takes a very light hand on the tools. It's better to extract just a little at a time to get it where it sounds the best. If you tray and remove all of the noise in one effort you may find that it creates distortions in the resulting audio track. I usually will repeat the process a couple of times, each time taking a very delicate approach to removing the noise. If you find that you've removed too much and the result sounds distorted, use the "Undo" button to go back and try again.

Automated Dialogue Replacement (ADR)

ADR is everything but automated. Sorry to say. However, it may save your scene for you. ADR is basically replacing the dialogue in a scene by having the actor re-record their dialogue in a studio setting. The new re-recorded dialogue is then used to replace the dialogue from the original scene. I know what you're thinking that you can't afford to do ADR in a studio for your film. Wrong. A temporary ADR studio can be setup just about anywhere. All it takes is a very quiet room with EVERYTHING shut off (air conditioners, furnaces, etc.), a large screen monitor or TV, a copy of the sides for the actor, a good microphone, microphone stand, a field recorder, the latest DVD version of your film, and a good DVD player that allows you to shuttle back and forth on the DVD.

Schedule the actor(s) that you need the ADR from for a few hours and assemble a small crew of the director and someone to run the DVD player. The trick to ADR is to get the actor back into their frame of mind when they shot the scene so the tone of their dialogue is correct. The actor watches the large screen and reads their lines, trying to sync up with the mouth movement of their character in the film. They will have to do at least half a dozen times for you to have good material to work with. Once they get the tone and timing correct, you are done.

Back in editing, the editor will bring in the ADR tracks and using the best synced version along with the best tone of the actor, they will add it back into the editing timeline. Since the voice track from the ADR session will be clean, this will mean that it will lack room tone. The room tone already existed in the sound recording from the location but will not now exist in this new ADR track. Remember the room tone that I told was so important to get at each location? Well, this is where it comes in. The editor will need to add the room tone from that location underneath the new ADR track so that the scene sound track doesn't sound devoid of room tone.

Most likely, the new ADR track will not perfectly match, especially if the actor has never done ADR, and will need tweaking by the editor. The editor will bring the new ADR track into a sound editing application (like Audition or SoundBooth) and remove pieces of the soundtrack between each word until it matches the movement of the actor's mouth. It's very tedious but it works. If you need a longer pause between each of the actor's words, you can copy a small part of the track between each word. By pasting this back into the timeline between each word, you increase the pause between words. Figure 66 shows how to select the audio track timeline between words using Audition.

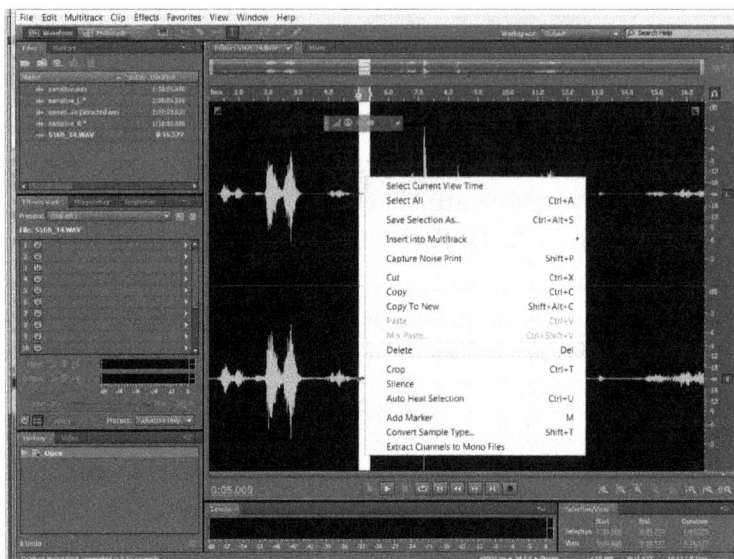

Figure 66-*Deleting Space between Spoken Dialogue*

Using your mouse, select a portion of the timeline that you want to copy or delete. Then by right-clicking the mouse, select "Copy" or "Delete" from the drop-down options.

Scoring Your Film

The music score behind the film can add a lot to it. Some of the most memorable films have a great score that burns them into our memory. The shocking shower scene in Alfred Hitchcock's *Psycho* or the simple but horrifying melody of the shark approaching in *Jaws* makes them unique and epic. Usually these are created by talented composers who create original melodies that drive the action on the silver screen. Depending on your budget, there are several options when looking to compose a soundtrack for your film. If you have a large enough budget for your film, you can pursue experienced composers in the industry who work on major films. Most likely you won't have the budget to hire film composers like Danny Elfman or John Williams but there are many composers across the country and around the world that will work with your budget or even compose for free for exposure. The easiest way to look for a composer for a low budget film is to post a wanted ad on music composer web sites.

There are web sites dedicated to music composers and they usually have a board where you can post a notice. For our last two films, I solicited on these web sites and have always gotten over fifty responses back from composers interested in doing the scores for the films. Most will be glad to send you a music sampler CD or a link to a site where their work is posted. The first time (our first feature) I found a composer in Canada who did a fantastic job on our film and the second time I solicited, I ended up with a composer who wrote one melody piece for our last film. I ended up doing the score myself but used his composition for a couple of key scenes. I'll discuss how to do your own score later.

The composer will need at the least a rough cut of your film to start. If they are composing an original score for your film, expect this to take several months. You'll need to negotiate a price with each composer. However, don't assume because they call themselves a composer that you can just hand over your film and receive an Academy Award winning score. I worked with several composers on our last film, but they could just not deliver anything that worked for me. You need to ask them to provide a sample score for one scene and see if it works for your film. If it doesn't, just politely tell them that you don't feel that it's right for your film project. The score should hit the emotional points in each scene (drama points or funny points) and emphasize them. If you feel that the score doesn't hit the emotional highs and lows on target, then you need to pass on that composer and look for another. Do NOT sign a contract or agreement with them until you are 100% convinced he/she is the right composer for your film. What's nice is that you can work with composers from anywhere in the world. Composers can create soundtracks from the rough cut that you send them and then send back the WAV or MP3 files for integration into the edit.

I would try to work with composers who don't use synthesizers but real instrument samplings. The sound is a much better quality when the composer has access to real sounding instruments rather than synthesizers. If you can afford it or are a good salesman, having an orchestra perform the original score will take the music to a new level. Every city usually has an orchestra. Look for arts organizations in your area and a point of contact for their orchestra. They will most likely charge you to work on your film. If you have the budget to have an orchestra perform the composer's score, remember that you will need to get a studio quality version recorded. Make sure you have a plan for recording it and what type of format you need it recorded in (WAV or MP3) and the equipment you will need to record it (recorder and microphones).

If you find the right composer, negotiate whatever you can. Perhaps your budget allows you $10K for the score. Then write a work for hire agreement that provides all the rights worldwide and document the price agreed upon. If you don't have the funds in your budget, then agree to a deferred price and include that in your agreement. Do not pay an up-front fee. Only pay when the agreed upon sound track is delivered. Also make sure that you write in your agreement that you have the right to modify the sound track as needed and that the composer has created an original sound track and is the author of that music. You may bring in the soundtrack and realize that changes are needed. Make sure that you have these rights included in your agreement. The soundtrack should be delivered in stereo and in a format that meets the requirements for your editing platform (i.e., WAV or MP3, and 48Khz, 24 bit sampling).

What you can't do when creating a sound track is use unauthorized or unlicensed music in your film. All music must be licensed from the source. You cannot just use hit songs or music that you find on the web. This is illegal and it can not only cause legal issues such as copyright violations but can also cause your film to be yanked from the market. There are plenty of options that are free or inexpensive that are legal for developing a sound track for your film. Some of these are:

- Composers
- Open source or royalty free music
- Upcoming local bands
- Music score software (i.e., Pro Scores)
- Music applications

We've talked about composers and the options depend upon your budget. There are also many sources on the web that provides already developed music scores that can be licensed for film. These usually are canned tracks that can be purchased and applied to your film. They usually come packaged by genre (sci-fi, drama, comedy, etc.) and have usage and licensing fees attached to them. Make sure to read the fine print and ask questions about using for your film. Some sound pretty good and some can be somewhat campy sounding. You can check them out and judge for yourself.

Local up-coming bands are a good source for music for your indie film. Many times, these bands see this as a good promotional activity to showcase their band's music. For our short we found a local band that provided much of the music that we used in the film. In our film, *The Darkening*, we found a popular band in Chicago that not only provided music but were also showcased in a club scene in our film. They had a good screen presence and worked perfectly for our film. Make sure that you write an agreement for bands just as we discussed for composers. If you don't know any local bands or don't have contacts, you can contact local sound recording studios and put the word out that you are looking for a local band for your film.

I used Pro Scores by Video Copilot for our last film. Pro Scores is a library of samplings and full scores that sound rich and use real instrument samplings. You can arrange the instrumental sounds into your own arrangement and create professional sounding sound tracks. It's very reasonably priced ($100 when I purchased it) and doesn't require any background in scoring or creating music. If you have limited funds, it's a good place to start. Did you know that Quentin Tarrantino does his own sound tracks by using music from composers to master his own sound track. If you are talented and have music composition skills, you can also elect to create your own music from a variety of software applications on the market. I have not used any myself, but if you are musically inclined (I'm not), this may be an option for you.

So you have your soundtrack and it's been mastered by a talented composer and delivered to you. You'll want it sent as separate WAV or MP3 files that are sequentially numbered from the first scene to the last scene. You want separate files (tracks) so you can adjust the dB level of the individual sound tracks up or down as you feel necessary. If one huge file (track) was delivered, all scenes will be at the same dB level. If you need to adjust the volume for just one scene, you will have to split the tracks to do it or adjust the volume of the whole film. If one long file for the entire film was delivered, you can also break it into sections for each scene. Breaking it down in this manner will not only allow you to control the volume but also let you fade in and fade out (beginning and ending) the music for the scenes. If you need to tweak individual cues or notes in the soundtrack, use an application like Adobe Soundbooth© or Adobe Audition© to import and edit the file.

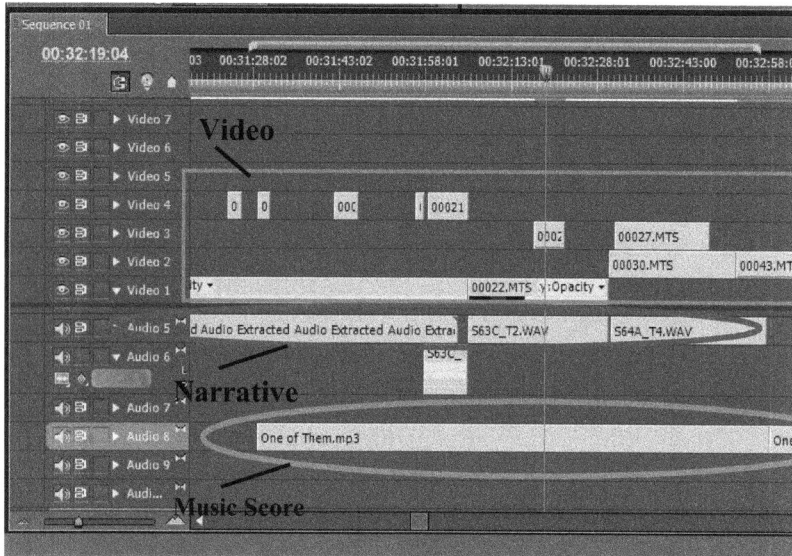

Figure 67-*Adobe CS5 Editing Timeline*

Figure 67 shows the editing timeline, to include the video, narrative audio, and the music score. Note in this timeline, we see one of the music tracks used "One of Them."

Removing Pops and Audio Transitions

Your audio track for the film will consist of hundreds of pieces of audio since each scene has its own audio track that must be integrated into the whole audio track for the film. During playback the abrupt starting or ending of a track may cause a popping sound. To resolve this pop, you will need to transition the audio track. To do this, you'll need to add an audio transition to each of the pieces of soundtrack where the audio track starts and ends. See Figure 68. Note that on each audio track segment I have applied a Constant Gain from the audio transition from the tools panel. This is an effect listed under the Effects tab. Right-click with the mouse and drag to the beginning or end of each audio clip and release. You can adjust the size of the transition by moving your mouse cursor to the edge of the transition applied to the audio clip. A red bar with an arrow through it will appear (see Figure 68) at the edge of the end of the transition. Click and pull the mouse. This will change the length of the audio transition.

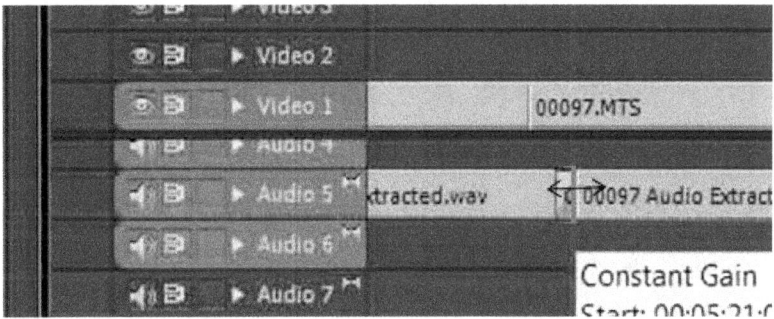

Figure 68-*Audio Transition Adjust*

This audio transitioning will remove the pops from the audio track. As you can see in Figure 69, it's a tedious task but will improve the quality of the sound of the film.

*Figure 69-**Sound Tracks with Audio Transitioning***

Creating & Exporting Dolby 5.1 Surround Sound

Again, here's where it pays to have a sound engineer on your staff because creating a true surround sound track for your film can be a daunting task. Surround sound not only improves your listening pleasure when watching a film, but many times you will find that it's suggested as a requirement when delivering your film to distributors. If you are doing a theatrical release of your film, it's a must.

You will find numerous discussions about surround sound channels and what should be allocated to the front speakers, rear speakers, center, and LFE among others. Typically it's suggested that the center channel be for narrative, the front left and right be allocated to the scoring of the film, and the rear left and right be allocated to the Foley and sound effects for the film. However, it comes down to some personal choice as well. I prefer my music on the rear speaker and my narrative on the front speakers. I then run my score on the LFE and put an additional voice track on the center. I'm sure there's a better solution than what I've chosen. It depends upon your skill level and resources for the approach you want to take.

First of all, you need to make sure that your editing platform supports Dolby 5.1 surround sound. Surround sound, at a minimum, contains six tracks. These are:

- Front left
- Front right
- Center
- LFE (Low Frequency Effects)
- Back (rear) left
- Back (rear) right

For CS5, you'll need to purchase the Surcode Dolby 5.1 plugin for Windows. Current pricing is around $250. Once you have installed the Surcode plugin and registered it you'll be able to export your film in Dolby 5.1 surround sound. If you have issues getting your Surcode plugin to work, the Surcode support is very good and will gladly help with any issues that you may have. I've used them myself and was very satisfied with their support after my drive crashed and I had to reinstall everything (youch!). Anyway, once you have it installed and working, you'll see a similar screen to the one in Figure 70 showing the surround sound icons.

*Figure 70-**Surround Sound Tracks***

Be aware that if you originally setup your project sequence for stereo tracks it won't work for surround sound. When you first created your film project in CS5, it asked you for setup info that included the type of sound tracks to create. See Figure 71.

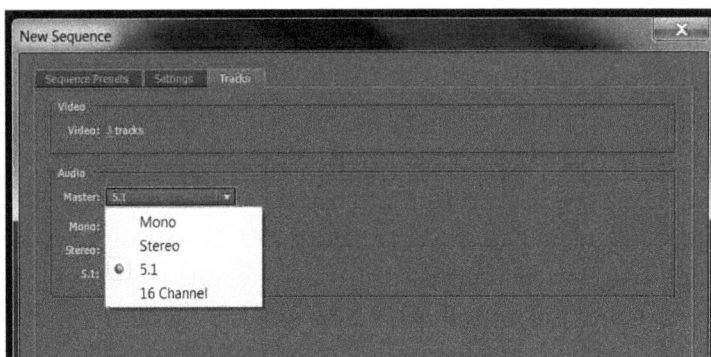

Figure 71-New Sequence Audio Setup

If you didn't select "5.1" for your original sequence setup, you'll need to create a new sequence for your film. Don't panic. Adobe Premiere CS5 allows for multiple sequences in a project. Simply go to "File" on the top toolbar and select "New" then select "Sequence" to create a new one. Once you've created your new sequence you can copy your entire audio and video editing timeline into your new sequence timeline. This is the only way to safely make a copy of your timeline without losing any of your settings. I used this and it worked perfectly.

Where did the six surround tracks come from? Good question. In my editing timeline for the audio tracks I had as many as nine levels of audio. I had narrative audio that we captured on the set, Foley sounds, room tone that we captured on the set, and multiple layers of music scores. By selectively turning on or off audio tracks, I can choose to export an audio track composed of all of my music tracks into a single stereo track (wav file) from CS5. I'll call this my music stereo track. To generate this, I turn off all other audio tracks except the ones that I want to export. See Figure 72. By clicking on the speaker icon on the associated audio track, I can turn the audio track on or off. When the speaker icon is visible, this means that the audio track is active. When the speaker icon is not visible, this means it's inactive. In Figure 71, I have all of the tracks associated with the score turned on.

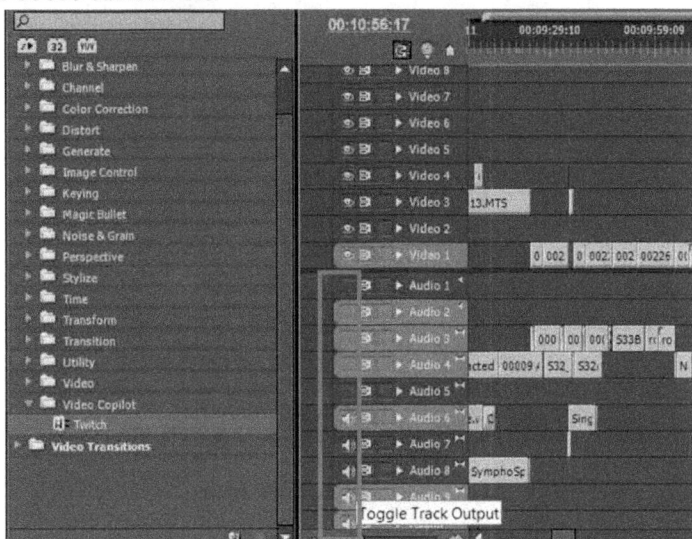

*Figure 72-**Creating Surround Sound Tracks***

I will then go to "File" and then "Export" to select a stereo only export (turn off video) of the audio tracks associated with the scoring.

I will then do the same for my narrative audio tracks. Turn all tracks associated with any audio narrative on and the rest of the audio tracks off. Export the narrative audio as a stereo track also. If you have all of your Foley sounds on dedicated tracks, you can export them out as a stereo track. I actually exported all of my Foley and narrative as a single stereo track. I did this because a lot of my Foley was captured on the set and is multiplexed into my narrative tracks. I didn't want to spend three months pulling out all of my Foley from my sound captured on the set to create separate Foley tracks. As a smarter solution, I'd suggest thinking of ways to capture Foley separately on the set for surround sound purposes.

Once the separate stereo tracks have been exported from CS5, open up these stereo files in Audition or SoundBooth (or whatever your flavor is). See Figure 73.

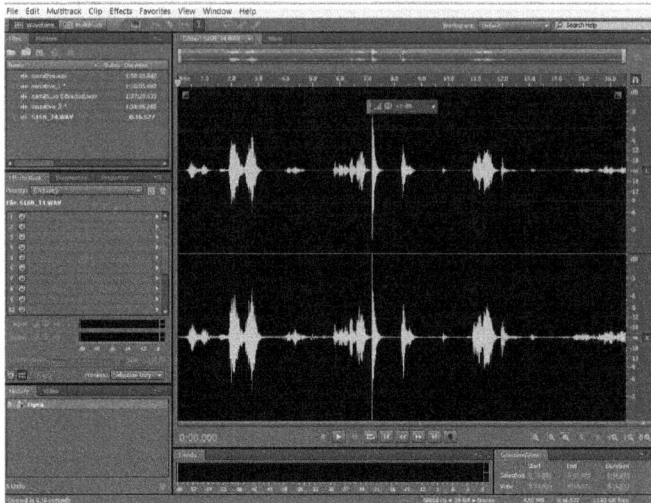

*Figure 73-**Stereo Narrative Sound Track***

Go to "Edit" and "Extract Channels to Mono Files" to extract the stereo channels to two separate mono files. This creates a left and right mono channel.

Once you have done this, with your music track and narrative audio track, you'll end up with four separate channels. Import these files back into CS5 and use the left and right narrative mono channels for your first and second channels. I use a narrative mono track for my center speaker and a mono scoring track to throw against my LFE. As I mentioned, you may want to separate out your Foley and SFX sound and allocate to a different set of speakers (like rear). Also remember that if you have the time, most of the audio applications today have panning features wherein Foley sounds can be panned from one speaker to another. Not being an audio engineer, I opted to do a pseudo surround sound track.

Creating a Telephone Voice

If you have a scene in your film where one of your characters is talking to another on the phone, you can choose to cut back and forth between the actors to show them talking on the phone or you can choose to stay on one character and hear the other part of the telephone conversation as voice-over. If you choose to hear the voice-over, you want it to sound more like a telephone voice than their normal voice. Because of the narrow bandwidth of phone communications, the voice does not normally sound as rich or deep in base because of the narrow frequency range of telephones. So in creating a telephone voice, you basically limit the frequency response. In Adobe Audition, there is a menu selection for a telephone voice that does this automatically. You simply highlight the section of the audio track (or select all) that you want to sound like a telephone voice and it applies the filter. See Figure 74.

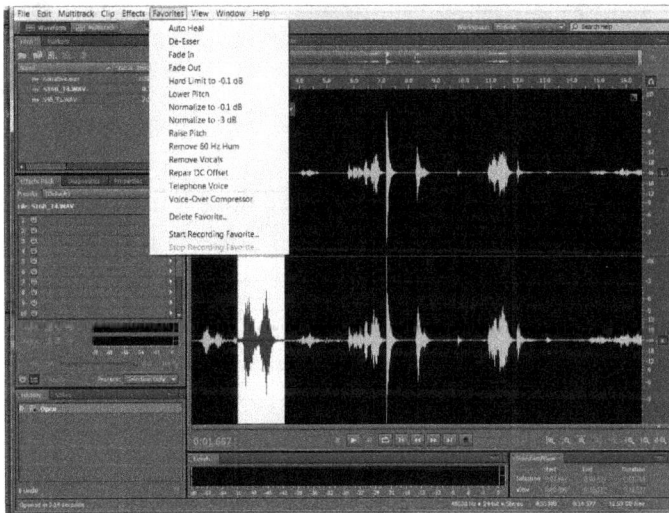

*Figure 74-**Automated Selection of Telephone Voice***

If you want to modify the frequency response, you select the "Effects" option from the top toolbar then select "Filter and Echo" from the dropdown menu and then select "FFT Filter" to bring up FFT Filter menu. Select the "Presets" at the top of the FFT Filter window to display the available presets and select "Telephone Receiver."

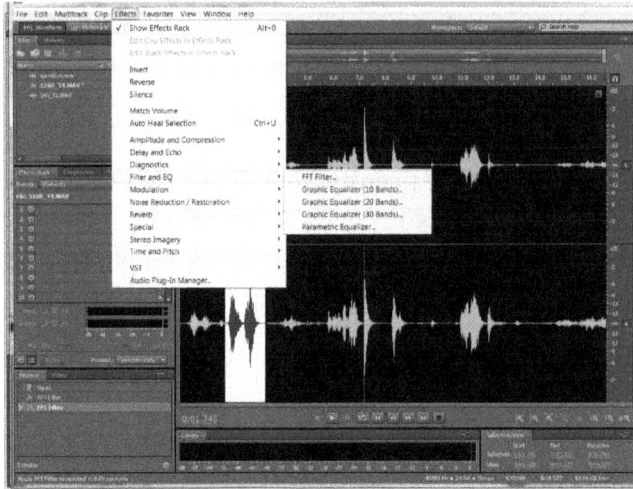

Figure 75-FFT Filter Selection

This plays the frequency response diagram shown in Figure 76. Note the frequency response for a telephone voice is around 400Hz to 2KHz. The frequency response (and the way the telephone voice sounds) can be modified in this window by using your mouse to move the frequency response points.

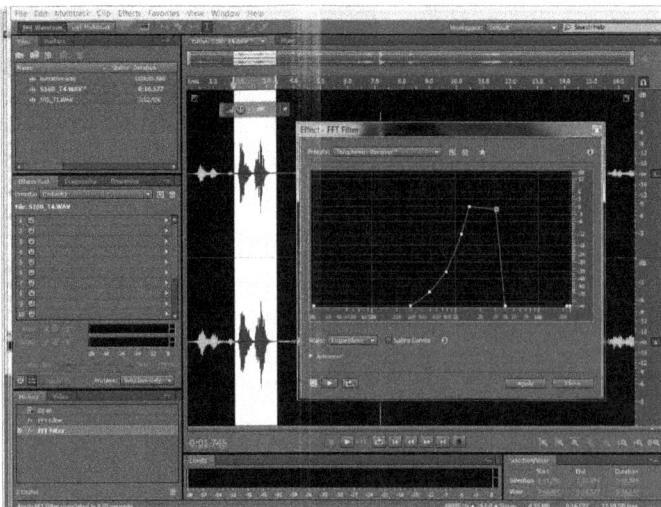

Figure 76-FFT Filter Frequency Response Graph

Adobe Soundbooth also has options for creating a telephone voice. Then again if you want a real sounding telephone voice, you can always record the actor's dialogue off of the phone and use that. Another option.

Colorization and Crushing Blacks

Okay, I've mentioned this before, but I'll mention it again. The DP (or cinematographer) should white balance the camera for each location to ensure that the colors are true. If you don't the editor will have the task of colorizing the scenes. Colorization, as many things in film, is an art. It takes years of experience to become a pro at it, but with the tools that are included with the editing applications today, even the novice editor can do color correction to scenes that have issues. In Figure 77, we shot a scene right at sunset and forgot to white balance. Naturally, the scene has some hue issues, but using Colorista (comes with Magic Bullet) I was able to get the skin tones back to something acceptable (see Figure 78). I used Colorista to remove some of the orange hue from the scene.

*Figure 77-**Before Color Correct***

*Figure 78-**After Color Correct***

Since our last film was a suspense horror film, I wanted the opening sequences to look dark and also decided to do them desaturated of most color. Saturation is one parameter of Colorista that I used to get this effect. I desaturated the image (removed color) in Colorista. Saturation went from normal "0" to a more negative number (-100) here. The image in Figure 79 is raw, without any video effects applied but just as it was shot.

*Figure 79-**Normal Saturation and Contrast***

Figure 80 is the same shot desaturated and with the blacks crushed. By crushing blacks, I mean that I decreased the brightness from "0" to a more negative number. This becomes more of the look that I was after.

*Figure 80-**Desaturated and Crushed***

Special Effects (SFX)

If you planned on having special effects in your film, you should have shot the scenes on the set that required special effects. Hopefully, you took my advice and took some work-around shots in case the special effects work falls through. For Hollywood films, SFX is just another budget item, but for indie filmmakers if we get to post and the SFX work falls apart or increases in cost, we don't usually have the funds to deal with it. Just have a backup plan to work-around SFX just in case. Then if it goes bad, you can still get your film finished. This section assumes that things went well and you were able to find someone with experience in SFX and it fits into your budget.

There are web sites out on the Internet where people in the special effects industry hang out and post work for hire ads. Normally, the site will want you to join before you post it. Do it. It's free and fairly painless. On these sites, they'll provide guidelines in offering work to these talented folks. There's usually some minimum pay amount that they suggest that you offer for work but offer whatever you can afford. Make the work you're offering sound challenging and fun. You'll get some bites.

When you start getting bites, make sure to check them out by asking for links to their work or references. Most of the visual artists that contact you will most likely be out of state and you'll end up having to figure out a system for them to get paid and you to get your product. If you stick to respectable sites and artists who have worked on major films, you shouldn't have to worry that it's a ripoff scheme of any kind. If you're on a pressing schedule, you'll probably need a drop box to exchange files back and forth. www.dropbox.com has free dropboxes that start at 1 Gbyte (I believe). Whenever someone joins the dropbox to download files from you, they add additional storage to your dropbox. I used it to work with our SFX person in LA. We were lucky enough to find a visual effects designer for our last film that worked in the industry. Naturally prices vary with the type of special effects and the number of scenes that need the SFX. If you need to have actual CGI graphics created (such as prehistoric beasts or aliens) this can get very expensive. If your needs are just composited special effects (like fire, explosions, ghosts, etc.) you can usually negotiate prices within your budget.

The editor will post the scenes on the dropbox site (or snail-mail them) for the visual artist to work with. Once the artist does the composite, they will post the draft version back onto your Dropbox site. Most artists will encode information onto the image for protection. Once you are happy with the product, these are removed for the final, after payment. See a SFX shot we worked on our last film in Figure 81.

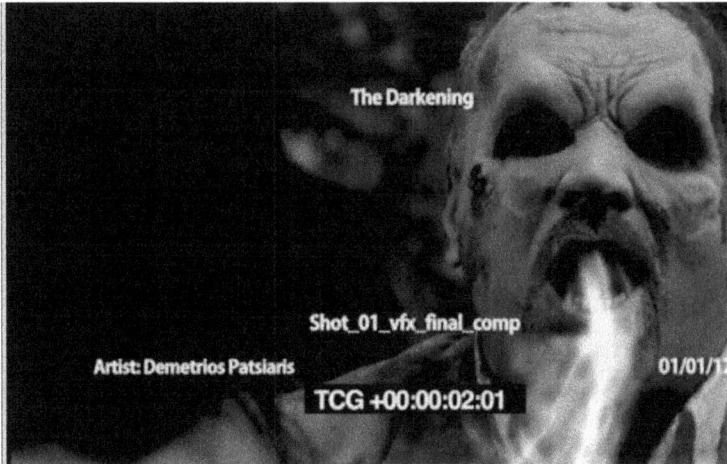

Figure 81-SFX Composite - Draft

The editor will import the newly composited SFX shot back into the editing timeline to see if it works or needs any changes. The editor should be open with the SFX person about what's required in the shot so that the film company gets what they need for the film. SFX artists are proud of their work, and since they will have their name on the credits, they want it to work for the film. Make sure that you write a contract for the SFX artist's work and that they provide the title they want to use in the credits and the name they want used in the credits.

Opening and Closing Credits

First of all, many of the distributors you finally end up doing business with will have a requirement that your titles be **title safe**. So what is it? Title safe is when titles do not extend beyond a safe zone of the screen where they will be cut off. They must not extend too far into the outer zone of the viewing screen. Because of the way they may be displayed on smaller screens, they may get cut off. Most editing applications, when building titles, will have a visible border area that defines the title safe area. Figure 82 shows the outer boundary of the image size with another border inside that defines the safe title boundary for the closing credits.

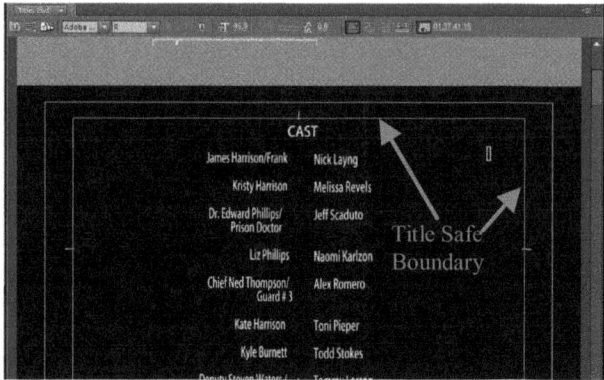

*Figure 82-**Title Safe Boundary***

To create a rolling credit like the one above, simply select "Title" from the top main menu of Adobe CS5 and select "Default Roll" from the dropdown menu. A configuration screen will appear for setting up the credits for your film. Once you select the info for your film, a main screen will appear for inputting your credits. Here you can select the font style and color. If you need to add a logo, such as MPAA (if you got it rated), you can add a logo that actually crawls with the text. To insert a logo, right click on the screen. A menu will appear. Select "Logo" then select "Insert Logo." This will take you to a browse window where you can select the logo for import.

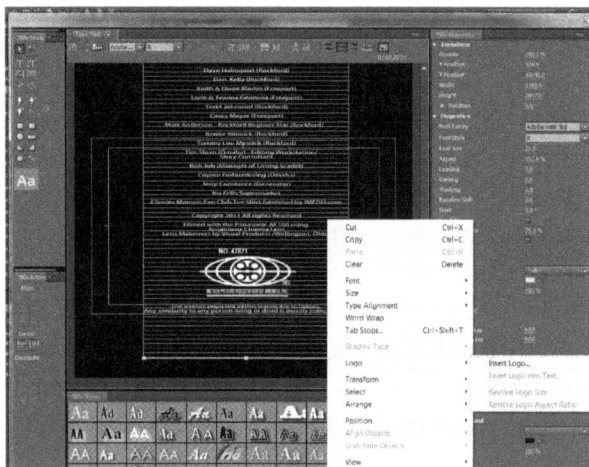

*Figure 83-**Rolling Credits Screen***

Make sure that you identify all cast and crew and contributors for your film in the credits and have the proper title and position identified for their role in the film. Make sure that you do not add too much black screen after the credits end or at the beginning of your film. Many distributors require that the black screen before the start of the film and after are around three seconds. You don't want to have twenty or thirty seconds of black screen before or after the film.

For my opening credits, I used Adobe After Effects to create the simple and clean opening credits. I created a new composition and tweaked the text so it had a slight glow to it.

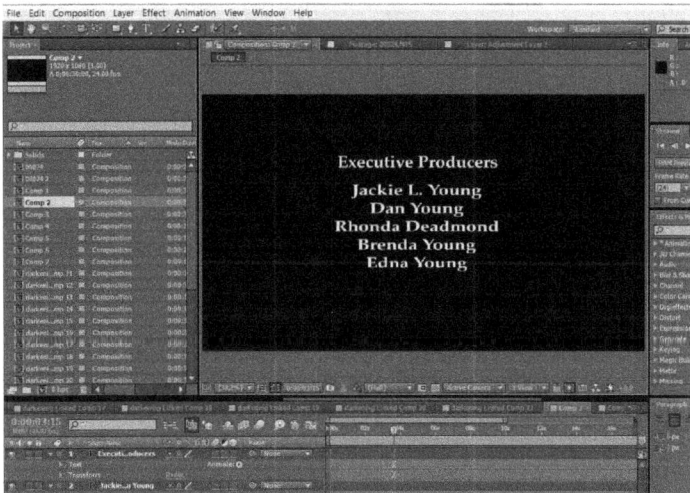

*Figure 84-**Executive Producer Opening Credit in After Effects***

For fancier titling, Adobe After Effects has a ton of presets to choose from for lettering.

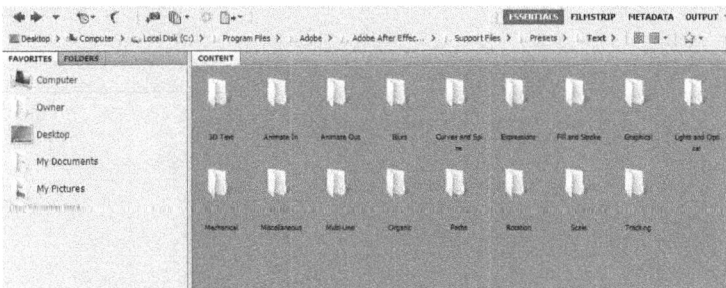

*Figure 85-**Adobe After Effects Text Presets***

After you have created the title, select "Composition" from the top menu and select "Add to Render Queue". This adds it to the queue at the bottom of the main screen. Once you have created all of your titles for the film, you can go down to the render queue and submit all of the titles by selecting the "Render" button. Adobe After Effects delivers the product in ".avi" format.

Once the titles have been rendered out, the editor selects these files and imports them into the editing timeline. Again, the editor should be sure to keep the opening credits within the titling safe boundaries, see Figure 86. Note the two boxes outlined in white. The inner box is the title safe boundary.

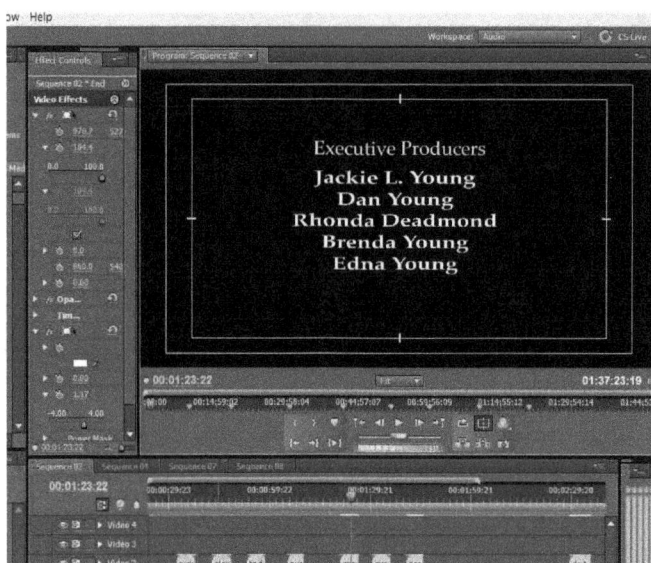

*Figure 86-**Opening Credits Title Safe Boundary***

Codecs and Exporting HQ HD Products

Codecs are program modules that "compress/decompress" video/audio. For Adobe CS5, to generate a compatible Pro Res (Apple) high quality (HQ) high definition (HD) product requires an Avid ® Codec. Avid codecs are free and can be downloaded from the Avid site. The Avid Codec plug-in for Adobe Premiere Pro CS5 includes codecs for various resolutions and data rates. The Avid code uses an Apple QuickTime wrapper (selected in the CS5 "Export" window) along with a "codec" dropdown window. The codecs are arranged by resolution (i.e., 1920x1080 23.98 frames, or 1920x1080 24 frames, etc.) and may come in 8-bit or 10-bit flavors.

Whether you create products for film exhibition (theater), DVD, VOD, cable, or free TV, they each will have their own format requirements (specs) for delivery of the film to them. Generally, they will provide both SD (standard definition) and HD specs for submitting in SD or HD. Below are the HD specs for delivering the film to a cable broadcaster for VOD.

High Definition Progressive (HDp):

- Video Codec: MPEG2
- Bit-rate: 80 Mbps; (min. 50 Mbps if A/V quality approved)
- Bit-rate mode: CBR
- GOP: I frame only
- Resolution: 1920x1080
- Scanning: Progressive
- Frame Rate: 23.98 (23.976)
- Profile/Level: 422@HL
- Chroma Format: 4:2:2
- Display Aspect Ratio: 16:9
- Closed Captioning: CEA-708 NADBS
- Container: MPEG2 Transport (.ts or .m2t) Preferred .mpg (Program Stream), .mxf, .mp4, .mov

Although this spec calls for a MPEG2 codec, if you provide a codec that is comparable in quality and data rates, they will generally accept it. We are delivering our film in QuickTime (.mov) using an AVID DNxHD (Digital Nonlinear Extensible High Definition) 175 10 Bit codec. The DVxHD can be enclosed in a QuickTime wrapper and has a high data rate. If you have a Pro Res HD HQ spec to meet, you will need to find software or a company that can convert your format into a Pro Res product. Figure 87 shows several screens on how to select a high quality HD codec during export of a film. From the format drop-down menu select "QuickTime."

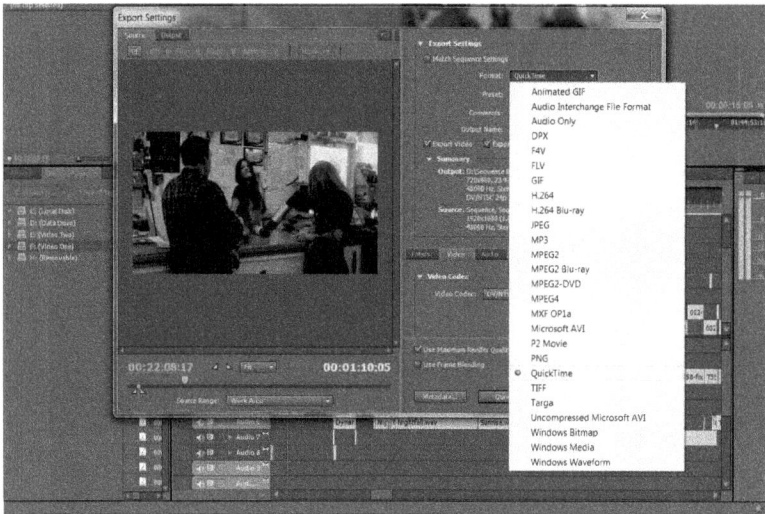

*Figure 87-**Selecting the Format***

Under the "Video" tab click on "Video Code." This will open up a selection of codecs available under the QuickTime format. Note the Avid selections. These are not available prior to downloading and installing the Avid codec for Premiere Pro from the Avid site. The codec is free to download.

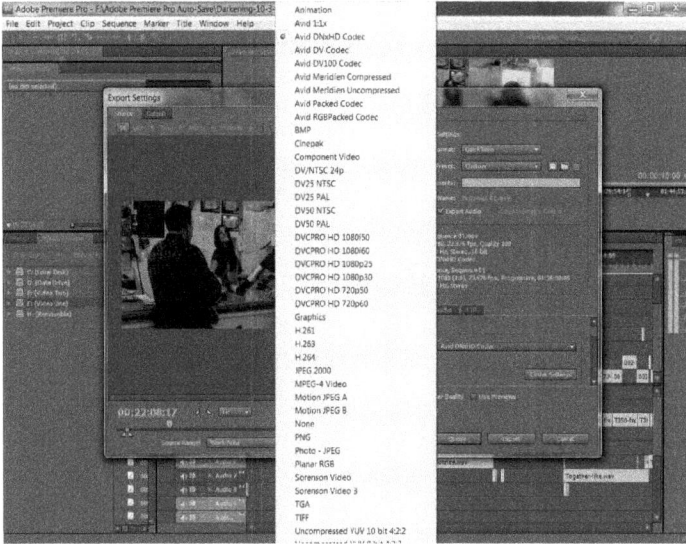

*Figure 88-**Selecting the Codec***

Once you select the Avid codec, click on the "Codec Settings" button to display the available Avid DNxHD codecs. See Figure 89.

*Figure 89-**Avid DNxHD Codec Options***

The listing provides for both 8-bit and 10-bit choices. Since we are delivering a 1920x1080 HD product at 23.976 frame rate, the options are:

- DNxHD 36 – (8-bit) lower bandwidth and size Avid codec compression for HD
- DNxHD 115 – (8-bit) medium bandwidth and size Avid codec compression for HD
- DNxHD 175(x) – (8 or 10-bit) higher Avid codec bandwidth (x = 10 bit), good Avid codec for broadcast
- DNxHD 444 – (10-bit) highest Avid coded bandwidth (440Mbit/s at 10 bit depth) for broadcast

The DNxHD 444 codec will generate a rendered file of over 700 GBytes for a 90 minute film. However, I'm told by Pro Res experts that it's very close to Pro Res quality. Be prepared to generate near 500 GBytes of data for the Avid DNxHD 175x rendered product. Therefore, you'll need to deliver the final product on a digital USB 3.0 (or FireWire) drive to accommodate the massive size of the file.

Exporting in Surround Sound

Since we are talking about codecs and exporting the best product that we can, let's talk a little about exporting sound as well. Just like Avid codec plug-ins help us to export high quality (HQ) HD products, so does Surcode Adobe plug-ins for Dolby 5.1 surround sound help us to generate better sound than just stereo. Although the Surcode plug-in is limited to 5.1 (six channels) and doesn't do Dolby 7.1, it meets most requirements for high quality film products and is affordable to the indie filmmaker. With Surcode installed, Adobe CS5 will export Dolby 5.1 Surround Sound (six tracks) although at times it isn't obvious. When using the QuickTime wrapper to export our Avid DNxHD product as we discussed earlier, when selecting the audio export options, there are minimal options for audio to choose from but one of those is a "5.1" selection under the "Channels" drop-down choices. See Figure 90.

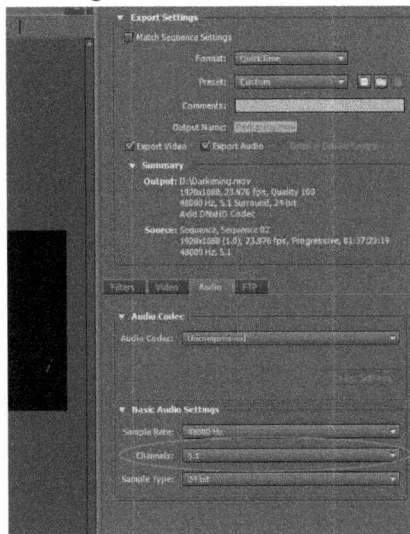

*Figure 90-**Audio Setup for QuickTime Export***

Although the settings are minimal, it does work and does create six channels of Dolby surround sound export in the QuickTime file. However, when creating other non-Apple exports, you'll find more than enough settings for generating your 5.1 Dolby surround sound tracks.

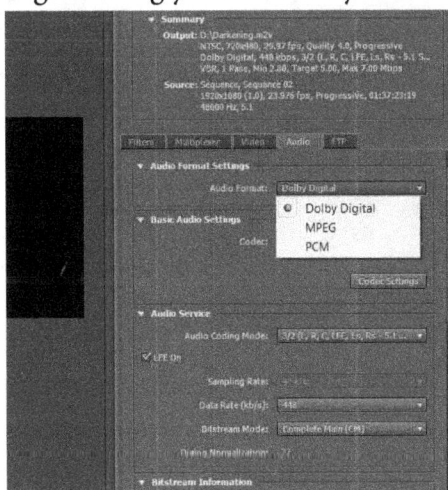

*Figure 91-**MPEG2-DVD Export Audio Setup***

By selecting Dolby Digital from the "Audio Format" drop-down selection and clicking on "Surcode for Dolby Digital" a huge variety of additional setup parameters are displayed. The figure below shows the additional Surcode Dolby Digital surround sound parameters displayed when scrolling down. Note that one of the parameters is data rate.

I usually try to max out data rates, but when creating a high quality DVD you may find that with higher data rates the files are so large that the DVD does not contain enough space for both high quality video and high quality audio, so you will be making decisions and tweaking data rates for both until you find the optimum size and quality for your DVD.

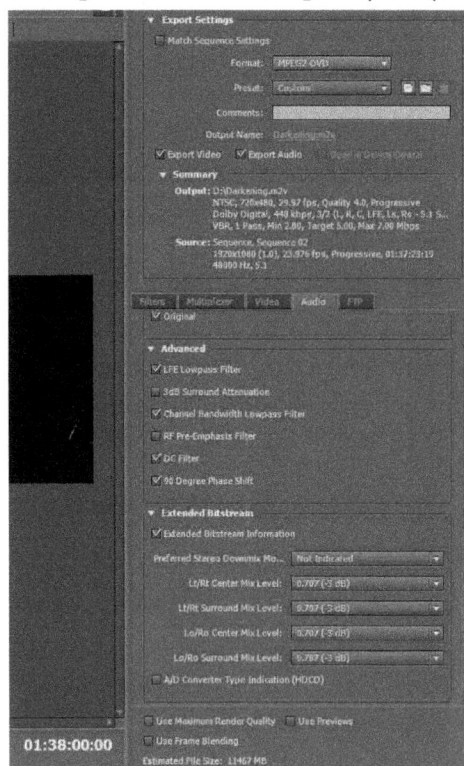

*Figure 92-**MPEG2-DVD Export Audio Setup Cont'd***

Creating DVDs

The DVD market isn't as thriving as it once was due to the introduction of video-on-demand (VOD. However, the market still exists and there are still opportunities to create revenues from the DVD market. Several of the DVD markets attainable for indie filmmakers are Amazon.com, Netflix, and Redbox among others.

Adobe Encore is a very rich DVD creation software application and a whole book could be dedicated to DVD development, but in this book I will only focus on some highlights of DVD development using Encore. Please search out the Adobe site and YouTube for instructional videos on Encore. The learning curve is actually not too steep.

By selecting the "Flowchart" tab at the top of the main screen, you can display the flow of the DVD and how all elements are linked together. The figure below shows how all of the elements are linked together. We typically will have a "main" DVD screen that the viewer first sees when the DVD begins. From the main menu, we link to other menus if we have chapters or other content. Normally, a DVD is divided into chapters. Each chapter may be from up to fifteen minutes long. The links must not only point at chapters and other content but provide a return path when the viewer exits. The DVD needs to have return paths set up. Where it returns is up to you, but it should make sense to the viewer logically, such as returning to the last menu that the viewer interacted with. See Figure 93.

To create the menu, I imported an image from the film and a knife jpeg file and added some glow to it in Photoshop. I then saved it out as a .psd file. I imported the file back into Adobe Encore as a menu file Select "File", "Import As" and select "Menu" to bring it in as a new menu. I used the knife icons as a link to other menus and chapters. I only create one of the knife icons in Photoshop and once I have it in Encore, I can copy and reuse other menu selections.

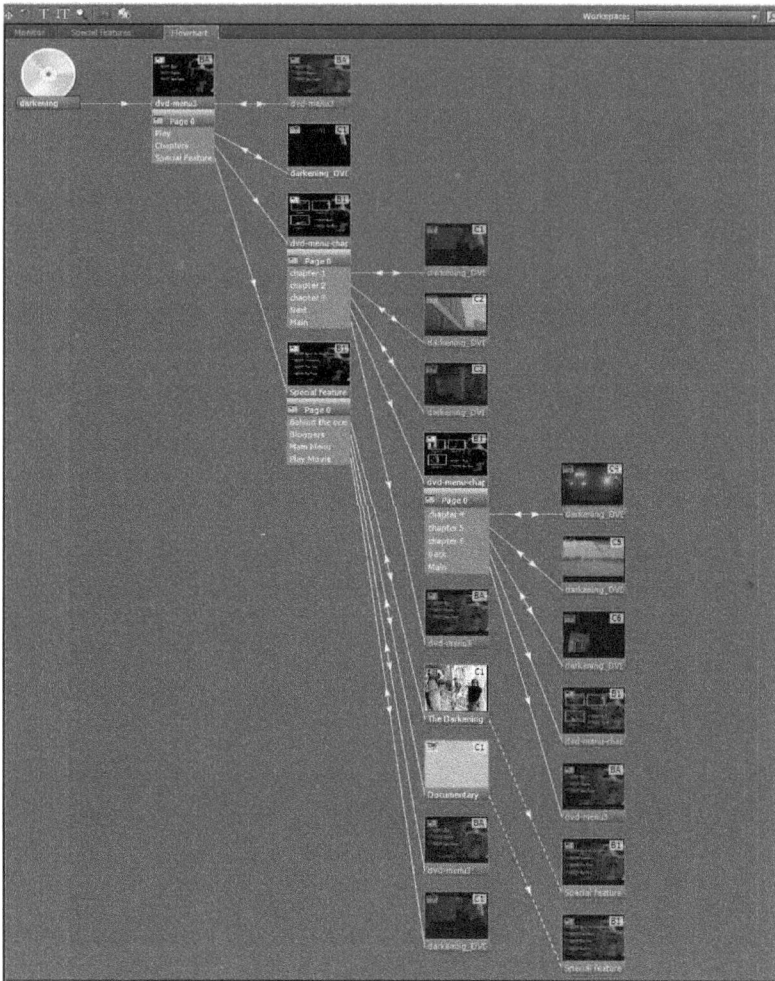

*Figure 93-**DVD Flowchart (Links)***

The DVD has three timelines; One for the movie on the DVD (called "*Darkening* DVD" here), the documentary, and the slide show (called *The Darkening* here). Each has its own timeline selectable by clicking on the appropriate tab. I created chapter points for the DVD about every fifteen minutes or six chapters. Chapter points are easily created by right-clicking on the timeline on the lower half of the screen and selecting "Add Chapter Point" or selecting "Add Chapter Points at

Intervals" to automatically insert chapter points at timed intervals. The white triangles on the timeline are chapter points. For the structure of the DVD, I chose a main page that directs the viewer to either play the DVD, go to a chapter selection page, or to go to a special features page.

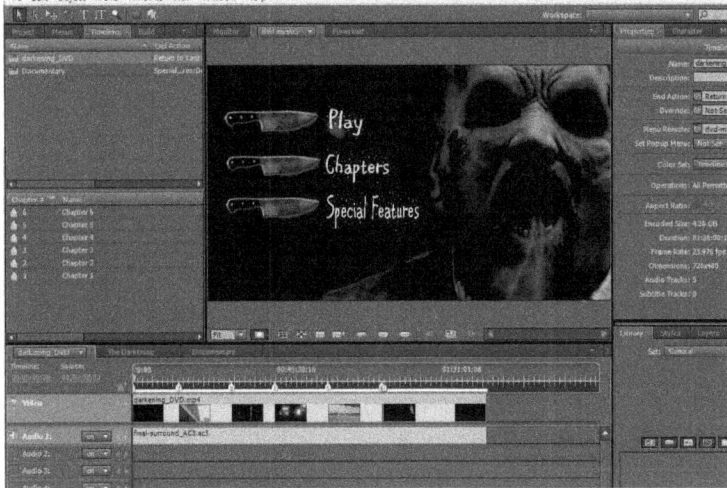

Figure 94-The Darkening DVD Main Menu Page

The chapter page also allows you to go to the next set of chapters (4-6) or to the special features page.

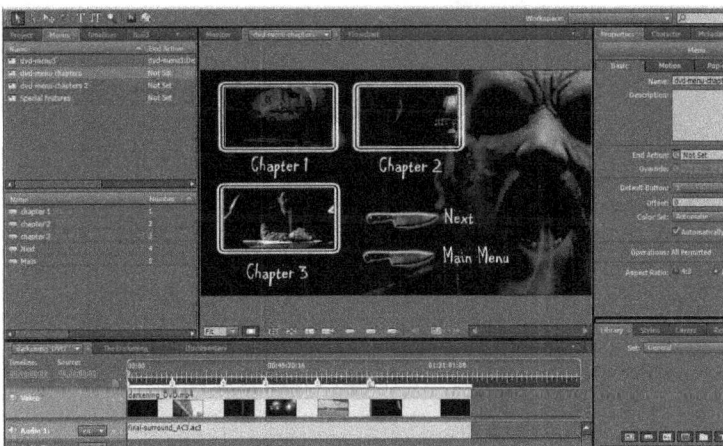

Figure 95-"The Darkening" Chapter 1-3 Page

The 4-6 chapter page allows viewing by chapter but also has a back button that links to the previous chapter page or links back to the main menu.

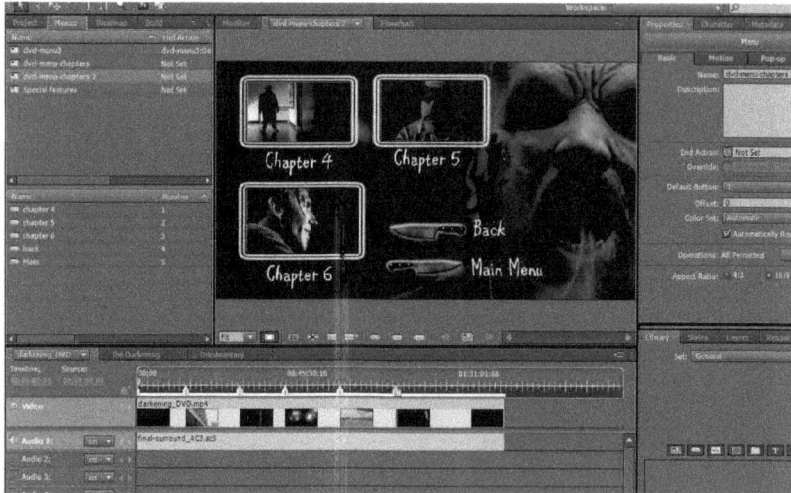

Figure 96-"The Darkening" Chapter 4-6 Page

The special features page provides links to the "Behind the Scenes" slides, the documentary, the main menu, or plays the movie.

Figure 97-"The Darkening" Special Features Page

For the images in the chapter icons, I imported shots from the film into Photoshop, added a border, and saved them out as menu files. I then re-imported them back into Encore as menu items and linked them to specific chapters.

Working between Photoshop and Encore allows you to create menu icons from any image from the film and allows you to link them to functions within the menus. Once the graphics have been inserted into the menus, you can right-click on the icon image to specify the link to the proper page.

*Figure 98-**Specifying Link***

About Files and Transcoding

One thing that Encore does is **transcode** most of the video and audio files. It's a form of compression that is used to condense the files down for the DVD size requirements. I noted that when a surround file gets transcoded, it doesn't play back in the final DVD correctly. The solution is to bring in the audio file in AC3 format. Encore will see that it's AC3 and should tag it as "Don't Transcode." If it doesn't tag it as this, then right-click on the file (in the Project bin) and select the "Transcode Settings."   In the transcode settings under "Quality Preset" ensure that "Don't Transcode" is selected.

The video will automatically be transcoded and cannot be changed (At least I'm not aware of an option to not transcode). For DVDs to get the best quality, I import my video file as MP4 1280x720 @ 29 frames per second. Today, most DVD players can play 24 Frames Progressive and don't have an issue, but older DVD players have an issue with 24 frames per second and are expecting 29 frames per second. Since newer DVD players can handle both, it's better to go with the 29 frames per second so the DVD will play on new and old DVD players. I bring in the video file at a higher resolution although the output for standard definition (SD) is 740x480 because with the compression that Encore uses, it creates a better looking product when starting off with a higher resolution video than starting with a 740x480 video.

Building a DVD in CS5

Adobe Encore has a "Build" function that will create the actual DVD and burn it. The build window, selected by clicking on the "Build" tab is very intuitive and easy to use. There's a "Check Project" button that will bring up a screen to check the build. It identifies any missing links or required set commands. Some of the found errors will not affect the functionality of the DVD. I don't think I've ever had a clean project check. Since I use rewriteable DVDs, I always select the "Auto Erase Rewriteable Discs" button so that I'm not prompted as to whether to delete the contents of the disk.

Once you have created the DVD, it can be used as a master for DVD creation and distribution.

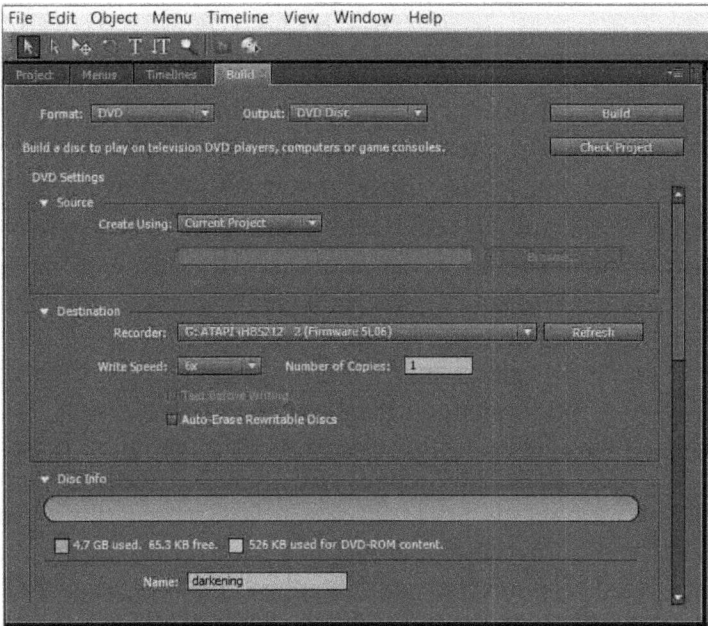

*Figure 99-**Adobe Encore DVD Build Window***

DISTRIBUTION

After completing the production phases of film production, as with the preproduction and production phases, the producer should report to investors the funding status. Again, if you are self distributing the film and have secured funding from the investors to pursue distribution, you will have funds allocated to the distribution of the film. As before, provide a regular status to investors on the status of distribution and funding.

If you haven't given any thought to distribution, then your film is a labor of love, you're making a statement, or you just don't care about profits. Personally, I look at filmmaking as the creation of products. If I don't make profits, then my company will most likely cease to make films. To get distribution for an indie film or a no/low budget film is extremely difficult. There is currently a flood of products in the marketplace. Recently, I heard of an interview with Stephen Spielberg where he said that he was lucky to have gotten his film about Abraham Lincoln released in the theaters and that it almost ended up on HBO. If it's tough for Spielberg, I don't have to tell you how tough it's going to be for an unknown or small indie film company. Okay, bad example, but you get the point.

There have also been changes in the market place as to how films are released in the last few years because of the explosion of video on demand (VOD). In earlier days, movies first had a theatrical release, went to DVD, then cable, and then finally reached standard TV broadcasters (free TV). With the introduction of VOD, everything has changed. Now it's possible to have a simultaneous premiere release at the theaters at the same time as a VOD release.

However, you may find that cable broadcasters will have heartburn with filmmakers releasing in the DVD or VOD markets simultaneously as the cable broadcast and may turn down a distribution deal because of it. If a theatrical chain discovers that you have released a film in a submarket like DVD, they will yank your film from their theaters. The point is that you need to make sure your **release windows** for your film make sense and you don't step on your distributor's toes. Release windows are planned or scheduled release periods in the marketplace of your film. Always plan on theatrical release first, if you can get it, and free TV last.

Indie filmmakers today can manage or be more involved with

the distribution of their film than ever before. In the past, a filmmaker completed a film and then turned the reigns over to the distributor. From that point forward, your film was in the hands of someone else, good or bad. And many times, most distribution contracts were for several or more years. So whatever deal that you had made, you were locked in until you had exhausted what life was in the film. Today, filmmakers have more choices for film distribution that includes flat-fee based service companies (as opposed to taking a percentage) that provide distribution services to filmmakers.

Although filmmakers have more options for distribution today, there are also more products in the marketplace than ever before so filmmakers should consider from the start whether or not they plan to self-distribute, use a distributor, or use a combination of both. Self distribution will require additional resources and funds. Look at the budget discussion on page 12, where we show the top-level budget diagram. If you have no plans for self distribution and plan on just handing your film to a distributor, then a lot of the additional expenses shown in the figure may not apply. If you plan on your own theatrical release, which is possible, you'll need additional funding and marketing. As a general rule, studios plan on budgeting Print & Advertising (P&A) that is half again the budget of the film. If the film is a $5 million film, then plan on a $2.5 million P&A budget. Okay. Now pick yourself up from the floor and listen. Changes in cinema, especially the conversion to digital cinema, and changes in how people get exposed to movie marketing (web and social media) have opened the doors for independent filmmakers to compete somewhat with major studios.

Marketing

Producers should have a plan for marketing the film early in preproduction when they are securing funding. Without marketing, you have no demand for your film and no way to recoup the investment in the film. Marketing creates demand and demand creates sales. Even films with big budgets start marketing the film early. If these films that usually have A-list actors and big budgets start early, what makes you think that you don't have to?

Actually, you have more work ahead of you if you have a lower budget film and only B-list actors or no actors for marketing the film. Make sense? If you have no marketing plan you are left at the mercy of a distributor, if you can get one, to market your film. As I mentioned early in this book, if you do not have attachments such as a name recognizable star or director, it's going to be difficult to market your film unless it is unique. Many indie filmmakers believe they can rely on Facebook, YouTube, and other social media sites to establish a presence for their film. Although this may get the word out, I'm not convinced it's a totally effective marketing strategy. I've yet to see convincing revenue figures on the return of this type of marketing for independent films.

Release Windows

The indie producer must look at the release of a film in its totality from a top down release window approach just as studios do and follow up with effective marketing/advertising in those market areas to get the full return of their film investment. **Release windows** are a systematic and scheduled approach to releasing a film. Each release window is for a specific type of market (theatrical, DVD, VOD, cable, TV, etc.). The release approach must reap the benefit of each market and when that market is saturated or exhausted, move to the next one. For instance, a top down release window model may be to first circulate through the theaters followed by the DVD release three months later. Afterwards, the film would be made available on VOD. After several months on VOD, it may go to a cable network and then released to the free TV channel. If I were to release the film on free TV, who would pay the VOD download fee of $4.95? Make sense?

However, the old standard release window model has been replaced by a more progressive model that allows a VOD release at the same time as a theatrical release. Distribution companies are discovering that there's a large market for VOD downloads that are currently playing at theaters and they can charge more for the VOD. It's all about revenue.

How can an indie film company afford what studios do to promote films? The answer is that they can't and it's not what you do but how you scale down the same process for a lower budget film. Indie filmmakers can follow the same model but scale down the marketing investment since they have less to recover than the studios. Indie filmmakers need to pay attention to what studios do for marketing and advertising and develop similar approaches…but on an indie budget. So first, try to get enough budget to have attachments even if they are B-list stars. Now you can at least market your product to some degree.

Secondly, take advantage of these attachments by giving them a small percentage (2% to 5%) of the profits so they'll have ownership in the film and will help you to market it by showing up at premiers, doing talk shows, talking to magazines and TV, etc. Be sure to include marketing funding in your budget so when you have a product you can market it. Look, getting money from investors is tough, may as well get what you need for all that effort. Believe me, investors WANT to get their money back. They want you to have a marketing plan and budget to get their money back. If you get picked up by a distributor, you can provide this piece of the funding back to investors if it isn't needed. But get it in your funding anyway just in case.

Trailers

Spend your marketing/advertising bucks where they are the most effective. The most effective advertising dollar that can be spent on film is right in the theater buying trailers during showings of similar films to yours (same genre and rating). This is usually the priciest advertising of all but it's the most effective. Arbitron Inc., a media and marketing research firm, did a study on the moviegoer's relationship with cinema advertising and its influence on young and affluent consumers. For the full report see the link in the back of this book. In summary, movie posters and trailers are highly effective on moviegoers.

Budget dollars to show your trailer at theaters where your film will be exhibited a month or two in advance. While we're talking about trailers, let me make a point. Trailers are critical to getting people to watch your film. Again, developing great trailers is an art. Most of us can cobble a trailer together but is it the most effective trailer possible? Probably not. Make sure to include funds in your budget to get a professional trailer done (no, not by your cousin or the guy that owns a video business down the street). Put an additional $5K to $10K in your budget to find someone in LA who works on big budget trailers to do yours.

Typically, Hollywood quality trailers costs between $50K and $100K so look for someone moonlighting for work. By putting the word out and talking to the Hollywood community, you can find a professional to moonlight doing your trailer. Again, look at the web sites out there for editing and visual artists in the LA area for someone to take it on. You'll get a much more professional product and you'll sell your film.

If you are successful with getting a theatrical release, even limited, this will greatly help you to promote your film in the other markets. Theatrical release is the best marketing possible for any film.

Booking a Theater

The key to getting theatrical exhibition of your film is to talk directly with the **booking agent** for the theater chain. This is the person who makes the deals for the movies the theater chain will show at their establishments. Warning! You must be absolutely prepared and know everything about the exhibition of a film. These companies DO NOT normally deal with independent filmmakers and you WILL have to sell them that you are worthy of a chance. But please, do your homework. You have to have the resources and money to get a Digital Content Package (DCP) done. Also, you have to have the money to buy Virtual Print Fees (VPFs) at $1,000 a screen. You HAVE to have a marketing strategy that aims at your target audience. Don't even call them if you don't.

You must also understand the delivery system (drive transport or USB drives) of the theaters and be able to deliver the correct method to each screen you get. You'll also need to have a printer that can deliver professional quality oversized posters to all of the theaters. Don't forget to get a MPAA rating at a cost of at least $3K. Trailers usually cost extra but you may cut a deal with the theater chain. Theatrical trailer fees are usually based on 70 cents per seat and are the absolute best advertising you can do if done right - aiming at your target audience for your genre and rating of film.

Following is a list of theater chains. By the time you read this, many will have been acquired by larger chains. However, if you don't have luck selling to the major chains (Cinemark, Regal, etc.) for theatrical exhibition of your film, you may have better luck selling to a smaller theater chain. When I talked to the big chains, they all agreed that if the film did well in a limited release, they would look at exhibiting the film. So starting with a smaller chain and doing well may be a way for you into the larger chains. Locate the main corporate phone number for the chain you want to pitch and ask for their booking agent. Then give them your pitch!

- Alamo Drafthouse Cinema - nine theaters, cinema/restaurant concept, operating in Texas and Virginia

- AMC Entertainment Inc - 4,610 screens in 307 theaters

- Allen Theatres - located in New Mexico and Cortez, Colorado

- AMC Theatres

- B&B Theatres - 31 theaters, family owned and operated chain in Missouri, Kansas and Oklahoma.

- Bel Air 10 Theater - independent movie theatre - 10 screens in Detroit, MI

- BIG Cinemas - 22 theaters, a division of Reliance MediaWorks Ltd and a member of Reliance ADA Group

- Phoenix Theatres - acquired in 2008.

- Big Picture Theater - located in Wooster, Ohio, and a non-profit theater.

- Bow-Tie Cinemas - 150 screens in 18 theaters

- Brenden Theatres - 7 theaters, located in California, Nevada and Arizona.

- Caribbean Cinemas - 35 theaters, located in the U.S. insular territory of Puerto Rico

- Carmike Cinemas - 2,277 screens in 244 theaters

- Center Cinemas - 3 theaters

- Cinebarre - 40 screens in 5 theaters cinema/eatery concept, operating in North Carolina, South   Carolina, Colorado, Washington and Oregon and expanding across the U.S.

- CineLux Theatres - 7 theaters

- Cinema Arts Centre - independent movie theatre - 3 screens in Huntington, NY

- Cinema West Theaters - 12 Theatres, 94 Screens in Northern California, as of December 11, 2009

- CinemaStar Luxury Theaters South California and Northwestern Mexico, Oceanside, CA based

- Cinemagic Theatres - 8 theaters in Minnesota, Iowa, and Wisconsin

- Cinemagic Stadium Theaters - 5 Stadium theaters in Maine, New Hampshire and Massachusetts

- Cinemark Theatres - 3,838 screens in 294 theaters

- Century Theatres - acquired in 2006

- Classic Cinemas - 13 theaters in Illinois

- Clearview Cinemas - 48 theaters in the New York metropolitan area

- Cobb Theatres - 16 theaters

- Coming Attractions Theatres - 18 theaters

- Dickinson Theatres - 367 screens in 37 theaters

- Showplex Cinemas, Inc. - acquired in May 2010 with 80 screens in 10 theater locations

- Dipson Theatres- 57 screens in 12 theaters

- Emagine Entertainment - 5 Locations, 66 Screens

- Entertainment Cinemas - 10 theaters

- EPIC Theatres - 7 theaters, 76 Screens. Located in Florida,

North Carolina and Pennsylvania

- Fairchild Cinemas - a movie chain based in Moses Lake, Washington. Currently, there is one 10 screen theater in Moses Lake, as well as a 12-screen theater built in Pasco, Washington and opened in April of 2007

- FunAsiA Theaters - operates the largest Bollywood Theater Chain (www.funasia.net) in USA and is part of Pyramid Saimira Group (www.pstl.in)

- Galaxy Theaters -currently 9 theaters with 84 screens in California, Nevada, Texas and Washington. Completely converted to digital projection (DLP)

- Georgia Theatre Company - 29 theaters with 288 screens in Georgia, Florida, South Carolina, and Virginia.

- Goodrich Quality Theaters, Inc. - 30 theaters in Michigan, Indiana, Illinois, and Missouri

- Grandview Theatre - single screen theatre in Grandview Heights, OH

- Great Escape Theatres - 25 theaters

- Harkins Theatres - 429 screens in 30 theaters

- Hollywood Theaters (formerly Wallace Theaters) - 546 screens in 49 theaters

- Kerasotes Theatres - 957 screens in 95 theaters

- Krikorian Premier Theaters - 7 theaters in the Greater Los Angeles Area

- Landmark Theatres - 220 screens in 54 theaters

- Locks Theatres, Inc. (also known as Celebration! Cinema) - 11 theaters in Michigan

- Mann Theatres - 54 screens in 7 theaters

- Marcus Theatres - 668 screens in 54 theaters

- Marquee Cinemas - 19 theaters

- Maya Cinemas - 2 theaters, one in Bakersfield, California and another in Salinas, California

- Megaplex Theaters - 93 screens in 6 theaters in Utah. Soon to be 108 screens in 7 theaters

- Metropolitan Theatres Corporation - 21 theatres with 104 screens in California, Colorado, Idaho, Utah, and British Columbia, based in Los Angeles

- MJR Theatres - 7 theaters in the Detroit Metropolitan Area

- Muvico Theaters - 154 screens in 9 theaters

- NAOS Entertainment - start-up Alabama chain with 1 theater, 8 screens as of September 10, 2007. Three additional multiplexes are under development. Based in Greenville, Alabama.

- ArcLight Sherman Oaks - formerly Galleria Stadium 16, was transformed to an ArcLight Cinema that opened in 2007.

- National Amusements - 450 screens in 34 theaters

- Cinema de Lux

- Multiplex Cinemas

- Showcase Cinemas

- Pacific Theatres

- Premiere Cinemas - 18 theaters

- Polson Theatres - 11 theaters

- Rave Cinemas - 930 screens in 62 theaters, acquired by Cinemark 2013

- Reading Entertainment

- Reading Cinemas - 8 theaters

- Angelika Film Center - 6 theaters

- Consolidated Theatres - 9 theaters

- Pacific Theatres - 15 theaters acquired in February 2008

- Reel Theatres - 6 theaters in Oregon, Idaho, and Utah

- Regal Entertainment Group - 6,761 screens in 545 theatres

- Regal Cinemas - one of three chains part of the 2002 consolidation

- Edwards Theatres - one of three chains part of the 2002 consolidation

- Sawmill Theaters - 6 Screen multiplex located in Payson, Arizona.

- Rogers Cinemas - 10 theaters, 48 screens in Wisconsin and Upper Michigan.

- Santikos Theatres - 8 theaters

- Southern Theatres - 18 theaters, 241 screens, located in Southeastern United States, created through a merger of Grand Theaters of New Orleans, Louisiana and AmStar Cinemas of Birmingham, Alabama. Based in New Orleans the chain has locations in Alabama, Florida, Georgia, Kentucky, Louisiana, Mississippi, North Carolina, South Carolina and Texas.

- Starplex Cinemas - currently operates 24 theaters and

222 screens

- Stone Theatres - 3 theater chain based in the Carolinas with current locations in Durham, NC, Myrtle Beach, SC and Hope Mills, NC.

- Studio Movie Grill - 8 theaters, cinema/grill concept, operating in Texas and expanding across the U.S

- Texas Cinemas - 3 theaters, 28 Screens, San Marcos and New Braunfels, Texas

- Trademark Cinemas - operates 6 theaters and 43 screens that are scattered across the eastern U.S. in New York, Rhode Island, Georgia, and Florida.

- Warren Theatres - owned and operated by Bill Warren, headquartered in Wichita, Kansas, operates four luxury theaters under the Warren Theatres brand, including three cinema complexes in Wichita, Kansas and one in Moore, Oklahoma.

A note about theatrical exhibition. Did you know to be eligible for the Academy Awards, your film MUST be theatrically exhibited in a theater in Los Angeles and a theater in New York? If you cut a deal with theaters, make sure you get a theater in each of these cities to be eligible. You never know what might happen!

Amazon DVD

Amazon.com via CreateSpace is probably the easiest to attain and the quickest to setup and get running to create revenue with DVDs. CreateSpace is a service of Amazon.com that allows for book, video, and audio product creation. The service has no fees but does take a large percentage of the profits. Filmmakers can make around $5 per DVD when the retail price is set around $20. CreateSpace provides easy to follow directions and templates for creating the DVDs. They allow multiple timelines if you have additional content such as special features, as well. The end product (DVD and case) look professional and I have not experienced any issues with compatibility.

Back to multiple timelines on a DVD. As I mentioned earlier, the DVD that I created had multiple timelines. When it creates directories on the DVD itself, it will make three separate directories and video files for these three timelines. When I shipped this DVD to Amazon, I had also requested that it be made available as a VOD through Amazon.com. Amazon said that they could not make it available as a VOD because of the multiple timelines. It could, though, be made available as a DVD with these multiple timelines since I included additional content. Here's the point, make sure that if you are going to deal with Amazon that you understand both their DVD and VOD requirements.

If you want to use Amazon for both DVD and VOD, and your product has multiple timelines, you'll need to submit them separately. Submit your DVD ONLY then open a new order with them for the VOD. If the format is a single timeline format, you can do both at the same time with no problem.

If you have a DVD project that has additional content and multiple timelines, there is a way to deliver the additional content and still meet the single timeline requirement at Amazon. By bringing all of the content that you plan for the DVD into the Adobe Premiere Pro CS5 editing timeline, you can generate a single MP4 file for use in Adobe Encore. You can add additional chapter points in Encore that take the viewer directly to the special features sections. By doing this, your multi timeline DVD and VOD product will contain the same content. By the way, if you create a DVD with the VOD files on it, make sure that you strip all of the menus from the DVD and make the DVD an "auto-play" DVD in Encore. To set the DVD to auto-play, select "Disc" and set "First Play" to Chapter One.

Netflix

We had our first feature film picked up by Netflix years ago on DVD, but things have changed since then. It was much easier than it is today, and they didn't have VOD available back then. If you do not go through a conventional film distributor who has contacts at Netflix it is somewhat difficult since they, like others, prefer not to deal with independent filmmakers. For bookkeeping and other reasons, they prefer to deal with distributors who have a good number of titles in their library.

If you decide to represent yourself, you'll need to make sure that you contact their DVD buyer for corporate. Don't waste your time trying to sell to everyone you talk to, just the buyer. When you finally talk with their buyer, the first step is to sell them on looking at a screener of your film. Send them a professional looking DVD. I'd suggest using Amazon's CreateSpace to make it. If you provide good artwork for the cover and label, you can create a professional looking DVD. Once they get back with you and decide to carry the DVD, you'll be able to get it in their library. This is the key to convincing Netflix to carry your title on VOD. Currently, it is extremely difficult for indie filmmakers to sell Netflix on VOD without first having the title in their DVD library.

Family Video

Family Video is one of the larger video store DVD rental companies still operating with more than 750 stores (as of today). Their main office in Glenview, Illinois has a DVD buyer that still accepts screeners for indie films. When you're dealing with any company, always verify the buyer's name and address before shipping a screener. They expect you to send a store-ready DVD with artwork on the cover for the screener. If you can't get them to cut a deal for your film, request that they test market it in some of their stores to convince them it will move. I suggest that you send them ten copies for marketing at a minimum to prove your film will generate revenue.

Distribution Contracts

To me, this is the scariest part of making movies. You put in years of hard work and money in your film and now you must turn it over to a company that will help you get your film seen by the public and hopefully get your investment back. And believe me, it's not an easy task. I didn't say it was impossible, just difficult. You'll see enough legalese in distribution contracts to choke a horse. As I've mentioned before, it always helps to have a lawyer guide you through film contracts. If you don't, the next best thing to make sense of it is to ask questions. If you don't understand it, ask them to explain what the clause in the contract is stating.

Generally, distributors will ask for a certain amount of exclusivity to markets and a specific length of time to saturate that market. If for instance, you sign a contract that states that a broadcasting company has exclusive rights in the broadcasting market for 18 months and wants a three year contract, then you cannot sell the rights to another broadcaster in that country until the 18 months has expired. Usually distribution contracts are written for licensing in specific geographic areas like the U.S, Canada, etc. Make sure you understand what geographic area the distribution is for and what exclusivity they want. Make certain you understand the following requirements that you must meet:

- Film format (standard definition, high definition) and codec requirements
- Sound requirements (Surround Sound 5.1?)
- Error & Omission (E&O) Insurance, is it needed?
- Closed Captioning requirements
- Cue sheets (music) requirements
- MPAA rating requirements
- Copyright requirements

Many distributors will send the delivered film to a lab for a quality check (QC) to ensure it meets requirements. Determine if there are any fees and what happens if you don't meet the requirements. Some distributors want to have the freedom to fix these problems in the lab and bill you for the changes. Make sure that these are reasonable fees and that work doesn't get done without your prior approval or opportunity to fix the problem yourself.

Someone once told me that distributors exist because they have the connections and you don't. I agree. Most of us don't. But some distributors have a reputation for generalizing expenses for handling films for clients and taking hefty percentages and then leaving the client with very little for the amount of effort they have put into their film. Most of the distribution contracts I have read are written exclusively for the distributor with the filmmaker having very few rights or say-so in the distribution of their film.

Look for distributors that don't ask for too much exclusivity in the markets (just what they need) and don't ask for exceptionally long contracts. Three years is plenty. If they haven't done anything with it in three years, they are not going to do anything. A seven year contract will kill your film. There's not much you're going to be able to do with it after seven years. Don't sign anything that seems unreasonable or is a lopsided contract in favor of the distributor.

Now if you are considering self distribution, you'll have to develop relationships and contacts with distributors who will work with independent filmmakers. The advantage with self distribution is that it allows you more control over the destiny of your film. The drawback is that distributors already have established contacts in the industry and have more clout with exhibitors and companies (DVD suppliers, VOD, cable, TV) that are looking for films to acquire.

The good news is that more than ever before, companies have sprung up that can help independent filmmakers reach their intended audience. Even some of the companies out there looking for films to acquire are working with independent filmmakers to some degree.

Companies like Cinedym (digital content supplier) and Gravitas work with indie filmmakers to reach the theatrical and VOD markets and beyond. Smaller indie-oriented companies like Distribber, an Indiegogo company, and Distrify are perfect fits for indie filmmakers and can cut through the massive onslaught of distribution contracts. They also offer several distribution markets that can enable indie filmmakers to get their film out there and generating some level of revenues.

Smaller indie-oriented distributors like Distribber focus on video-on-demand markets like iTUNES, Amazon.com, HULU, Netflix and cable broadcasters who deliver VOD content. Some of these smaller indie-oriented distributors have minimal contracts or none at all (the fee based ones).

There seems to be a move in the industry towards film acquisition companies working only with larger distributors that can provide a library of film content to choose from and seeking films that have had some form of theatrical release. This may be an attempt to cut through the massive amount of independent films flooding the distribution channels due to the digital camera revolution that has put the prosumer line of digital film cameras in the hands of filmmakers from Maine to LA. Distributors are trying to weed out the "YouTube" type films hitting the market.

No matter where you end up, make sure you understand the terms of the distribution contract and whether the distributor is a large distribution company or a small indie-oriented distributor. Like I said, if you don't know, ask!

Cue Sheets

If you've never worked with cue sheets before, let me try to explain. I was exposed to the **cue sheet** when I was reviewing requirements for a distribution contract. It listed cue sheets as a condition for broadcast. Broadcasters are obligated to put funds into a pool that go to performing rights organizations for musicians who belong to those organizations. The musician can receive a small percentage of those funds. However, production companies must let performing rights organizations know what songs, for how long, and what musicians and publishers are included in their film products so the musicians can get a piece of the pie based on how much music they contribute to the whole. All broadcast companies, as well as any companies that play music in public, pay annual fees to their local performing rights organizations. The cue sheet documents include:

- Cue title (song title)
- Use (when and where in the film)
- Time (the length of time for each song used in the film)
- Composer affiliation (the performing rights organization they belong to)
- Publisher affiliation (the performing rights organization they belong to)

Developing and Delivering a DCP

If you plan on a theatrical release, you'll need to know about **digital content packages (DCP)**. You DO NOT need a DCP for anything but theatrical exhibition, so if you haven't secured theatrical exhibition, don't pursue DCP creation. Save your money. DCPs are used to broadcast your film on the silver screen and supposedly provide the highest quality product that you can deliver.

The concept is to deliver a format that the modern digital cinema systems can ingest and understand. This happens to be a Linux type compatible drive that can either be inserted into their rack or a USB portable drive. However, it does have a Linux structure and uses JPEG 2000 compression for the images.

When you create a DCP, you are exporting the highest quality "still" images of the film for each frame of the film. Typically these are generated as TIFF images and has an accompanying audio track that is separate and of the highest quality (5.1 surround sound minimum). These images are used in the creation of the DCP. There is more to it and it involves an investment in DCP generation software and hardware. DCPs can be huge files and can approach the terabyte range. If you are supplying a movie trailer, the trailer also has to be in DCP format. There are numerous companies out there that create DCPs for filmmakers and prices vary starting around $1,300. If you need multiple copies and drives for theater distribution, these can also be duped by the DCP creator at a lower price than the creation of the original.

There is also open source software available for those who want to do it themselves, but remember that developing DCPs can be tricky and any problems with the creation is amplified by the projection of your film on the big screen. For the price, it's worth having a professional tackle the DCP creation. Normal lead time on creation of a DCP is usually a week. Most DCP creators are willing to provide a quicker turn-around for an additional price.

A word of warning, as with anything in film, make sure that you have a good process developed for the DCP creation wherein you can preview an intermediate delivery prior to the actual shipping and release of the film at the theaters. When it's shown on the big screen, it's too late to find out that you aren't satisfied with the end product.

Here's how to stay ahead of this so that doesn't happen. Once you have delivered the drive with the DCP materials (like I said, a boat-load of TIFFS and soundtrack) and your DCP creator has created the DCP, have them ship a copy to you for a QC check. Call a local theater that has a digital cinema projector and negotiate a day when you can bring down the DCP to test on one of their screens. You'll need to contact the manager and sweet-talk them into giving you some time. I've done this and it's not that hard of a sell. You just need to schedule it when they aren't busy. Make sure you ask them what kind of transport they will accept, i.e., a disk drive that slides into their rack for downloading or if they'll accept a 3.0 USB portable drive. Keep in mind that the larger the file, the longer it will take to download. A whole film will take some time to download onto their system. If it's just a sample of the film, you may be able to put it on a 4 GByte thumb drive.

Make sure that it plays okay and that the sound is correct. If there are problems, this is when to find out. If there are, discuss this with your DCP creator to resolve them. Work closely with him/her to get the best product for theatrical display as possible. Your DCP creator can also help walk you through the conditions for your DCP. The following are requirements for DCP submission courtesy of SV2:

Visuals:
- Colorspace:
    - Visual should be in a specific colorspace. Examples: Rec709, sRGB etc. ProPhotoRGB is preferred.

- Preferred resolution:
    - Flat Aspect Flat -2K, 1998×1080 or 4K, 3996×2160 at 1.85:1
    - Scope - 2K 2048×858 or 4K 4096×1716 at 2.39:1

- Acceptable resolution:
    - HD Widescreen (1920 x 1080) at 16:9, this will

require scale and crop or leaving pillar-box bars on the side.

- Preferred format:
    - o 16-bit TIFF or EXR sequence, CinemaDNG, ProRes 4:4:4, Avid DNxHD Avid DNxHD 220 (10-bit)

- Acceptable format:
    - o ProRes 4:2:2, Avid DNxHD 220 (8-bit), QuickTime or AVI uncompressed (less color quality)
    - o HDCAM SR, HDCAM (extra fees for digitizing)

- Preferred frame rate:
    - o 24.000 or 23.976 fps

- Acceptable frame rate:
    - o 25 or 29.97 fps, these will require frame rate conversion which takes extra time and expense and reduces quality OR a venue that supports SMTPE DCPs which are not yet widely supported.

Sound (sound must be identical length to sound to the frame):

- Preferred config:
    - o Discrete channel 3.1 (left, center, right, LFE) or 5.1 (left, center, right, LFE, left   surround, right surround).
    - o 3.1 will be four files, 5.1 will be six files

- Acceptable config:
    - o Stereo Mix (this will result in unreliable playback volume but for a small charge can be multiplexed to 3.1 or 5.1

- Preferred format:

> o   48 Khz or 96 Khz/24 bit mono discrete channels, AIFF or WAV

- Acceptable format:
  - o   48Khz/16 bit embedded in visual file or as AIFF/WAV (a 16-bit will result in reduced dynamic range and more noise especially in larger venues.)

Once you have created the DCP, assuming you have negotiated the theatrical release with the theater chain (see section on Theatrical Release), you will ship the DCP out on dockable drives or portable USB drives. If you are asked to ship the drive with a docking station, you will need several components. Total cost is around $300. These are shown in Figure 100.

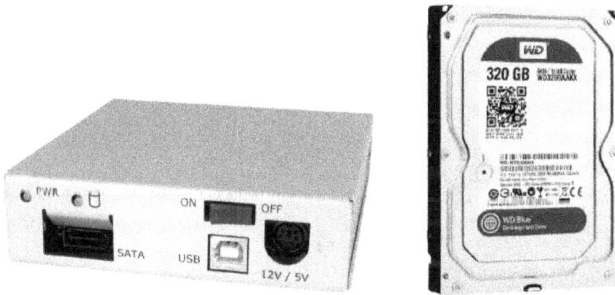

Docking Station and SATA Drive

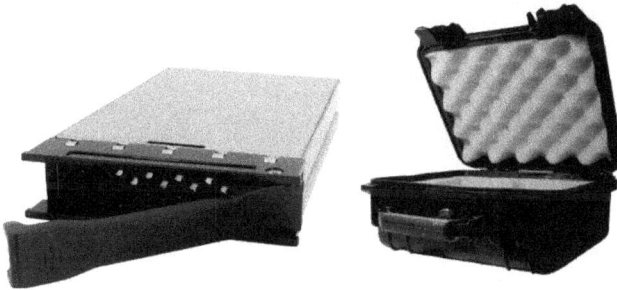

Drive Enclosure and Shipping Case

*Figure 100-**Components for Docking Station***

A cheaper solution is to use USB 3.0 (or 2.0) portable drives if the theater can ingest from these. These are much cheaper and can be picked up for around $60 to $80 per drive. How you deliver all depends upon what the theaters will accept. Now keep in mind that some of the larger chains also have an option to load the DCP onto their main server and to then make this available to the theaters throughout their chain. This is the most cost efficient method. Discuss this with the theater chain with whom you set up the exhibition deal to see what their preferred method of distribution is for their chain.

Use UPS or FedEx when shipping DCP drives to theaters. The package should include any specific directions to the projectionist. Since our rating for our film did not reach us before the DCP was created, we were forced to deliver the MPAA logo separately and needed to provide directions for displaying it. Once a film is rated, the MPAA logo MUST be displayed with the film. This was our way of meeting that requirement and meeting our DCP deadline. Figure 101 shows a sample letter to the projectionist which provided additional instructions for showing our film.

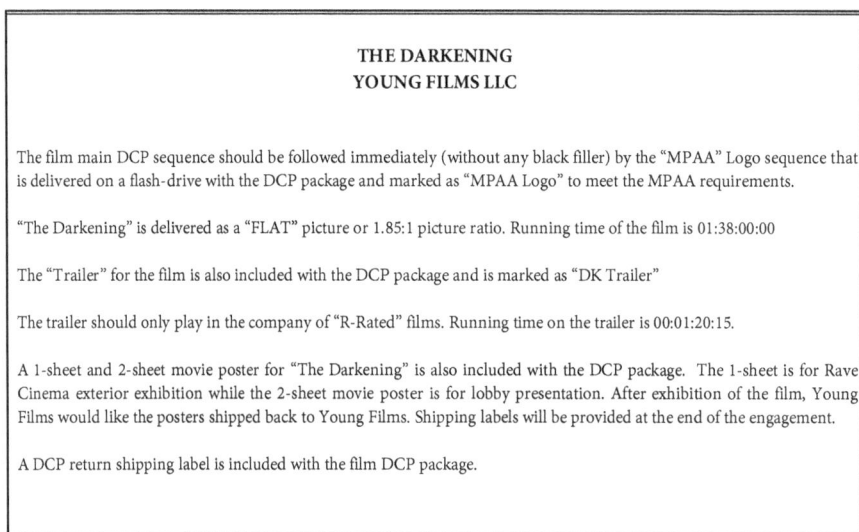

THE DARKENING
YOUNG FILMS LLC

The film main DCP sequence should be followed immediately (without any black filler) by the "MPAA" Logo sequence that is delivered on a flash-drive with the DCP package and marked as "MPAA Logo" to meet the MPAA requirements.

"The Darkening" is delivered as a "FLAT" picture or 1.85:1 picture ratio. Running time of the film is 01:38:00:00

The "Trailer" for the film is also included with the DCP package and is marked as "DK Trailer"

The trailer should only play in the company of "R-Rated" films. Running time on the trailer is 00:01:20:15.

A 1-sheet and 2-sheet movie poster for "The Darkening" is also included with the DCP package. The 1-sheet is for Rave Cinema exterior exhibition while the 2-sheet movie poster is for lobby presentation. After exhibition of the film, Young Films would like the posters shipped back to Young Films. Shipping labels will be provided at the end of the engagement.

A DCP return shipping label is included with the film DCP package.

---

*Figure 101-**Sample Letter to Projectionist***

If you'd like to have the drives shipped back once the DCP is downloaded, include specific directions to this effect with the return address and a pre-paid shipping label.

Closed Captioning

Closed captioning is a process wherein text is added to a film that depicts the narrative and sound effects for the hearing impaired. It must be located on the screen in a specific manner and format that complies with federal regulations. There are specific guidelines for this, so unless you are familiar with the federal guidelines you are better off hiring a service to insert the closed captioning. There are many of these companies around today and prices vary from company to company and how soon the closed captioning is required. Some companies will provide the filmmaker with a template of how to format the screenplay for the closed captioning creation. Closed captioning basically strips everything from the script except the dialogue and the characters' names. It then adds text and describes any sound effects important for the hearing impaired viewer's understanding of what's going on in the story (gunshots, a door closing, heavy music overtones, etc.).

The first thing a filmmaker should do when preparing for closed captioning is to ensure that the current script matches the film 100%. Sometimes during shooting, the words in the shooting script may end up changed by the actor. This is the importance of having a script person on the set. They should be monitoring this and updating the final script to match what was actually said in each scene. If the script girl stays on top of the script during production, the script will only need reformatting and cleanup to prep for closed captioning.

Closed captioning for a film can cost around $1,000 so be sure to include this in your budget if you are planning on a cable or TV release. Also be aware that some VOD suppliers such as iTunes will have to meet this federal requirement in the very near future. I'm sure other digital content providers are likely to follow. So plan on doing closed captioning at some point and make sure you have it in your budget.

Getting Your Film Rated

If you plan on releasing your film to the theater, most theater chains will be expecting that the film has been rated by the MPAA. Actually, the Classification and Rating Administration (CARA), an arm of the MPAA, rates your film. You will need to submit a form, a screener, and fee to get it rated. Also be advised that once it is rated, any advertising that you do for the film (trailers, posters, etc.) must be submitted to the MPAA for review and approval.

During this process, we discovered that on a movie poster for our horror film, we were not allowed to show blood on the knife. We had to bring in a graphic artist to quickly remove the blood before we shipped the movie posters to the theaters. The rating process takes time and depends upon how many other films are in the queue. Plan on at least six weeks to get your film rated.

*Figure 102-**MPAA Ratings-Full Rating Blocks***

G ⊕

PG ⊕
| DESCRIPTOR BOX |

PG-13 ⊕
| DESCRIPTOR BOX |

R ⊕
| DESCRIPTOR BOX |

NC-17 ⊕
| DESCRIPTOR BOX |

Figure 103-MPAA Ratings - Abbreviated Rating Blocks

Once your film gets rated, the MPAA will notify you of the rating and any special information that you need to provide in the rating block. Ours, for instance, was deemed to have violence (so they say), so the R-rating block had to include the words "For Violence." The MPAA will send the filmmaker the rating block art work to use for the film, to include a variety of green and blue MPAA screens for inserting into the film products.

When the trailer or full film is shown in public, they expect that the proper notification on green or blue screen is presented to the audience as well. Of course, if the filmmaker disagrees with the rating by the MPAA, they can dispute this and try to get the rating changed. The filmmaker also has the option of editing the scenes that generated the rating decision in favor of lowing the rating, but I'm sure that there are additional fees to have the film re-rated by the MPAA. Although I did not believe that our film deserved an R-rating, indie filmmakers usually cannot afford to protest ratings and to pay additional fees. Typical low indie films can cost around $3K to get rated.

The MPAA will also provide you with a copy of the Advertising Handbook that outlines the advertising rules that apply to your film. If you are self distributing your film, be aware that for a rated film, your are responsible to ensure that all advertising is approved by the CARA Advertising Administration before it is used to advertise your film to the public in any venue or medium. The intent is to assure that the print or visuals that are shown in a public venue that is seen by all ages, doesn't contain images that most parents would consider inappropriate for their young children. If the venue is more adult oriented, then the advertising would be approved with restrictions.

Error & Omissions (E&O) Insurance

The first question you may have is "do I need it?" It depends. Distributors ask for this so that they aren't liable for you forgetting to attain all rights for the film. As I have mentioned numerous times throughout this book, producers should ensure that everything in front of the camera (and behind) is covered with a contract, agreement, or license. By not securing these rights, the producer leaves himself open for a lawsuit. Distributors surely don't want a film where the rights have not been secured properly by the producer. Even when you have supposedly done everything right, there is always a chance that something was missed or not correctly covered. The E&O provides insurance against having missed (omission) or not correctly (error) covered all rights and licenses required for the film. However, the basic assumption is that the producer made due diligence to get these in the first place.

The E&O is not an insurance policy against the producer not having made the proper attempts to secure all rights. However, many distributors will enter a contract with a producer with the understanding that he/she acknowledges that they are totally responsible to attain all the rights and have done so. If you find that a distributor cannot make a deal without the E&O, you will need to purchase the E&O insurance.

Typically, insurance companies provide a variety of film insurance packages to filmmakers and are easily found on the web. They are usually the same company that you purchased your location liability insurance from and can provide you a quote. Generally E&O insurance will costs around $2,700. The E&O provided will require a title search, usually around $250, and a letter from a lawyer that summarizes the title search findings, another couple of hundred bucks. Once you have the title search and letter, this and a fee will get you the E&O. Filmmakers with limited budgets usually try to avoid E&O if possible. The best defense is to make sure that all rights and licensing has been done correctly then with or without E&O, you can sleep at night.

Virtual Print Fees (VPFs)

Before the age of digital cinema, when all movies were shot on 35mm or 16mm film, copies of the master print for the film, called dupes, for duplicate, were made and shipped to theaters for theatrical distribution. This dupe or as the industry called them "print" cost around $1,500 to $2,000 each to create. So the cost of theatrical exhibition included the print costs per screen for a film's release. With the digital cinema, came a new way of delivering the "print" to the theaters. The film reels (prints) were no longer needed since the film could be ingested into the digital projection system via a hard drive or digital stream (satellite or modem).

However, to recover the costs of digital conversions, a third party for licensing the new virtual digital print was created to help offset the equipment costs (a digital funding company) associated with the digital conversions which ran between $70 to $100K per screen. This new virtual print fee for this digital delivery was somewhat less expensive, $900 to around $1,100, depending upon which deployment phase, I or II, the theater chain belonged to.

Cinedigm, located in LA, is one of several companies that collects these VPFs for exhibition in association with the Access Digital Cinema Phase II, Corp (ADP) for films shown in the digital cinemas in the US and Canada. Depending upon which theater chain your film is deployed (exhibited) under, your rate will vary between the two prices previously cited above. The role of companies like Cinedigm in this process is to collect the fees for the exhibition at the theaters. The theater chain will refer you out to the digital funding company for collection of the fees.

The filmmaker will be required to sign a contract with the digital funding company agreeing to the fees per each engagement of the film. When filmmakers purchase a VPF, it covers an engagement period for the exhibition of the film per each screen. A single VPF covers a single screen. Once the fee is paid the theater operators may show the film as long as they desire. I can tell you right now that it will ONLY show as long as the theater is making money on your film or in other words they are filling seats. If a blockbuster comes along, you can bet they will most likely pull you from that screen in favor of the blockbuster.

Movie Posters

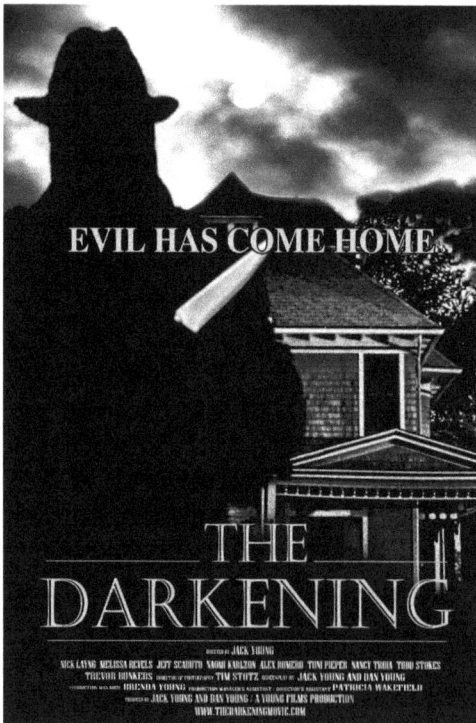

Figure 104- The Darkening Movie Poster

Second to showing trailers at the theater, the most effective way to promote your film is with a movie poster in the lobby of the theater. Getting the movie poster right, again, is an art form. There are some amazing movie posters by such artists as Drew Struzan (artist of the *Star Wars*, *Back to the Future*, and *Indian Jones* posters to name a few) that are works of art. Unfortunately, to have him do your poster will cost you at least $10,000.

Believe me, I know. I contacted him and got a pricing. Most of us indie filmmakers certainly can't afford Drew, but we still need to shop around for artists that can help us to develop an effective movie poster for our films. Movie posters, once developed, can help us promote our film on the web and other avenues that require artwork. Figure 104 shows a poster that we did for our last film.

Since we knew that haunted house themes on movie posters work with horror film fans, we wanted to creep up the house in the poster to create this surreal depiction of the house from the film. We shot an actor in full costume against green screen, added the foreboding sky, added some titling and a tag line, and had our poster. Design a poster that captures the essence of your film and looks professional. The PG-13 eventually changed to an R-rating, after the MPAA rating, and the blood was removed from the knife to comply with the guidance from them. Movie posters come in a range of sizes and are called **sheets**. Some are listed below:

- One sheet - 27 x 41 inches

- Two sheet - 41 x 54 inches

- Three sheet - 41 x 81 inches

- Six sheet - 81 x 81 inches

- Twenty four sheet - 246 x 108 inches

For printing posters for the lobby of theaters for a theatrical exhibition, you want to go with at least the two sheet or larger poster to even compete with the studios advertising in the lobby. You'll also want to provide a one sheet poster for the theater to post in their exterior display cases. I'd suggest that indie filmmakers do a follow up phone call to the managers to check that your posters have been placed.

Also try to get the theaters to put up your movie posters as early as possible before the release. You want the traffic in the theaters to see that your movie is coming at least a couple of weeks prior to it showing. For some reason, theaters seem to forget to give the indie filmmakers the same attention as they do to studios. At one theater, they had forgotten to put up our poster until we asked them to on the night it premiered. Posters should be shipped in circular cardboard tubes to protect them during shipment. If you want your posters back after the theater engagement, you'll need to provide a pre-paid FedEx or UPS shipping label and instructions enclosed with the poster.

Distribution Summary

Distributors do attend festivals and do look for product to pickup. However there are tons of festivals and distributors do not go to all of these. They mostly circulate at the larger festivals like the Sundance Film Festivals, the Austin Film Festival, Tribeca, and other select few. Film festivals are a good way to shop your film to distributors only IF they actually go to the one you have your film entered into. Research the film festivals to find out which are being attended by large production companies and distributors who are looking for films to acquire. If you search Google on film acquisitions and film festivals, you should come up with acquisitions that have occurred at film festivals. Enter your film into these.

Once you have exhausted the film festival circuit (if you are lucky to get in), then you must decide if you are going the conventional route for distribution and pitching distributors or are doing self distribution. If you have followed my advice and have attached some level of name recognizable stars to your film, you may get lucky and land a distribution deal. Be advised that distributors will look at your film from a marketing angle and determine its selling points like the name recognizable stars in it, and whether it's unique compared to the mountain of films available in the market place.

Also be aware that distributors have overhead and expenses that will be deducted along with their take (at least a 30% cut). You go to distributors because they have the clout and connections in the industry to get your film to buyers whereas most indie filmmakers do not. Read distribution contracts very carefully and if you can afford one, have an entertainment lawyer review it before you sign. Many distribution contracts can run anywhere from 3 years to 7 years and can have varying levels of exclusiveness. This means that they have exclusive rights preventing you from making other deals. So be sure before you sign that you don't have any heartburn with the terms of the contract.

If conventional distribution is not for you, you can tackle self distribution. If, again, you've followed my advice and have budgeted in marketing/distribution monies into your funding plan, you can put into effect your marketing/distribution plan based on some form of a windows release model for optimum revenue generation. If you have a limited marketing budget, opt for a limited release. Even a limited release adds value to your film when pitching it in the other markets. Use some form of a roll-out plan if the film does well (Roll out means to expand to additional screens if the film is doing well. See appendix D for the Phased Rollout model). Once you have played out theatrical, move to a DVD release or VOD release, followed by cable/TV markets.

Aggregates

Filmmakers may have a hard time pitching their film projects to distibutors if they don't have established relationships with distributors or a catalogue of films. Today, major VOD distributors (like NetFlix, iTunes, and VUDU (Walmart)) do not like to deal with smaller independent filmmakers who they don't have established relationships with and only have one film. Filmmakers can approach "Aggregate" companies (Like Distribber) who have these established relationships and represent numerous filmmakers (aggregate). These aggregates either charge a flat fee (Like $ 250 to $ 5K per VOD market) or percentage (like 15%) off the top.

International Distribution

Based on a study (*The determinants of foreign box office revenue for English language movies by Journal of International Business and Cultural Studies, Texas A&M University*), U.S. domestic box office is a significant predictor of foreign box office success. So the best way to achieve success in international distribution is to have a successful domestic release. Domestic releases are releases within your own country where the film was produced. International distribution is distribution that occurs outside of your country. For instance, Canadian distribution is considered international when the film is produced in the domestic U.S.

International distribution is attained the same way as domestic (U.S.) distribution. The film company pitches foreign theater chain booking agents, VOD providers, and foreign cable networks/TV channels to acquire the rights for airing the film. Just as with domestic, you want to be pitching the "buyer" or content acquisitions person. The British Broadcast Channel (BBC) doesn't like to acquire movies for broadcast that haven't had a British theatrical release. The British theatrical chains also require the purchase of Virtual Print Fees (VPFs) the same as domestic theatrical chains here in the U.S. I can't attest to it, but their fees may actually be higher than in the U.S.

For indie filmmakers with limited budgets and funds, it's best to pitch only English speaking countries or where cinemas show English speaking films and do not require dubbing (a process where actors voiceover the English in another language). This would include countries like Canada, England, Australia, and so on. For American filmmakers, Canada would be the easiest target for international distribution. I would begin by targeting Lions Gate in Canada who does not only theatrical distribution in Canada but DVD release in rental stores as well.

The indie filmmaker can also approach places like the Movie Network in Canada who handle video on demand products and who are open to looking at foreign indie films. Some international distributors will ask for exclusivity in the market. This basically means that if you sign a deal with them for VOD on cable TV, you can't pitch other cable TV VOD to broadcast it until your exclusivity period expires (This could be 6 months to a year). Foreign distributors may also have different requirements from American distributors, especially for TV broadcast since television in foreign countries may use a different refresh cycle (50Hz versus 60 Hz) than in the U.S. (PAL versus NTSC in the U.S.).

Spend time looking at the best revenue approach and window release method for both domestic and foreign distribution. Always keep in mind that all anyone can ever say is "No" and every "yes" you get moves you closer to having a successful film. And always treat everyone professionally that you meet and do what you say you'll do.

IN CLOSING

So here's the speech. I began as a storyteller. I always had a wild imagination and it took me years to learn how to communicate those ideas on paper. Then I discovered screenwriting. It seemed to fit me and my storytelling. But I found it impossible to get my story on the big screen. My agent (I think he was kidnapped by aliens because he just dropped off the planet) once said that writing a hundred pages of words and having them told in a film on the silver screen would be the hardest thing that I would ever do. He was right.

I finally achieved getting my words on the screen in September of 2012 when our film was shown in a limited release by Rave Cinemas. It didn't play in many theaters and only ran for a little under two weeks, but my family and I did it. Today, it is possible to live your dream as a storyteller or filmmaker. You can have an idea, write it down, bring together others with a common interest, make that movie, and yes, take it to the silver screen.

We are the new breed of filmmakers. We don't have a screenwriter from Hollywood on contract. We don't have the fancy equipment (like a Panavision), or the funds (I had to hock my coat). Hell, most of the time, we don't even have a known actor. But we have heart and desire and passion just as any other filmmaker does. My last film took three years to complete because I had a full time job, a family, and a life to deal with at the same time. Your excuse can't be that you don't have the time. If you spent $20K on a new car, you could have spent $10K on a used one and got a loan for $10K to buy a camera and good lens. Find the time. Find the money. Find the passion. And make that damn movie that you've wanted to. You CAN produce a movie. Hell, I did it and so can you!

Good luck and happy adventures in filmmaking!

Bibliography

Arbitron, Inc: ***Arbitron Cinema Advertising Study***

filmmakermagazine.com: ***Quotes on Video-on-Demand (VOD)***

Mark Litwak; ***Contracts for the Film & Television Industry by Silman-James Printing***

Motion Picture Association of America: ***MPAA Theatrical Market Statistics 2011***

the-numbers.com, Nash Information Services, LLC (www.the-numbers.com)

Wikipedia Commons:

http://en.wikipedia.org/wiki/File:180_degree_rule.svg

http://en.wikipedia.org/wiki/30-degree_rule

(http://en.wikipedia.org/wiki/Depth_of_field)

http://en.wikipedia.org/wiki/List_of_large_sensor_interchangeable-lens_video_cameras

http://en.wikipedia.org/wiki/Clapperboard

AUTHOR BIO

Photograph by Timothy Sloan

JACKIE LYNN YOUNG earned a Bachelors of Science Degree in Technical Management from Bellevue University with minor degrees in Commercial Art and Electronics Technology. Jack has managed Young Films, LLC since 2001 when he wrote, executive produced, and co-produced Love Wine, a romantic comedy. Additional credits include The Darkening, a suspense/horror film (2012) that he wrote and directed, and the short film, Manimals, which he wrote, produced, and executive produced (1997). He also acts as manager on the Read-A-Movie™ series books and is author of many of the stories that appear in it. He is author of the screenwriting book, "How to Write a Screenplay in 3 Days: The Marathon Method." He was the coordinator of Nebraskans for Film (a local screenwriting group) for over four years and was a member of the Nebraska Writers Workshop (NWW), chaired by Sally Walker, for over five years. Jack has also appeared in Screentalk Magazine and is the author of over forty original screenplays. Jack works full time as a Logistics Engineer for a communications company and government contractor in Omaha, Nebraska where he resides with his wife and two children.

Jackie Young

Manager Young Films LLC

APPENDICES

APPENDIX A

Blank Budget

You should develop your budget in Excel. If you don't know Excel, find someone who is good enough to know how to insert formulas. Formulas will perform the calculations to streamline totaling up hours and budget dollars entered into the table cells.

Below is a description of the cell titles and calculations that you'll need to perform.

- **Director:** film director on the film project
- **Writer:** the screenwriter on the film
- **Acct #:** an accounting assigned series of numbers that compartmentalizes your budget expenditures. Includes a category number (i.e., 100) and a subcategory number (i.e., -001).
- **Description:** description of the film expense
- **Amount:** the numerical number of days or weeks that the resource is needed
- **Units:** the unit of measure such as hours, days, weeks, etc.
- **X:** used to indicate multiple units
- **Rate:** the hourly, daily, or weekly rate
- **Subtotal**: subtotals for line entries
- **Total:** total of line entries for each expenditure

If you have additional expenses not covered in the categories, add new categories and assign them a new category number. For instance if I wanted to add an IT person to handle loading digital media to the below-the-line expenditures, I'd create a category 170-009 and add the info for that person in the spreadsheet.

		Title:			Producers:		
Director:		Writer:					
Acct #	Description	Amount	Units	X	Rate	Subtotal	Total
100-001	STORY						
100-002	SCREENPLAY PURCHASE						
	purchase						
					Total for 100-001		
110-00	PRODUCER						
110-01	ASSOCIATE PRODUCER						
	tbd						
	tax						
110-02	SECRETARIES						
	t.b.d		Week				
	tax						
					Total for 110-00		
120-00	DIRECTOR						
			Week				
	fringes						
120-02	CASTING FEES						
	t.b.d		Allow				
					Total for 120-00		
130-00	CAST						
130-01	PRINCIPAL PLAYERS						
	lead 1		Weeks				
	fringes		deferred				
	lead 2		Weeks				
	fringes		deferred				
	lead 3		Weeks				
	fringes		deferred				
Subtotal	taxes		deferred				
							page 1

Acct #	Description	Amount	Units	X	Rate	Subtotal	Total
130-02	**DAY PLAYERS**						
	male support		Weeks				
	male support o.t.		Hours				
	female support		Weeks				
	female support o.t.		Hours				
	female minor support		Days				
	male minor support		Days				
	minor support o.t.		Hours				
	taxes						
	fringes		Allow				
130-03	**STUNTS & ADJUSTMENTS**						
N/A	coordinator		Weeks		-		
N/A			Allow				
	taxes						
					Total for 130-00		
140-00	**TRAVEL & LIVING**						
140-01	**PRODUCER'S TRAVEL**						
	producers' travel		Weeks				
140-02	**PRODUCER'S LIVING**						
	producers' living		Days				
	pm living		Days				
	assoc. prod. living		Days				
	producer's per diem		Days				
	pm per diem		Days				
	assoc. prod. per diem		Days				
140-00	**TRAVEL & LIVING (cont'd)**						
140-03	**DIRECTOR'S TRAVEL**						
	gas/mileage/airfare		Allow				
140-04	**DIRECTOR'S LIVING**						
	living		Days				
	per diem		Days				
							page 2

Acct #	Description	Amount	Units	X	Rate	Subtotal	Total
140-05	**CAST LIVING**						
	lead living		Days				
	lead per diem		Days				
	lead living		Days				
	lead per diem		Days				
	support living		Days				
	support per diem		Days				
					Total for 140-00		
	TOTAL ABOVE-THE-LINE						-
150-00	**EXTRA TALENT**						
150-01	**EXTRAS & STANDINS**						
	tbd		Days				
150-02	**CASTING AGENCY COMMISSION**						
	tbd		Allow				
150-03	**ALLOWANCES CAR**						
N/A	vehicle		Days				
					Total for 150-00		
160-00	**PRODUCTION STAFF**						
160-01	**PROD. SECRETARY**						
deferred	tbd		Weeks				
	taxes						
160-00	**PROD. STAFF (cont'd**						
160-02	**UNIT PROD. MANAGER**						
	tbd		Weeks				
	fringes						
	taxes		deferred		-		-
160-03	**1ST ASST. DIRECTOR**						
	tbd		Weeks				
	fringes						
	taxes						
160-04	**2ND ASST. DIRECTOR**						
	tbd		Weeks				
	fringes						
	taxes		deferred		-	-	-
160-05	**SCRIPT SUPERVISOR**						
	tbd		Weeks				
	fringes						
	taxes		deferred				-
							page 3

Acct #	Description	Amount	Units	X	Rate	Subtotal	Total
160-06	ESTIMATOR/PROD. ACCT.						
	tbd						
160-07	PRODUCTION ASSISTANTS						
	tbd	0	Weeks	0	-	0	
	fringes	0			0	0	
	taxes	0.15			-	-	-
160-08	ASSIST. DIR. TRAINEE						
	tbd	0	Weeks		0	0	
	fringes	0			0	0	
	taxes	0.15			-	-	-
160-09	PRE-PROD. EXPENSES						
	Location Surveys	Allow					
					Total for 160-00		-
170-00	CAMERA						
170-01	DIRECTOR OF PHOTOGRAPHY		Weeks				
	fringes						
	taxes		deferred				-
170-02	OPERATOR						
	tbd		Weeks				
	fringes						
	taxes		deferred			-	-
170-03	1ST ASST CAMERAMAN						
	tbd (Can.)		Weeks				
	fringes						
	taxes		deferred		-	-	-
170-04	2ND ASST CAMERAMAN						
	tbd		Weeks				
	fringes						
	taxes						-
170-05	FILM LOADERS						
	tbd		Weeks				
	fringes						
	taxes				-	-	-
170-06	STILL CAMERAMAN						
	tbd		Weeks				
	finges						
	taxes				-	-	-
							page 4

Acct #	Description	Amount	Units	X	Rate	Subtotal	Total
170-07	**CAMERA RENTALS**						
			Weeks				
	taxes						
	steady cam.		Weeks				
	taxes						
170-08	**CAMERA SUPPLIES**						
	misc.	Allow					
170-09	**LOSS, DAMAGE, REPAIR**						
	misc.	Allow					
					Total for 170-00		-
180-00	**SET DESIGN**						
180-01	**PRODUCTION DESIGNER**						
	tbd		Weeks				
	fringes						
	taxes		deferred				-
180-02	**CONSTR COORD/FOREMAN**						
	tbd		Weeks				
	fringes						
	taxes				-	-	-
					Total for 180-00		-
190-00	**SET CONSTRUCTION**						
190-01	**CONSTRUCTION LABOUR**						
	foreman		Weeks				
	labor		Weeks				
	taxes				-	-	-
190-02	**CONSTRUCTION MATERIAL**						
	set #1						
	set #2						
	set #3						
					Total for 190-00		-
200-00	**SET STRIKING**						
200-01	**LOC. STRIKING COSTS**						
	labour	0	Weeks		-	-	
	taxes	0.15			-	-	-
					Total for 200-00		-
							page 5

Acct #	Description	Amount	Units	X	Rate	Subtotal	Total
210-00							
210-01	**SET OPERATIONS**						
	1ST COMPANY GRIP						
	tba		Weeks				
	fringes						
	taxes						
210-02							
	2ND COMPANY GRIP						
	tbd		Weeks				
	fringes						
	taxes						
210-03							
	COMPANY GRIPS						
	tbd		Weeks				
	fringes						
	taxes						
210-04							
	CRANE/DOLLY GRIPS						
	dolly grip		Weeks				
	crane grip		Weeks				
	fringes						
	taxes						
210-05							
	CAMERA CRANES						
	tbd		Weeks				
	taxes						
210-06							
	GRIP EQUIPMENT RENTAL						
	tbd		Weeks				
	taxes						
210-07							
	GRIP PURCHASES						
	expendables	Allow					
210-08							
	CRAFT SERVICEMAN						
	head craft service		Weeks				
	assistant		Weeks				
	taxes						
	supply allowance		Days				
210-09							
	STANDBY SUPPLYMAN						
	tbd		Weeks				
	fringes						
	taxes						
	purchase allowance		Days				
210-10							
	STANDBY PAINTERS						
	painter		Weeks				
	fringes						
	taxes						
							page 6

Acct #	Description	Amount	Units	X	Rate	Subtotal	Total
210-11							
	FIRST AID - STUDIO						
	doctor on call		Weeks				
	nurse		Weeks				
	taxes						
210-12							
	DRESSING ROOM RENTALS						
	tbd		Days				
					Total for 210-00		-
220-00							
220-01	**ELECTRICAL**						
	GAFFER						
	tbd						
	fringes						
	taxes						
220-02							
	BEST BOY						
	tbd		Weeks				
	fringes						
	taxes						
220-03							
	LAMP OPERATORS						
	tbd		Weeks				
	fringes						
	taxes						
220-04							
	GLOBES/CARBONS/SUPP.						
	expendables	Allow					
220-05							
	ELECTRICAL EQUIP. RENTALS						
	equip & gen. package		Weeks				
	taxes						
220-06							
	LOC. GENERATOR OPER.						
	tbd		Weeks				
	fringes						
	taxes						
220-07	**ELECTRICAL (cont'd)**						
	LOSS, DAMAGE, REPAIR						
	allowance						
					Total for 220-00		-
230-00							
230-01	**SET DRESSING**						
	SET DECORATOR						
	tbd		Weeks				
	fringes						
	taxes						
							page 7

Acct #	Description	Amount	Units	X	Rate	Subtotal	Total
230-02							
	SWING GANG						
	crew						
	fringes						
	taxes						
230-03							
	SET DRESSING PURCHASED						
	allowance						
230-04							
	SET DRESSING RENTALS						
	allowance						
					Total for 230-00		-
240-00							
240-01	**PROPERTIES**						
	PROPERTY MASTER						
	tbd		Weeks				
	fringes						
	taxes						
240-02							
	ASST. PROPERTY MASTER						
	tbd		Weeks				
	fringes						
	taxes						
240-03							
	PICTURE VEHICLE						
	vehicle #1 Jeep						
	vehicle #2						
	taxes						
240-04	**PROPERTIES (cont'd)**						
	VEHICLE RENTALS						
	rental #1 Cube						
	rental #2						
	rental #3						
	rental #4						
	taxes						
240-05							
	ANIMAL HANDLERS/WRANGLERS						
	animal package						
240-06							
	PROP RENTALS						
	tbd						
240-07							
	PROP PURCHASES						
	allowance						
240-08							
	LOSS, DAMAGE, REPAIRS						
	vehicle repairs						
					Total for 240-00		-
							page 8

Acct #	Description	Amount	Units	X	Rate	Subtotal	Total
250-00							
250-01	**WARDROBE**						
	WARDROBE MAN						
	tbd		Weeks				
	fringes						
	taxes						
250-02							
	ASSIST. WARDROBE MEN						
	assistants		Weeks				
	taxes						
250-03							
	COSTUME DESIGNER						
	tbd		Weeks				
	fringes						
	taxes						
250-04							
	CLEANING AND DYEING						
	allowance						
250-05							
	WARDROBE RENTALS						
	allowance						
250-06							
	WARDROBE PURCHASES						
	allowance						
					Total for 250-00		-
260-00							
260-01	**MAKEUP & HAIRSTYLISTS**						
	MAKE-UP ARTISTS						
	tbd		Weeks				
	fringes						
	taxes						
260-02							
	EXTRA ARTISTS						
	assistants		Weeks				
	fringes						
	taxes						
260-03							
	KEY HAIR STYLIST						
	tbd		Weeks				
	fringes						
	taxes						
260-04							
	EXTRA HAIR STYLISTS						
	assistants		Weeks				
	fringes						
	taxes						
260-05							
	MAKE-UP/HAIR KIT RENTALS						
	allowance						
					Total for 260-00		-
							page 9

Acct #	Description	Amount	Units	X	Rate	Subtotal	Total
270-00							
270-01	**PRODUCTION SOUND**						
	SOUND MIXER						
			Weeks				
	fringes						
	taxes						
270-02							
	BOOMMEN						
			Weeks				
	fringes						
	taxes						
270-03							
	CABLEMEN						
	tbd		Weeks				
	fringes						
	taxes						
270-04							
	SOUND EQUIP. RENTALS						
	package		Weeks				
	taxes						
270-05	**PROD. SOUND (cont'd)**						
	PLAYBACK EQUIP. RENTAL						
	package w/operator		Weeks				
	fringes						
	taxes						
					Total for 270-00		-
280-00							
280-01	**TRANSPORTATION**						
	TRANSPORTATION COORD						
	tbd		Weeks				
	fringes						
	taxes						
280-02							
	DRIVER CAPTAIN						
	tbd		Weeks				
	fringes						
	taxes						
280-03							
	STANDBY DRIVERS						
	drivers		Weeks				
	fringes						
	taxes						
280-04							
	STANDBY VEHICLES						
	executive vehicle #1		0				
	executive vehicle #2						
	standard						
	standard						
	taxes						
							page 10

Acct #	Description	Amount	Units	X	Rate	Subtotal	Total
280-05							
	MILEAGE ALLOWANCE						
	allowance						
280-06							
	FUEL						
	allowance						
280-07							
	CAMERA DEPT.						
	truck rental		Weeks				
	taxes						
280-08							
	ELECTRICAL DEPT.						
	truck rental		Weeks				
	taxes						
280-09	**TRANSPORTATION (cont'd)**						
	GRIP DEPT.						
	truck rental		Weeks				
	taxes						
280-10							
	WARDROBE DEPT.						
	truck rental		Weeks		0	0	
	taxes						
280-11							
	ALL OTHER DEPT.						
	truck rental - standby		Weeks				
	taxes						
280-12							
	ALL OTHER TRANSPORTATION						
	tbd						
	taxes						
					Total for 280-00		-
290-00							
290-01	**LOCATION EXPENSE**						
	SITE RENTALS/PERMITS/LICENSE						
	site rental (include electricity)	Allow					
290-02							
	HOTEL & LODGING						
	key personnel		Days				
	crew		Days				
	location crew		Days				
290-03	**CREW'S TRAVEL**						
	gas/mileage/airfare		Allow				
290-04	**OFFICE RENTAL/FURNITURE**						
	location office						
							page 11

Acct #	Description	Amount	Units	X	Rate	Subtotal	Total
290-05							
	LOCATION SECURITY						
	police & fire		Weeks				
					Total for 290-00		-
300-01	**PRODUCTION DAILIES**						
	NEGATIVE RAW STOCK						
			Weeks				
	tax						
					Total for 300-00		-
310-00							
310-01	**FACILITIES FEE**						
	STAGE SHOOTING						
	studio	Allow					
310-02							
	STAGE HOLDING						
	studio	Allow					
					Total for 310-00		-
	TOTAL SHOOTING PERIOD						-
320-00							
320-01	**EDITING**						
	FILM EDITOR						
			Weeks				
	fringes						
	taxes						
320-02							
	OFF-LINE EDITOR						
			Weeks				
	fringes						
	taxes						
320-03							
	SPECIAL EFFECTS (SFX)						
	tbd		Weeks				
	fringes						
	taxes						
					Total for 320-00		-
330-00							
330-01	**MUSIC SCORE**						
	COMPOSER						
	music package						
330-02							
	POST PRODUCTION SOUND						
	SOUND TRACKS (Pop Music)						
	TBD						
					Total for 330-00		-
							page 12

Acct #	Description	Amount	Units	X	Rate	Subtotal	Total
340-00							
	TITLES						
	TITLES (MAIN & END						
	package						
					Total for 340-00		-
350-00							
350-01	CONVERSIONS						
	POST PROD. PACKAGE						
	complete package						
					Total for 350-00		-
	TOTAL POST COMPLETION						-
360-00							
360-01	ADMINISTRATIVE EXPENSES						
	MPAA RATING						
	TBD						
					Total for 360-00		-
370-00							
370-01	PRINT & ADVERTISING (P&A)						
	Adverising/Posters/Ads package						
	Virtual Print Fees (VPFs)						
	Digital Content Package (DCP)						
					Total for 370-00		-
	TOTAL POST PRODUCTION				POST		
	TOTAL ABOVE-THE-LINE						
	TOTAL BELOW-THE-LINE						
	ABOVE & BELOW-THE-LINE						
	TOTAL FRINGES				INCLUDED		
	Insurance						
	contingency	0%					
	Overhead	0%					
	Completion Bond	0.00%					
	GRAND TOTAL						-
							page 13

APPENDIX B

Blank Shooting Schedule

As I discuss in the book, a shooting schedule is critical for keeping a film shoot on schedule. I've seen other shoots that have tried to run without a daily schedule and it amounts to chaos. It becomes even more important when you are shooting a film with investor's money. When a film falls behind schedule, it will require more funding to complete. Investors will want to know why the film is behind schedule and running over budget. Although I funded our last two films, it was still important to me to run the production on schedule because I was using personal time off from my job to shoot the film. I wanted to come home with a film in the can.

Developing schedules isn't incredibly difficult, they're just time consuming. Figure to spend two or three weeks shaking out the schedule so it looks like it'll run. Also check my links in the back of the book for sites that have tutorial videos on developing a schedule. Figure you'll need a minimal of 16 days to shoot a 90 minute film and go from there. I'm including a blank schedule for you to play with. You can use the single page as a template to create additional pages for your film. Like I mentioned, we first did a master schedule that addresses all scenes at all locations and then we did separate schedules (same form) for each shooting location.

Just a note about other methods of scheduling. There are physical methods of scheduling a film. You can buy a board version that has paper strips that you write the scenes on and these can be found for sale on the Internet. We bought one originally and they are very expensive. I put the schedule together using this method and when I took the works to the designated production manager (My sister) she actually gasped and complained how difficult it would be to carry the board version around from set the set and suggested the electronic version (Excel Spreadsheet). Once we built the spreadsheets and started using them, we'd never go back to paper.

Breakdown Page	Day or Night (D or N)	Scene No.	Extras (E)	No. of Pages	Vehicles (V)			

Title:
Director:
Producer:
Production Manager: Brenda
Asst. Dir.:
Cinematographer:
Script Dated:

Character	Artist	No.

APPENDIX C

Contracts

As a final warning, I want to remind you (if you can afford it) to have a lawyer review your contracts. Always only ask for the rights that you need and try to be straightforward with your language and clearly state what you need from that person performing the service. The contracts presented here are only examples and should only be a starting point for you to build the type of agreement or contract that you need. Names and personal information were removed for privacy laws. As with any contracts, you may have to negotiate some for a fee. For example you may have to negotiate payment with some locations. First try and sell them on the credit in the film and a free DVD. If so, include any of these details in the contract.

I've included a sample contracts for:

- *Location Agreement* - This location agreement was used to secure rights for shooting outside of an airport. You'll note that any rights granted are only for the exterior of the airport. If you write one of these for shooting in the interior, make sure that this is laid out in the agreement and the rights for anything shot in the interior are granted.
- *Product Placement Release* - The product placement release should be used if you plan on showing any name brand products in your film. We used a grocery bag (Mother shopping in film) and needed clearance.
- *Music Agreement* - A composer wrote and scored a piece for the film and this agreement assigns us the rights from the composer.
- *Cinematographer Work-for-Hire* - This contract assigns us any rights assigned to the cinematographer.
- *Letter of Intent* - Letters of intent are just that, an agreed upon intent for the actor to work on the film. It doesn't guarantee anything other than intent.

STANDARD LOCATION AGREEMENT

Name of Production:
The Darkening

Name of Production (the "Company"):
Film Company Name Here
Street Address Here
City, State & Zip Here

Address of Property
(the "Premises"):   Removed_____

                            Removed _____

                            Removed _____

"Owner" Contact:_____
Phone: _____

This Location Agreement ("Agreement") is dated as of _ _____ and entered into by _____ (collectively "Company") and _____ ("Owner") (Or Representative) in connection with the Premises. The terms and conditions follow:

1.   Owner hereby grants to Company the right to enter upon the Premises bring personnel and equipment on the Premises as described in Exhibit 1 and have non-exclusive use of the Premises, as described below, on a _____(the "Term"). Premises as described in this agreement refer to the exterior of the airport terminal.

2.   Owner, to the extent it has the right to do so, further grants to Company the rights to:

A.   photograph, reproduce and replicate the real and personal property, only exterior of the Premises (including the name, trademark, signs, and identifying features thereof); and

B.   use the photography and sound recordings (or any part thereof) made by Company in accordance with this Agreement in connection with the Picture as described in Exhibit 2 and/or in connection with the exhibition, advertising, and exploitation of the Picture in any media, now known or unknown at any time in any part of the world in perpetuity;

C.   solely with respect to aspects of the photography and sound recordings made by Company in accordance with this Agreement in which the Premises cannot be identified, re-use such aspects in any manner as Company may elect in any media, now known or unknown at any time in any part of the world in perpetuity.

3.   In the event Company desires to photograph retakes or other scenes in accordance with this Agreement (for example, in the event of damaged or imperfect film or equipment), Company may re-enter and use the exterior of the Premises for such period as may be reasonably necessary therefor, commencing at a mutually agreed upon date and time within twelve (12) months after the end of the Term.

4.   Owner makes no representation or warranty of any kind regarding Company's rights to carry out the activities set forth in Paragraph 2 above, and assumes no liability to Company or any third party with respect to claims arising from Company's actions pursuant to this Agreement. Company agrees to indemnify and hold the Removed, and employees harmless from any third party claim, demand, cause of action, liability, loss, damage, cost or expense, including attorneys' fees and court costs, which directly or indirectly arises out of or is in any way associated with actions of Company pursuant to Paragraph 2 of this Agreement. Owner does represent and warrant that it is the sole and exclusive owner of the Premises.

5.   Company and Owner acknowledge that the Premises shall remain open to the public during the Term. Owner agrees that it shall use best efforts to keep the public away from the filming area, and Owner agrees that Company shall have the right to control the flow of vehicular and/or pedestrian traffic during filming.

6.   In full consideration for all of Owner's obligations under this Agreement and the rights being granted to Company by Owner, Company agrees to acknowledge the Owners involvement in the production of the film with screen credit as agreed to upon by the Owner and promotion of their involvement on the film's web site (www.thedarkeningmovie.com). Company has provided a description of its anticipated usage in Exhibit 1 attached hereto for the purpose of clarification of personnel and equipment to be used on premises.

7.   At any time up to the date that the Premises are actually used by Company as contemplated herein, Company may elect not to use the Premises by giving Owner notice of such election, in which case neither party shall have any obligation whatsoever.

8.   Company agrees to leave the Premises in as good order and condition as when received by Company, reasonable wear, tear, force majeure and permitted use excepted, and Company shall have the right to remove all of its sets, structure, and other material and equipment from said Premises and shall make all good faith, reasonable efforts to do so in a timely manner.

9.   Company shall not construct, erect, build or fabricate any structure on the Premises or add any props, temporary or permanent, to the Premises for any purpose.

10.   Company and Owner agree to jointly inspect the Premises prior to and following Company's use, specifying in writing all existing damage, if any. Owner agrees to submit in writing within thirty (30) days of vacating the Premises a detailed list of all apparent property damage for which Owner claims Company is responsible and shall permit Company's representatives to inspect such damage.

11.   Company shall not be obligated to make any actual use of photography,

recordings, depictions, or other references to the Premises in any motion picture or otherwise.

12.   All rights of every kind in every media (whether now known or unknown) in and to the photography and sound recordings made by Company in accordance with this Agreement shall be solely owned in perpetuity by Company. Notwithstanding the foregoing, nothing in this Agreement shall cause Owner or any other party to forfeit or transfer to Company any rights associated with the Premises that Owner or such other party had or acquires apart from this Agreement.

13.   This Agreement shall be construed and enforced in accordance with the laws of the State of Illinois applicable to agreements of this nature and Owner hereby consents to the jurisdiction and venue of said State.

14.   This Agreement is entered into as of the date indicated below, represents the entire agreement between the parties, and may be amended only in writing signed by the parties.

15.   This Agreement may be executed in one or more counterparts, each of which shall be deemed an original, but all of which together shall constitute one and the same Agreement.

16.   The Company will show proof of Location Liability Insurance in sufficient amount two (2) weeks prior to commencing at the Owner's location.

ACCEPTED AND AGREED:

"Owner" or representative Printed Name: _____

Signature: _____ Title: _____

Date: _____

Company Representative Printed Name:_____

ACCEPTED AND AGREED:

"Owner" or representative Printed Name: _____

Signature: _____ Title: _____

Date: _____

Company Representative Printed Name:_____

Signature: _____ Title: _____

The location agreement also had an exhibit attached. The exhibit is nothing more than an extra page of information that provides details about what we plan to do at the location. It includes a copy of the scene(s) we are shooting and a list of the people that will be on the set at that location. Note that we provided a summary of the scene, a list of equipment, the number of those in the crew, and the length of time that we need to shoot the scene.

Exhibit 1

Description of scene, personnel, and equipment on the Premises during the Term:

Doctor Phillips, a psychiatrist, picks up his wife at a local airport.

Film crew of ten plus six actors will arrive and need use of the Unloading area in front of the entrance to the terminal.

Equipment will consist of a film camera and lenses, lighting, and a dolly and track system.

The scene is estimated to take approximately 2 ½ hours to setup and shoot.

PRODUCT PLACEMENT RELEASE

Name of Production:
The Darkening (the "Picture")

Name of Production Company (the "Company"):
Film Company Name Here
Street Address Here
City, State & Zip Here

Product Name Owner
(the "Owner"):   Removed_____
    Removed_____
    Removed_____
    Removed_____

Contact: Removed

Vice President & C.O.O.

Phone: Removed

This Product Placement Agreement ("Agreement") is dated as of   1-05-2012   and entered into by __Young Films LLC_____ (collectively "Company") and Removed Supermarket ("Owner") (Or Representative) in connection with the Removed product/brand. The terms and conditions follow:

The Owner grants to you, your successors, licensees and assigns, the non-exclusive right, but not the obligation to use and include all or part of the trademark, logo, or identifiable characters (the "Mark(s)") associated with the above listed product(s) and/or service(s) in the Picture, without limitation as to time or number of runs, for reproduction, exhibition and exploitation, throughout the world, in any and all manner, methods and media, whether now known or hereafter known or devised, and in advertising, publicizing, promotion, trailers and exploitation thereof.

The Owner warrants and represents that it is the owner of the product(s) or direct provider of the service(s) as listed above or a representative of such and has the positive right to enter into this agreement and grant the rights granted to Young Films LLC hereunder. In full consideration of the Owner providing the product(s) or direct provider of the service(s) to Young Films LLC, Young Films LLC agrees to accord the Owner screen credit in the end titles of the positive prints of the Picture in the following form" Grocery Bags furnished by Removed Supermarket."

1.   The Owner understands that any broadcast identification of its products, trademarks, trade names or the like which they may furnish, shall in no event, be beyond that which is reasonable related to the program content. In return for being able to include the product in the production, the Company agrees not to disparage the product or the Owner

2.   I represent that I am an officer of the Company and am empowered to execute this form on behalf of the Company.

3.   I further represent that neither I nor the Company that I represent will directly or indirectly publicize or otherwise exploit the use, exhibition or demonstration of the above product(s) and or service(s) in the Picture for advertising, merchandising or promotional purposes without the express written consent of Removed Supermarket.

4.   ACCEPTED AND AGREED:

5.   "Owner" or representative Printed Name:

_____

Signature: _____ Title: _____

Date: _____

Company Representative Printed Name: _____

Signature: _____   __ Title: _____

Date: _____

MUSIC AGREEMENT

Name of Production:
The Darkening (the "Film")

Name of Production (the "Producer"):
Film Company Name Here
Street Address Here
City, State & Zip Here

"Removed" (The "Composer")_____

The Darkening Theme Song (the "Song")

Music Publishing and Performing Rights Royalties: The Composer "Removed" will own 100% of all worldwide music publishing rights for the Song as described herein. Producer agrees to specify "Removed" as 100% writer for the Song used in the film.

Ownership of Sound Recordings: The Composer will own 100% of all worldwide master rights to the Song used in the Film.

Originality and Copyright Considerations: The Composer of The Song "Removed" certifies that the Composer wrote, composed, arranged, adapted, scored, produced, recorded, completed and performed the Song described herein as an independent contractor engaged by Producer. The Composer certifies that the Song is wholly original, except to the extent that it is based on or uses material in the public domain or material furnished to the composer by Producer, and that the Composer is the author at law thereof and owns all right, title, and interest in and to the Song and the results of the Composer's services rendered in connection therewith, including without limitation all copyrights and renewals and extensions of copyrights therein.

Synchronization and Master Licenses for Song: The Composer shall grant Producer and its successors, assigns, and licenses the irrevocable right, privilege and authority to record, copy, sell, distribute, and use the Song subject to the terms of the Synchronization and Master Licenses supplied with this document.

Warranty and Certificate of Authorship: The Composer represents and warrants to Producer that (i) The Composer has full right and legal capacity to execute and fully perform this Agreement and to make the grants, assignments and waivers contained in it, (ii) that the Composer warrants and confirms they are the sole writer of the original musical compositions ("Song") delivered to Producer for use in the film and that the Song will not be copied from or based on, in whole or in part, any other work; (iii) to the best of the Composer's knowledge as far as the Composer knows or should have known in the exercise of due diligence and prudence, nothing in the Song does or will infringe on any property right (copyright, trademark, patent right, right to ideas and the like) or personal right (defamation, false light, moral right and the like) of any person or legal entity; and (iv) there is no pending or threatened claim, litigation, arbitration, action or proceeding with respect to the Song. The Composer will indemnify and hold harmless Producer, its affiliated companies, successors and assigns, and their respective directors, employees and agents, from and against any claim, loss, liability, damages or judgments, including reasonable outside attorneys' fees, arising from any breach of the above representations and warranties.

Compensation: The Producer agrees that for compensation, the Producer will provide screen credit during closing credits in the following form:

"Removed Song composed by Removed"

The Producer also agrees to send the Composer a Blu-ray and standard DVD version of the film when the film is completed.

The Composer will execute, acknowledge and deliver such additional instruments as necessary to confirm the intent of this Agreement. This instrument is the entire Agreement between the parties and cannot be modified except by a written instrument signed by the Composer and an authorized officer of the Producer. This Agreement shall be governed by and construed under and in accordance with the laws of the State of Nebraska applicable to agreements wholly performed therein.

Agreed to and accepted by the following parties on this 29 day of January, 2012.

Producer (Removed) _____ Date_____

Composer (Removed) _____ Date_____

Below is a contract for a cinematographer. Note that we added bonus clause that allowed the cinematographer to use our equipment for a specific length of time as a bonus. On indie films, filmmakers may come up with creative ways to pay back to those that help with production. With limited funds, this was a way for us to give back something.

Cinematographer Work-for-Hire Agreement

Name of Production:
The Darkening (the "Picture")

Name of Production Company (the "Producer"):
Film Company Name Here
Street Address Here
City, State & Zip Here

Cinematographer: Removed

TERM:

The Cinematographer's services shall commence on or about _____, 2011 and ending on or about _____, 2011. Cinematographer also agrees to be available for pick shots as needed for completion of the film. The Producer will give reasonable advanced notice prior to the pickup shots required.

COMPENSATION:

In full and complete consideration for the services to be rendered hereunder, Cinematographer shall be compensated the sum of $ Removed during the term and a deferred salary of $ Removed. Producer also agrees to allow the use of the camera, lens, head, and tripod by the Cinematographer after production is completed until the end of the year (December 31st, 2011) in exchange for work performed (as a bonus). The Producer agrees to report per an annual basis on net profits available to payout deferred salaries.

1)   SERVICES: During this engagement, Cinematographer will render services whenever and wherever Producer may require, in a competent, conscientious, and professional manner, meeting the needs of the Producer in all matters, including those

involving artistic taste and judgment. The Producer shall have no obligation to actually utilize the Cinematographer's services, or to include any of Cinematographer's work in the Picture, or to producer, release, or continue the distribution of the Picture.

2)   RIGHTS: All results and proceeds of Cinematographer's services hereunder shall constitute "a work made for hire" for Producer, and Producer shall be considered the author thereof for all purposes and the owner throughout the world of all the rights therein. Producer shall have the right to use and license the use of the Cinematographer's name, photograph, likeness, voice and/or biography in connection with the Picture and the advertising, publicizing, exhibition and/or other exploitation thereof, including, without limitation, in connection with "behind the scenes" and "making of" films and featurettes.

3)   CREDIT: Provided that Cinematographer fully performs   all services and obligations hereunder and is not in default hereunder, he/she shall be entitled to receive credit on screen substantially in the form:

CINEMATOGRAPHER

In the main titles of the Picture, or in the end titles if no main titles are used or if only cast credits or production/presentation/film by credits appear in the main titles. Producer shall make reasonable efforts to accord Cinematographer credit on screen immediately following the Production Designer, subject to the requirements of the Picture's distributors. All paid advertising credit shall be subject to the customary exclusions of the Picture's distributors. All aspects of Cinematographer's on screen and paid advertising credit shall be in Producer's sole discretion. No failure by Producer or its assignees or licensees to comply with the credit requirements hereof shall be deemed a breach of this Agreement, subject to distributors' customary exceptions and exclusions.

4)   DVD/Blu-ray: Cinematographer shall be provided with one (1) copy of the completed Picture on DVD and/or Blu-ray disk as soon as it is available.

5)   ASSIGNMENT: Producer may assign its rights hereunder to any person, firm, or corporation.

6)   CINEMATOGRAPHER'S REMEDIES: Cinematographer recognizes that in the event of a breach by Producer of its obligations under this Agreement (including, without limitation, breaches of the Agreement rising out of credit obligations), the damage (if any) caused to the Cinematographer thereby is not irreparable or sufficient to entitle Cinematographer to injunctive or other equitable relief. Cinematographer therefore agrees that Cinematographer's rights and remedies shall be limited to the right, if any, to obtain damages at law, and that the Cinematographer shall not have the right in such

event to terminate or rescind this Agreement or to enjoin or restrain the distribution or exhibition of the Picture. Neither the expiration of this Agreement, nor any other termination thereof shall affect the ownership by Producer of the results and proceeds of the services supplied by Cinematographer, or any other rights granted herein to Producer, or alter any of the rights and privileges of Producer, or any warranty or undertaking on the part of Cinematographer in connection with such results and proceeds.

7)   MISCELLANEOUS: This Agreement shall be deemed to be made in the state of Illinois and shall be construed in accordance with the laws of Illinois applicable to contacts made and performed therein. Notwithstanding any other provision of this Agreement, Cinematographer's sole remedy for breach by Producer of any provisions of this Agreement shall be the right to pursue an action at law for damages. In no event shall Cinematographer seek or be entitled to recision, or to injunctive or other equitable relief, and the termination of this engagement or this Agreement for any reason shall not affect the Producer's right to the result and proceeds of Cinematographer's services hereunder. Producer shall have the right to assign this Agreement to any person or entity, and the benefits of this Agreement shall inure to any such assignee. Cinematographer shall, upon request, execute, acknowledge and deliver to Producer such additional documents as Producer may deem necessary to evidence and effectuate Producer's rights hereunder. Cinematographer hereby grants Producer the right, as attorney-in-fact, to execute, acknowledge and record any and all such documents.

This Deal Memo supercedes all other agreements between the parties, either oral or written, and constitutes the full agreement between the parties unless amended to the contrary in writing and signed by both parties.

Agreed to: _____ Cinematographer :_____

Agreed to: _____ Producer: _____

Title:

Production Co:

Letter of Intent example:

Note: This may also be called a "Letter of Attachment". Both are a committment from an actor to attach to a film project. Figure to pay the actor 20% of their salary down to sign this letter (roughly).

Letter of Intent

_____ (hereinafter "Actor") hereby expresses interest in playing the role of _____ in the film project of the working title _____ under development by_____, LLC (hereinafter "Producer") subject to Actor's availability and the future agreement to terms of employment between Actor and Producer. This letter does not bind either Producer or Actor to an employment contract, but grants Producer permission to use Actor's name and likeness in the pre-production development of this project and in seeking financing for this project, for a period not to exceed one year.

Actor: _____ Date _____

Producer: _____ Date _____

Title:

Production Co:

APPENDIX D

Theatrical Release Phased Rollout Model

This section describes a model for a phased rollout for theatrical release. It's intended only as a model for indie filmmakers who are self distributing their film at the theaters. The approach must be carefully implemented and should not be attempted by indie filmmakers who do not completely understand the risks associated with film distribution. Keep in mind that when exhibiting a film at the theaters, you need to be aware of all costs associated with a release. Not only do we have to deal with VPFs, we also need to transport the DCP to the theater. As discussed earlier in the book, some theaters may require a drive that fits into the rack and includes a transport, while others can accept cheaper USB drives. These both have associated costs from $ 80 to $ 300.00, depending upon the transport. You'll also need to provide posters (see section on movie posters) that will add costs. The model discussion in this section only uses VPF fees in the calculations in demonstrating how the model works. Consider all costs associated with a theatrical release when implementing the model. Young Films is not liable for those who do not adhere to proper implementation of the model.

During the limited theatrical release of our last film, we acted as our own distributor and were able to get a deal for limited release (4 theaters) with one of the top ten theatrical chains in the U.S. I developed this model in hopes of propelling us forward with an option to acquire additional screens if the film did well. Being a first time distributor of a film for theatrical release, we were not prepared to support the film with the required marketing push or promotion (yep, lack of funds. Remember the "big" picture the producer must have?), so we did not move past the first phase. You MUST be prepared (or have the funding) to mount the required promotions for your film to have this plan succeed. However, this section details the model that I created to conduct a phased rollout of your film at the theaters.

Typically the standard release model for films is as so (VOD has created alternative release windows):

- Movie is first released through movie theaters
- After approximately 4 months, it is released to DVD
- After an additional number of months it is released to Pay TV and VOD services
- Approximately two years after its theatrical release date, it is made available for free-to-air TV

The most important release is the theatrical release. This is when the film can not only make the most money (generally) but it also provides marketing of the film to the general public that is hard to duplicate. If the film can get a foothold in the theatrical release, this paves the way for not only opening additional theater screens (if it does well) but gives the film legs to crossover into additional markets.

Many films enter into the theatrical release market via the "Limited Release" approach. This is a safe way to test the market to see if there is any interest in the film. If it does well, then additional screens can be secured to generate additional revenue. Blockbusters will forgo this approach and usually open with a minimal 1,000 screens. But for indie filmmakers, the limited release approach allows entry into theatrical release with minimal investment in screens (which I earlier stated cost $ 1,000 each for the Virtual Print Fees).

For a savvy indie film producer with access to funding (angel investor or revolving credit line) there is a way to roll out your film from a limited release to additional screens while reducing your risk of investment. I call this approach the "Phased Rollout." A Phased Rollout approaches theatrical release in a systematic and reduced risk method. The figure below shows how by securing a revolving credit line using your bank can supply the additional funding needed to open additional screens if, and ONLY IF, the box office receipts (revenue) are there to back the revolving credit line. The risk reduction is based on the fact that you DO NOT purchase additional screens ($ 1,000 each) unless the film is doing well and backed by receipts.

There are several important pieces to this model. First a note of warning! Young Films is NOT promoting that you go to your bank and back a loan with your personal property to buy screens. If you do this without good box office numbers, you will run the risk of losing your money and will be in hock to the bank with no revenue to pay back the revolving credit. Young Films is not liable if you incorrectly approach the use of this model. If you agree and accept the liability, then please read on.

First of all, banks understand that when you back loans or credit lines with sales (in this case box office sales) then the chances of you repaying that credit line are very good. A lot of businesses borrow money against sales and projected sales. It's the way businesses operate. Secondly, theater chain management is willing to provide you with the box office sales numbers on a week by week or day by day basis if you need those numbers. They usually pay the distributor 30 to 45 days after the box office receipts come in. This model also assumes that you are acting as your own distributor for your film. As I mentioned earlier in the book, a filmmaker can act as their own distributor for their film. You just need to do your homework and be able to sell this to the theater chain. So if we can get numbers from the theater on the box office receipts after the film opens, we know how much revenue (This is based on the deal that you cut. Typically, the distributor will get 45% of the BO receipts, but adjust accordingly) that we have coming. Set as a rule that you will only use 50% of the generated revenue to purchase additional screens. This is because of two reasons. One, you will need to pay taxes on the revenue and if things go bad during any of the phases, you won't lose all of the revenue that you have accrued.

Since most indie filmmakers probably won't be able to secure more than $ 25K to 50K of revolving credit, you'll need to pay off the revolving credit as soon as possible. Once it's paid off, you can reuse the revolving credit to buy additional screens (if it's still doing well at the BO). Also not that once you have paid off the revolving line of credit on time, the bank may be willing to raise the limit on your revolving line of credit. Also note that a revolving line of credit won't cost you anything if it's not used.

The figure below shows a model that begins with the investment for 4 screens. This initial funding needs to come from you or private investors. Remember that you want the bank funding to be backed from ticket sales. In the initial phase, all of the investment is at risk since you don't know how the film will play and whether you will have any ticket sales. The revolving line of credit is ONLY used after the initial phase. So let's say that the film plays well (Because you have done marketing, right?) and the film plays for 2 weeks. The following calculations are made based on having a 25% turnout for a theater that holds 175 seats, and that you will have only 5% of that during weekdays and that you get somewhere between 3 to 5 showing a day (I use 4 showings here). I also use $ 4.00 as the 45% of the door for calculating your earnings per seat.

4 showings daily (weekend) x 40 seats per theater x 4 screens x 8 days (2 weekends x 2 weeks) x $ 4.00 = $ 20,480.

After two weeks, if you have these numbers being reported back from the theater chain, you would ask for an additional ten screens ($ 20,480/2 = $ 10, 240 to invest in screens). At this point (knowing you have the ticket sales) you would use the revolving credit line to secure the screens. Once you receive the 45% payout from the theater chain, you then pay off the revolving credit line. Now you have an additional 10 screens to add to the previous 4 screens and are now playing at 14 screens. You also still have $ 10K retained in earnings.

For the next two weeks, you are playing at 14 screens and would then reevaluate the performance in the same way to determine if you should open additional screens.
4 showings daily (weekend) x 40 seats per theater x 14 screens x 8 days (2 weekends x 2 weeks) x $ 4.00 Plus 3 shows daily (weekday) x 8 seats (remember that theaters only get about 5% of the business weekdays) x 14 screens x 20 days (5 days x 2 weeks) x $ 4.00 = $ 71,680 (weekends BO) + 32,080 = total $ 103,760.

Now you have another $ 50K to reinvest in screens ($ 103K/2). However, these tickets sales MUST BE confirmed before using the revolving credit line to purchase additional screens. If, and ONLY IF, you have these numbers, purchase additional screens (Remember to only use up 50% of what ticket sales are reported to you from the theater chain).

The figure shows purchasing up to 100 screens, but this depends on how the film is doing and you only reinvesting 50% of the "reported" box office sales. You can see that once you start adding screens after the initial limited release, how ticket sales can start to accumulate. However, if you have not done any marketing or promotion on the film, do not expect to get these kinds of numbers. If people don't know the film is playing, they will not most likely find the film or come to see it. Remember that.

By promoting your film, starting with a small limited release, having a plan to roll out your film to additional screens, and having some form of funding available (private or credit line), and carefully only investing what is backed by "real" box office profits, you can expand your film release and earn real profits on your film at the theater.

Phase 1 Roll -Out 4 Theaters (September 7 th)

Angel or Personal Funds

Purchase VPFs

Screen 1   Screen 2   Screen 3   Screen 4

Ticket Sales Numbers

This phase will cost you between $ 8K and $ 10K ($ 4K for VPFs and $ 4-6K for marketing)

Revolving Credit Line

Use BO Receipts to back Revolving Credit Line

Box Office Receipts (45% of door)

Purchase VPFs

Phase 2 Roll-Out 10 Additional Theaters (September 28 th)

Screen 1 Screen 2 Screen 3 Screen 4 Screen 5 Screen 6 Screen 7 Screen 8 ... Screen 10

Ticket Sales Numbers

This phase will cost you between $ 18K and $ 20K ($ 10K for VPFs and $ 8-10K for marketing)

Revolving Credit Line   Payoff Revolving Credit   Box Office Receipts

Purchase VPFs

Phase 3 Roll-Out 100 Additional Theaters (October 12 th)

Screen 1 Screen 2 Screen 3 Screen 4 Screen 5 Screen 6 Screen 7 Screen 8 ... Screen 100

Ticket Sales Numbers

This phase will cost you between $ 180K and $ 200K ($ 100K for VPFs and $ 80 - 100K for marketing)

Revolving Credit Line   Payoff Revolving Credit   Box Office Receipts

Purchase VPFs

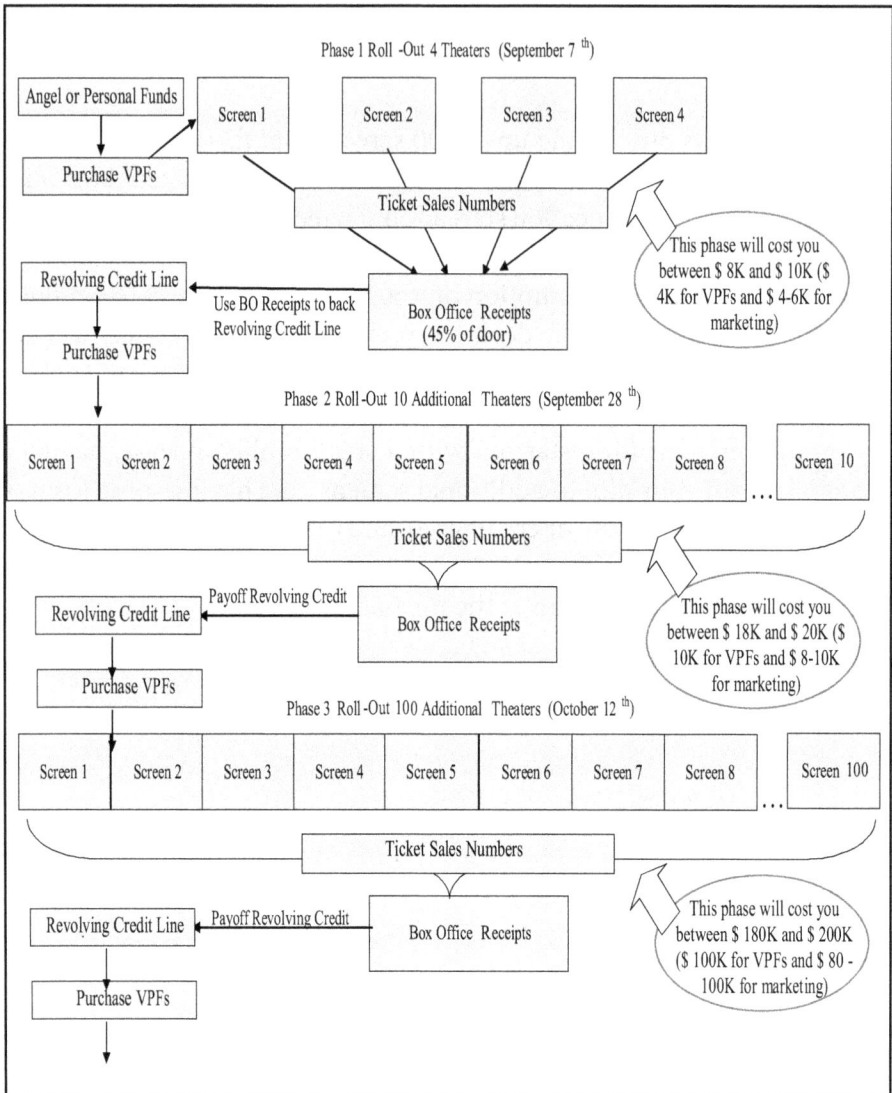

Theatrical Release Rollout Using Investor Funds

Let's talk a little about how investors can play a role in our phased rollout theatrical release. As I've mentioned, a producer should have a vision for not only production of the film but beyond to distribution. Times are changing and the indie producer must be creative to take advantage of it. I also mention in this new scheme that when you're securing funding, consider pitching the investor on the concept that to get their investment back, distribution of the film and marketing funding are essential to this end.

The problem with using investor money to fund this phased rollout is that not only do investors want to get their investment back; they'll want a percentage on top. Otherwise, why would they invest? If you set the production up correctly and have star (A, B, or C-List actors) attachments, you'll want to budget the film so you have enough production value to take it to the theaters. Let's say that you budget it at $ 1 Million. You may have ten investors that invest $ 100K each. Since you'll want to try and keep at least 51% ownership of the film (a majority), then you have 45% of the profits to play with. If you offer them 2.5% to 3.5 % of the profits, that'll leave you 15% to 25% to offer as incentives to actors should you need to offer additional incentives to bring them onboard. The point being here that investors and actors will be expecting a percentage of profits from the film beginning after the first initial release.

The producer should sell investors on theatrical exhibition and how it is probably the best shot at getting the kind of revenue that will not only recoup their investment but make them a profit. If your budget is $ 200K or $ 400K, pad in half again that much for theatrical distribution and marketing. If the budget is $ 200K ask for an additional $ 100K to open at 50 theaters with an additional $ 50K for marketing. If the budget is $ 400K, ask for an additional $ 200K to open at 100 theaters with an additional $ 100K for marketing and promotion. This indie approach mirrors how Hollywood actually releases and promotes their movies. Studios spend half again the budget of a film on promoting it. Again, this takes us back to the fact that if you do not promote your film, nobody will come to see it. Unfortunately, the old adage that if you build it they will come, is NOT true. If you build it and tell everyone that you built it, then PERHAPS they will come.

Now here's where the phased rollout changes a little with investor money. If you open at 100 theaters and do well, you'll want to take some of that profit (remember the 50% rule) and open additional screens. Since you are actually playing with the investors profits here, make sure that your investor is onboard with you using profits to expand to additional screens. It would be wise to write this into the contract as well. Investors may be reluctant with reinvesting profits back into additional screens so you may have to approach each phase rollout with them, giving them the details of each phase (ticket sales) and then getting their buy-in on the purchase of the additional screens. The point that I'm making is that when you are playing with money from investors, you need to make sure that you have their support.

Pitch it this way – After the first phase of release at the theaters, investors recoup their investment. The decision to move to phase 2 is based on whether this was paid back and if there is enough profits to fuel an additional 50 to 100 theaters. If you have deferred actors, they must be paid their 2.5% (If that's the deal) before going to phase 2. Investors must realize that if funds remaining are used to fuel additional screens, this could result in less profit for them, if audience participation is lower than expected.

Here are some scenarios to consider when working with investors and if you have deferred percentages for actors:

If the investor decides to take a share of the profits from phase 1 and decline phase 2, the producer can put up the funds from its profits and takes the risk. The investor does not receive profits from the second phase of theatrical showings if they are not invested. The investor may then be approached and be involved in phase 3 of distribution whereas a final group of screens are opened.

If no investor chooses to finance additional screens (including the producer) no phase 2 or phase 3 will be attempted.

Investors may choose to participate in all 3 phases by allowing the profits to be used to fuel all phases of theatrical release. They will then participate in the profits on all phases.

The investor is automatically granted profits from phase 1 per the contract. Phase 2 and phase 3 are choices the investor makes as supplemental agreements to the contract.

The films print and advertising budget only defines funds that support phase 1. If a film is successful, it is normal for film distributors to open additional screens. If a film is not successful, it is not unusual to close screens that aren't performing. Opening additional screens is an obvious response to a film performing well at the box office but requires additional funds. These funds are not requested by the distributor; however, it is more sensible to use ticket sales revenue to buy additional screens.

The investor may sign up pre-decided to support all phases of exhibition or elect to choose whether to continue after phase 1. The producer/distributor will disclose sales numbers and investment options after each phase allowing the investor to decide whether to conclude their investment and collect their returns after each phase. The producer would reserve the right to continue investing in additional screens and phases with or without investor participation.

Because actors are NOT investors, they would receive their 2.5 % of profits during each and all phases. Deferred salaries are paid out during the first phase. If after the first phase, once all deferred payments have been paid out and investors have received their investment back and their interest, there is not enough profits left for additional screens, the producer can choose to not continue with additional phases. This decision would be made solely by the producer.

However, the producer should discuss the options with investors and make a decision based on the feedback from the investors and how the film is performing at the box office. Investors deciding to support phase 2 activities are deferring their 2.5% return on investment until the next phase of profits (Phase 2). Since phase 2 doubles the number of screens, in theory it should double the sales and therefore double the profits.

APPENDIX E

Battle Plan

Okay, so what the heck is a battle Plan for films? You've probably never heard of one before. That's because I created it. Actually, it's really only a place to write down your thoughts in some formal way so that you can focus on the issues with getting the production off the ground and running. It's also something that you can share with your team that has the beginnings of a plan to get it done.

Although I didn't include it, I also had an appendix that had listings of all of the equipment (hardware and software) that I was currently looking at renting or buying. I would grab a screen shot or download the JPEG along with a quick summary (specs) and pricing. I didn't include that here because I didn't want to deal with the rights on all of the brand names.

Below, you'll find the ramblings of a mad producer as he tries to sort through the issues in a sort of organized way. I hope that it gives you an idea on how to organize your beginning thoughts about putting together a production.

Looking back at our original battle plan, it did give us some direction but some of the things we thought we could or would do, changed. We did purchase an HVX200 camera and tested it. We soon realized that it would never pull off what we wanted. So we sold the camera and shopped for another that could do the job (AF100). Anyway, what I'm saying is that it's only a plan to get you started in the right direction.

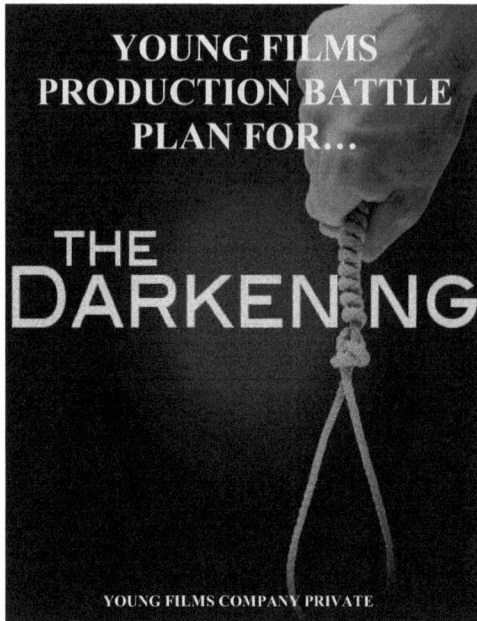

Battle Plan Cover Page

INTRODUCTION

I thought it appropriate to call this a "Battle Plan" because production of a feature film is similar to fighting a battle on several different fronts. It is a large collaborative effort that requires a wealth of people, resources, and money. When shooting an independent film, with limited funds, it becomes even more difficult. This plan is divided into Preproduction, Production, and Post Production, the three main activities in producing any film.

PREPRODUCTION

This is the current phase of the production of "The Darkening." Preproduction runs up until the shooting of the film actually starts (this is considered production). Preproduction starts with the selection of a screenplay for the film. Once a screenplay is selected, the selection of the type of technology that the film will be shot on becomes the next crucial choice. Today, there exists a variety of choices for independent film from 35MM to Super 16, to High Definition (HD) digital cameras. Filmmakers have moved away from film because of the expense of purchasing film and lab costs associated with processing the film and conversion to digital for editing. The choice in technology is based on the workflow desired. Workflow not only involved the type of look of the imagery produced by the camera, but the format (DV, HD) desired for the output product, the method in which the imagery is stored (short term and long term), and the format that is needed for a specific digital editing workstation.

EQUIPMENT

It was decided early on that the film would be shot in digital format using a high-end prosumer digital camera. The company will be using a Panasonic HVX200 digital camera equipped with a Letus Extreme Depth of Field (DOF) 35 MM adapter. It will be captured as 1080P 24 frames per second (24p). The DOF adapter allows the use of additional 35 MM lenses to create the depth of field imagery that more closely resembles typical 16 MM and 35 MM film shot feature films. The camera records the film to a digital P2 card and can record about 60 minutes on 32 Gigabytes of P2 storage (2 16 GB or 4 8 GB P2 cards). This is approximately the amount of HD digital data that is shot in one day of shooting. Each day, the cards are dumped to a standby laptop (Dual Core) that is equipped with a 2 Terabyte portable hard drive and a P2 card reader. A laptop with Dual-Core processors and 2 GByte of RAM is required (Needs to be purchased). Folders are previously setup on the 2 TB drive for each day of shooting for each card to dump. Folders are named Day1_P2#1 and Day1_P2#2, Day2_P2#1, Day2_P2#2, and so on for 16 days of filming. So there are 32 separate folders pre-created for dumping daily footage. After shooting, the terabyte drive is moved to an editing suite where the data is offloaded for editing. The camera will also be equipped with a Focus Puller to allow the Director of Photography (DP) to adjust the focus if the lenses with a "Whip."

Crucial to filmmaking is audio. Audio is recorded on the set using a portable field recorder. Young Films currently owns two Tascam DA-P1s and two shotgun microphones. The two Tascams will be sold off to allow upgrading to the Tascam HDP2 field recorder (The newest version of the Tascam field recorder). The Tascam DA-P1 records to DAT tape which is not conducive to the desired workflow (Digital). The newer Tascan HDP2 records to digital cards similar to the P2. They, too, must also be dumped to a larger drive periodically through the shoot.

Lighting is another crucial element for any film being shot today with hopes of marketing to distributors and theaters. Lighting greatly improves the quality of the film and attaining the "Film" look. We currently have (2) 650 Watt Halogens, a 300 Watt Halogen, and a 2,000 Watt Halogen light for lighting scenes. We also have a soft box, a circular reflector, and numerous smaller fluorescent lights (150 Watt).

The company will also be using an Indie style dolly and tracks for "Dolly" shots and a Jib Arm that allows the camera to be extended up into the air for overhead shots.

Rounded out the equipment list are: (2) 10' x 12' Painter canvases (to be purchased) for blocking out unwanted sunlight, glares, and wind during filming. A windblocker (Windsock) will also be purchased to fit over the microphone in exterior shots to block disturbance to the sound during audio recording. A boom pole (already purchased) allows for the shotgun microphone to be extended over the actors for recording sound. Already purchased sandbags are used to secure equipment like light stands (Purchased) and the Manfretto tripod with fluid head.

Since the film has several scenes that require green screen effects, we have purchased a 10'x20' foot and 8'x8' green screen. A harness and block and tackle may need to be purchased to create the "Falling" into darkness effect shown in the movie. The actor is suspended in the air with his arms outstretched as if he's asleep and falling through the blackness. This is captured against a green screen with a mild fan blowing his hair gently.

Another scene that may require the use of green screen is when we see the stranger in the hooded black rain coat. Since the audience shouldn't know (early in the film) that the man in the rain coat is actually James (or Frank) it becomes extremely difficult to hide his identity from view. However, by using a green screen hood, the face of the actor is green-screened out and a swirling black mass put into the chromo-keyed face of the actor. Then when we see glimpses of the actor under the raincoat hood, it's not easily identifiable as our lead character. The other option is to use a green screen face paint (or Chromo-key green color). A trial size of lime green face paint was purchased for testing.

YOUNG JAMES GLOW

When the Young James later appears to the older James, he has a shimmering ghostly glow as if he's forcing himself across time and space to help his older self. This effect is done with Red Giant software (Holomatrix) but requires that the actor playing Young James (Trevor) shoots his scenes in front of a green screen. The actor's figure is then later moved and placed in other scenes and appears with a eerie glow.

HOME-MADE CONTRAPTIONS

Several of the scenes have a special effect of a room that is spinning behind the actor. This is done by filming the actor in front of a green screen and then adding the spinning room during editing. The spinning room will be shot with a HD Camera that is suspended from the ceiling that spins. The spinning will be achieved by building a box for the camera that has a cable attached in the center that allows the camera to slowly spin during filming. The box will be designed by the DP (Dan). Another device (To be made by Dan) is the "Creature" viewpoint platform. This large flat platform supports the camera while two men move forward with it creating the look of a creature searching the neighborhood for a new host.

EQUIPMENT TRAINING

Dan Young, the DP or Cinematographer on the film, will be attending training from a well-seasoned Cinematographer in September on the Panasonic HVX200 in Chicago. Each training session will last a full weekend with Dan returning for follow up training as needed.

Our company has looked at available equipment in the industry and for the money, we feel the equipment choices that we are making align with the company's goals and budget requirements. Young Films hopes to upgrade equipment in the future, but feels the equipment identified will produce a quality Indie film look and feel for this genre.

ACTING

One of the biggest efforts of making a film is selecting the actors. Young Films has decided to use all local actors from the local area to fill all actor positions. Earlier this year, Young Films held auditions in Rockford Illinois to find these actors. All of the major actors have been identified but a few of the bit roles remain. On Saturday August 14th, the first rehearsal for the film was held. This was no more that a table reading of the complete script and a chance for everyone to meet. Monthly rehearsals will be held until we are 2 months away from shooting and then it will be stepped up to twice a month. Rehearsals in September and October of 2010 will focus on Act I (First 32 pages of the script). November and January (December skipped due to the Holidays) will focus on Act II (with 3 to four rehearsals), and February and March focusing on Act III. April will have final rehearsals and fine tuning in preparation for the shoot in early May (First 2 weeks of May 2011). The rehearsals will not only focus on the actors knowing their lines but provide exercises in developing natural sounding dialogue, finding the proper emotional levels for scenes, and learning how to "Step On" other actors lines when needed.

NOTE: Let's don't forget to find a double for Nick (Who plays James/Frank).

The double must look like Nick from the back. We'll use the double when James and Frank are in the same scene. Also need a girl with the same build as Robin to play the girl crossing the street. Also, make a note to talk with Nick and have him put on a little weight and grow out his hair a little. We also need to find someone to do the voiceover for Dr. Michaels.

PROPS/COSTUMES

As with any film, there are always props and costumes. A horror genre film adds additional requirements as well (blood, scars, lazy eyes, bad teeth, etc). This film has a chief and deputy, guards, a doctor, and other characters that require authentic costume pieces. We have already purchased Airsoft pistols, holsters, badges, a sheriff and deputy hat, belts, handcuffs, doctor's smock, fake baseball bat, fake kitten, dulled butcher knife, and a stethoscope. Still to be purchased are several guard uniforms and a prisoner jumpsuit (orange). Many of the actors will be bringing their own clothes to shoot in. This creates a problem in itself although it saves the company money in costumes for actors. Actors will be told to bring 4 to 5 sets of clothes, preferably in the color range of gray, blue, black, etc. No bright colors. Hollywood uses a very selective color pallet for wardrobes for films. For the horror genre, the best rule is to use very selective drab colors. This is a dark film and should fit the look of the horror genre.

The company has two smoke machines and will also purchase a lightning (Lightning scene when Doctor murders wife) machine of the grade used for major exhibitions (fun parks, etc). The cost of the machine is project at around $ 200.00.

The character of Kyle Burnett has a "Lazy" eye. It droops down to one side giving him an eerie look. One of his ears also protrudes out farther than the other. A makeup person will need to work with the company to create these effects. The Young James is also cut across the throat by our killer, Kyle Burnett. Our makeup person will need to discuss with us the method to be used to create this bloody effect. Later the older James is shown with a scar on his neck. Although this should be an obvious scar, it should look authentic (Not Halloweeny). There are several other makeup special effects required such as: a kitten's guts spilling out scene, several dead body scenes (pale makeup), a protruding knife scene, a gunshot scene (James shot in the back), Kate Harrison bound scene, an others. These will need to be discussed in detail with the makeup person. Perhaps the toughest is the bound scene. Although Kate must look like she's suffocating from the bound ropes, it must not present a danger to the actress. Therefore, a prop must be developed that looks like bound ropes but is harmlessly draped around her neck.

Below is a complete list of all props required (This section was previously listed earlier in the book – removed):

LOCATION INSURANCE

Most locations won't sign a Location Agreement without us providing location insurance. I got a quote for $ 650.00 for $ 1 Million dollars of liability coverage for a 2 week shoot. We can add a statement to our location agreement that we will show proof of location insurance 2 weeks prior to shooting.

PRISON SCENES

It is essential that the prison scenes appear realistic. It's hard to accomplish this without expensive sets or a real prison location. We are in discussions with the Illinois department of Corrections for using Joliet prison. Originally, we thought we only needed a master shot (Exterior of building) but after rethinking the scenes, we do need to shoot from the interior. We'll need to negotiate this. We may also be required to do some level of painting to prepare it for the shoot. Six actors (Doctor Phillips, James, Kyle Burnett, Kristy (As receptionist), Ned (Playing guard), and Deputy (Playing other guard), will need to be at the prison location to shoot this.

PRODUCTION

During production a good sized cargo van will be required to transport all of the film equipment. Young Films plans on buying a used cargo van (2005 if possible) in February 2011 timeframe to be used for this purpose. Transportation will also be required for transporting actors from the central headquarters to the locations. Dedicated drivers will be needed during production. A gas fund will also need to be setup for supplying gas funds for these vehicles.

Production (The Shoot) runs smoothly when the schedule is derived from a production board (We have one in draft form). Scenes are ordered together by location and a schedule derived from this. Since each scene strip on the board has a corresponding production sheet, information such as actors, props, vehicles, and costume can be attributed to each scene strip on the board. Therefore, with scenes grouped by location, it can easily deduce as to which actors are needed on which days. Young Films needs to order 2 to 3 additional "flaps" or a 3-fold production board to accommodate the remaining scene strips. Once this is completed, the scene strips should be grouped by location. Once this is done, a schedule should be typed up of the entire 16 day shoot. Once this is done, actors can be notified on which days to report and what scenes on what day we will be shooting.

When determining how many scenes to group at one location, the rule of thumb is to schedule roughly 7 pages of shooting per day. To calculate the total number of pages, the production manager should total all of the scene lengths notated on each of the scene's production page. The total should not exceed roughly pages.

7 pages x 16 days = 102 pages shot

Actors should receive a Call Sheet for every day of shooting. On the Call Sheet it provide information about what scenes will be shot, when they are being shot, where they are being shot, and any special conditions such as weather or what they should wear.

It is also important to note that during shooting, the director owns the set. The Production Manager runs the "Production" elements such as what resources are needed for each scene and where those are coming from. The Director's Assistant is the link between the director and production manager. The grips and gaffers take direction from the director and director of photography (Guy behind the camera). So lights and cabling go where the DP says they go. The director will also work directly with the sound engineer (Guy recording sound) to make sure he is ready to record and is getting proper sound. The boom operator (guy holding the microphone) reports directly to the sound engineer. If there is a "script" person, they will also double as the "Clapper" person. This person reports to the director and it's their responsibility to keep track of scenes and takes and to record changes to the script and to also double as the "Continuity" person. A continuity person is responsible for ensuring that continuity is maintained from scene to scene.

It's critical that when on location filming that all appliances and equipment such as refrigerators, air conditioners, fans, etc at a location be turned off. Devices that have motors generate noise that is easily picked up by the microphone. During filming on the set, 60 seconds of "room tone" will be recorded after the final scene at a location. Room Tone allows for adding in ADR or voiceover in post and matching up with previously recorded soundtracks. The room tone is what lies beneath recorded dialogue on location.

It is also critical while filming that HD and audio tapes/P2 Cards that come off the camera or sound recorder be immediately tagged as "Full" and have the write protect IMMEDIATELY set. This prevents accidentally deleting or overwriting the tape or P2 card. A permanent marker should be used to put an "E" (Empty) on one side of the P2 card cap and an "F" (Full) on the other side so that the condition of the tape or P2 card is always identified.

At the end of the shooting day, all equipment should be properly placed in a specific storage bin in the cargo truck so that it can be easily found the next day when needed. There should be a place for every piece of equipment and each piece of equipment should be accounted for each day. An inventory list should be used to properly check and account for all equipment, props, and costume pieces.

FOOD

If we do not feed the actors, they will not be happy campers. So, Young Films must do the best to provide nourishment on the set and liquids to drink. We estimate roughly $ 2,500 for food for 16 days. Since shooting will be schedule to begin at roughly 1:00 PM daily and extend to around 11:00 PM, we should schedule a supper break at 6:00PM and a snack at around 9:00 PM. The Production Manager (Brenda) and Director's Assistant (Patty) will query the actors for food and drink choices and develop a menu for the shoot.

MUSIC/BANDS

Dan is in discussion with local bands to find one that will be showcased in the "Club" scene and to possibly do some music for the movie (Soundtrack?). Bands love movies because if a movie, by chance, does take off, their popularity will go off the charts. This is a great opportunity for us to get free music and provide a chance for stardom to an unknown band. By the way, Young Films used local bands for music in both Manimals and Love Wine.

POST-PRODUCTION

Here's where we make this film shine. In the past few years some really great software has exploded onto the market place. Special effects wizards and film editors who used to work for some of the biggest special effects houses (Like George Lucas's Industrial Light & Magic) have been hired by software giants to create software for the desktop that does what only what the big special effects houses used to do. This software (Magic Bullet for one) allows filmmakers to add the correct coloring and film effects to make films look like big Hollywood blockbusters. One of the secrets is in using the same color palettes that Hollywood uses for big movies. Now, on the desktop, film editors can apply the same color palette to get the same look as studios.

For special effects, new companies have sprung up that allow every effect from fire, to smoke, to gunshots, to you name it, and it's Hollywood studio quality. Our film will be shot in High Definition (1080P 24P, and 720P for slow-motion or other variable rates) and have that big Hollywood look applied in post production. For post production, however, our current editing workstation (HP Dual Core Windows Vista PC) will need to have the motherboard upgraded to a Quad Core (4 CPUs) and additional memory. The 2 Terabyte drive used for image storage used on the set can be easily connected to the workstation for post production work. The new motherboard and memory upgrade will cost around $ 300.00. Additional software (Like Magic Bullet) will also need to be purchased. The estimated cost for this is an additional $ 1,000.

DISTRIBUTION

The main reason we decided to do a horror film in the first place is because they are MUCH easier to get picked up than ANY OTHER film. Lions Gate (Toronto and LA) picks up horror films for distribution to movie rental houses like they're going out of style. Conservatively, we can expect sales in excess of $ 20,000 with video rentals (Mark did $ 18K on a $1,000 budget horror film). We, Young Films, have already worked with NetFlix and they are easy to get distribution with. They picked up Love Wine and purchased over 150 copies at retail (around $ 3,000 worth). We also have contacts at Oberon Entertainment in Omaha who have West Coast connections and they have turned on these contacts for us in the past. We also plan to make our rounds at the Film Festivals and plan on premiering the film in Rockford. We also plan to market our own DVDs at the film festivals and premier as well as making it available on our own web site. Initially, we plan to produce 1,000 high quality DVDs. The sale of the initial production would generate $ 20,000 in revenue.

In total, we expect to generate around $ 45 to $ 50K, conservatively. This will not only pay back investors, but allow actors to be paid and generate enough revenue to upgrade equipment and plan for the next film production in 2012.

INTERNET PRESENCE

For "The Darkening" Young Films is getting a lot of assistance with Internet marketing from Myke Wilson. Myke has stood up a Facebook site, a "www. theDarkening.com" site, and he and Sue Cook have also stood up a Twitter page. With all of the buzz and interest this will generate, we can expect to exceed our own expectations on sales for the film. Who knows, with enough buzz created, it may even be picked up for theatrical distribution (I know. Don't get too cocky).

PRODUTION MEETINGS

Production meetings are a great way for the crew to discuss and resolve production issues. We plan on starting up weekly production meetings soon. During the production meetings, we will take up Action Items. Action Items will document tasks that are outstanding or need additional attention. They will also be assigned to a specific person and have a due date that action can be expected.

I hope that this "Battle Plan" helps to put the entire production crew on the same page. If you have any questions, please bring them to the production meetings where they can be addressed.

Thanks,

Jack Young, Manager of Young Films LLC

APPENDIX F

Film Investor Prospectus

If you want to have enough budget to produce a quality film, you'll need to go to investors. These investors that you need to seek out should be qualified. What I mean by qualified is that they are not your aunt or uncle or old lady down the street who is rumored to have millions stashed in her mattress. They are typically business men or women who already have investments and know the risks involved with investing large amounts of money.

When you find these people, you do not want to shoot from the hip and waste their time. Their time is worth money. You must always think from their perspective. What are they getting from this investment in your film project? Your best hope is to seek out investors who are looking for tax shelters and have an interest in the arts or films. Perhaps they just love movies.

I have lost count of the number of business plans and pitches to investors that I have written. This is one of my best pitches and I want you, as a producer seeking executive producers, to get a feel for what you need to include in your investor prospectus. Once you get the general idea, you can tailor the prospectus for your film, budget, etc. On my "Actors" slide, I actually include actor's photos and names of those we are pitching to get attached to the film project. If the prospectus stays private between you and those you are pitching and never ever gets published, there should not be any legal issues with using their likeness. I have removed the photos and names from the one shown here since that in itself could pose issues with those whose pictures were used. So they have been removed.

Paper- -hearts

My Hero

Just when you think your life is over, the magic begins...

FEATURE FILM PROSPECTUS

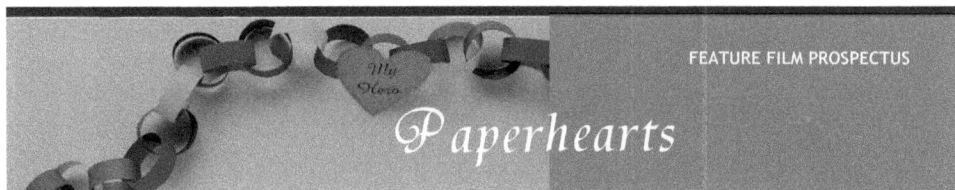

FEATURE FILM PROSPECTUS

Paperhearts

DIRECTOR
JACK YOUNG

WRITERS
JACK & DAN YOUNG

PRODUCER
DAN YOUNG

PRODUCTION MANAGER
BRENDA YOUNG

PRODUCTION ASSISTANT
PATRICIA WAKEFIELD

Young Films LLC

PRESENTS

INVESTMENT COVER LETTER

PRODUCTION BUDGET FOR "PAPERHEARTS" IS $ 1065,000

SHOOTING FORMAT IS RED HIGH DEFINITION

SHOOTING PERIOD IS APRIL AND MAY 2013

PRODUCTION LOCATION IS ROCKFORD, ILLINOIS

9 WEEKS PRE PRODUCTION SCHEDULE

TWENTY FOUR (24) PRODUCTION DAYS

12 WEEKS POST PRODUCTION SCHEDULE

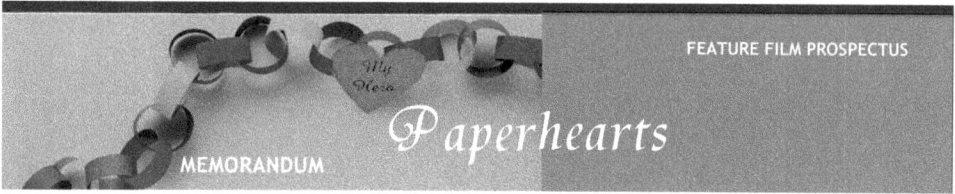

MEMORANDUM

Paperhearts

FEATURE FILM PROSPECTUS

This memorandum does not constitute an offer to sell, or a solicitation of an offer to purchase securities. This business plan has been submitted on a confidential basis solely for the benefit of selected, highly qualified investors and is not for use by other persons. Neither may it be reproduced, stored or copied in any form.

Paperhearts is the tale of a group of elderly residents of a retirement home who, with the aide of an aged "B" Movie film director, make a movie in an effort to bring two young hearts together.

Paperhearts is an amazing story that children can bring their parents and grandparents to. It is full of heartfelt drama and humor for the entire family.

"Just when you think your life is over, the magic begins...

2

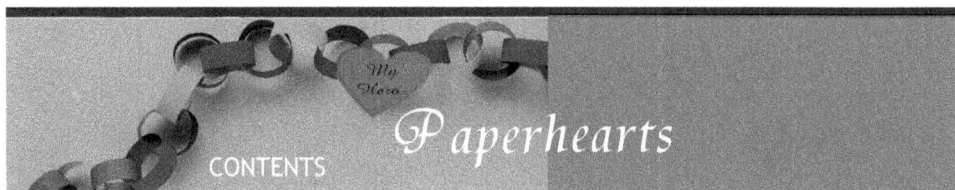

CONTENTS

Paperhearts

TABLE OF CONTENTS

APPENDICES

3

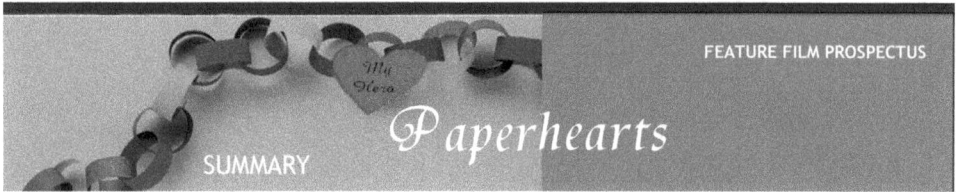

EXECUTIVE SUMMARY

Director/writer Jack Young has been writing screenplays for over two decades, with over forty written. Jack, a former member of the *Nebraska Writers*, also coordinated a screenwriting group for over four years, working with other screenwriters to polish and perfect their screenplays. Also the author of *"How to Write a Screenplay in 3 Days: The Marathon Method"*, a book that Lew Hunter, The Chairman Emeritus and Professor of Screenwriting, UCLA Department of Film and Television, called *"A unique look at the creative process behind screenwriting and a great book for the beginning screenwriter"*, Jack understands the essentials in screenplay development.

Writer turned director, Jack and Dan (co-writer and Producer) work closely with actors to ensure the story is faithfully told and the dialogue and acting are at the very best. With three films under their belts, the Young Films team has worn every hat in film production from casting, to auditions, from writing to directing, to editing and music composition all the way to theatrical distribution. Young Films has established solid contacts in the film industry from Special Effects technicians in Hollywood, to music composers in Canada, to contacts at theatrical distributors such as Rave Cinema, to Video on Demand (VOD) distributors such as the giant Gravitas Ventures, the number one VOD distributor in North America. Young Films prides itself on the solid relationships it has built with your average owners of locations that we use in our films, to city and county governments in Illinois who provide critical support for film production by closing roads for shoots and approving permits.

Young Films brings the bar up on each and every film production and each time develops new contacts and relationships that take us further in the development of quality feature films. We have also learned lessons along the way on what doesn't work and with this latest plan, you'll see lots of innovative approaches to resolve issues that can prevent a film from being successful and profitable. Hold onto your hats!

> *"Independent films are now a sought after alternative class invest-*
> *-ment, though it is often difficult to find good unbiased information*
> *on the topic. Independent films in certain genre and budget size can*
> *often prove to be excellent investments when properly managed*
> *within tried and true structures."*
>
> *Bx.Businessweek.com (Business Exchange)*

4

FEATURE FILM PROSPECTUS

*P*aperhearts

SYNOPSIS

SYNOPSIS

An ensemble cast of residents of a retirement home who show us that even with the elderly there are wonderful events that occurred in their lives that make them who they are and special. Sometimes it's easy to forget the moments and events until they are called upon and challenged near the end of our journey. What could be a solemn and melancholy story, becomes one of hope for the eternal heart in all of us. It calls to memory a successful and endearing film "Cocoon" that also has an ensemble cast of elderly. The film also includes several younger actors cast in the lead roles of Jenny, Thad, and Tim, and a recognizable older actor playing a famous director from the 1950s, Rolly Woods, well know for his "B" horror films.

Ben, the grandfather of Jenny, celebrates the New Year with his very dearest friend J-Dub (John Wilson), a retired school bus driver. It's shortly after, that John dies leaving Ben very depressed and lost. When his granddaughter Jenny falls for an actor that she'd seen in a local Indie horror film, Ben fails in being there for her and allows her to give up going after the one that she feels is her soul-mate.

When a new resident moves into Ben's old friend's room, Ben resents it and automatically has distaste for the stranger. The man, Rolly, and Ben don't hit it off, but Ben finds that Rolly may be the answer to helping his granddaughter finding true love. By concocting a fake movie studio and crew, Rolly and Ben draw in the young actor, Thad, into a fictional film they are making in an effort to bring the two together. When the news leaks out that Rolly is making a comeback movie, and actors show up for the fake audition, Ben and Rolly are trapped and must actually make a film. As the residents plunge into the film, led by Rolly, Jenny and Thad share a kiss in a scene in what appears to be true love. When Ben overhears Thad and Jenny discussing LA and realizes that Tim may be secretly in love with his granddaughter, it appears that the plan may have gone asunder. As events play out, Ben gives the paper heart and chain to Jenny and tells her to give it to the one that has her heart. As Jenny decides between Thad and Tim, we discover that Rolly is dying. Will the crew finish their movie and will Jenny find true love?

5

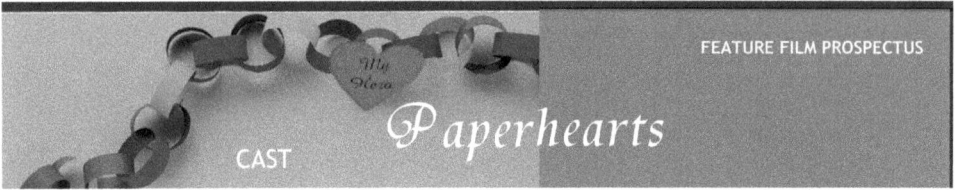

Paperhearts

CAST

CAST

Every filmmaker that has ever made a film has faced this irrefutable fact at one time during their career. Without star attachments, whether they are an "A" film star or "B" film star, almost ALL distributors will walk away from ever spending money or effort in the project. Why? Because, as they tell you, they CANNOT promote a film that has no attachments to promote, like an actor or director that is recognizable by the general public. Occasionally, a film does get through, but usually it's because of some genius marketing behind it or because of a unique message it may have. However, this is NOT the norm and as a general rule, if they can't market it, they don't want to waste their money and effort.

I have heard this numerous times on our other film projects. Although major distribution companies liked elements of the film (story, etc), they said that they had to turn it down because it didn't have anybody in it, plain and simple.

So, one simple method to reduce the risk of not meeting distribution company's expectations is to make sure to budget in recognizable stars into the film. Ours is unique in that the majority of our cast is elderly and for that reason, we would be shopping for a cast of stars who are not considered "A" actors any longer. However, many of these actors are still recognizable and still good at their craft. Our budget provides funding for several recognizable stars from Hollywood. Of course, this is always negotiable and we'll need to negotiate their salaries and ensure that the film does not go over budget. Our intention is to use a casting agency to help identify the perfect and affordable cast for this film.

6

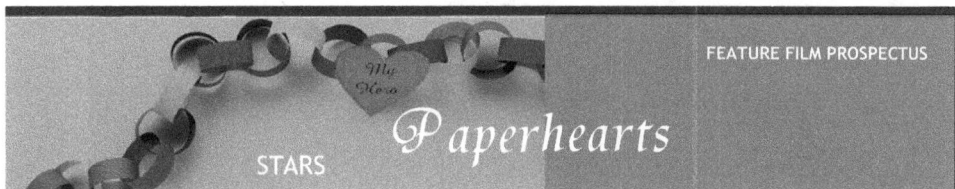

FEATURE FILM PROSPECTUS

Paperhearts

STARS

STARS AND MOTIVATION

_____ - As
"Rolly Woods"

Young Films has learned after many conversations with distributors how important "Star" power is to them. It allows them to develop a marketing plan based on those attachments. Another important aspect to attaching name-recognizable actors to films is that it allows the use of the stars in promoting the film at the theater. Talk shows are eager to promote name-brand stars on their shows, which can reach theater goers and promote the film. Young Films will not only pursue these attachments but develop a plan to promote the actors on national talk shows to promote the film.

_____ - As
"Ben Kelly"

Understanding that our limited budget may not entice the name-recognizable star in Hollywood, Young Films has incorporated additional incentives in its profits sharing approach to not only entice actors but to motivate the actors to promote the film to the public. Young Films will offer each participating "Principle" actor 2.5% of Box Office net profits.

Young Films' budget provides funding for TV talk show appearances that covers first class air travel, hotel accommodations, and meals while in New York city promoting the film.

Below are some of the actors we are considering.

_____ - As
"Smitty"

_____ - As
"Ben Kelly"

_____ -As
"Rolly Woods"

7

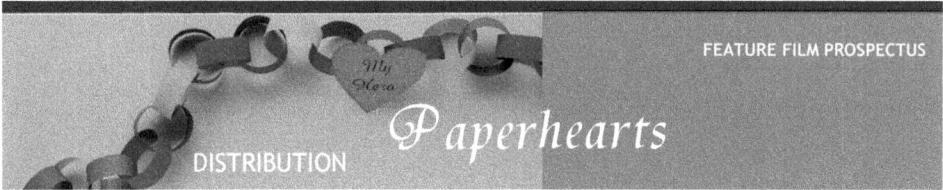

FEATURE FILM PROSPECTUS

DISTRIBUTION ℘*aperhearts*

"Investors have an active role in our profits scheme rarely offered to investors!"

Theatrical Release

One of the biggest challenges for a filmmaker is to achieve a theatrical release of their film. Most independent filmmakers will four-wall a theater to release their film. This means basically that they are PAYING the theater to show it and usually it's very expensive and is usually only a one or two night showing. It is NOT an official theatrical release by any means. Young Films has had an actual limited release of its last film "The Darkening" at theaters and understands the process of achieving theatrical release. Young Films has developed solid contacts that have asked us to come back for the release of our next film. Yes, Rave Cinemas, where we did a limited release at 4 theaters for 2 weeks, has asked us to bring our next production to them.

Many filmmakers are happy to get a DVD release or to have their film shown at festivals. Here's the beauty of theatrical release. The theaters payout in 30 days! That's right. By taking the film directly to the theater, Young Films cuts out the middle man, the distributor, who gets a whopping 30 % of the profit from the theaters. Young Films positions itself to receive 45% of the box office receipts and has no middle man to share the profits with. So Young Films is not only a production company, we are the distributor as well. Young Films is willing to share 2.5% of its net profit from theatrical release with each investor (2.5 % for each $ 100K). Each $ 100K investor will receive the entirety of their investment back from film profit then receive 2.5% of the theatrical release net profits.

Other Forms of Distribution

Young Films has established relationships with companies that distribute films in all types of media. One such company is Gravitas Ventures which provides Video On Demand distribution throughout North America and is the largest supplier of VOD products in the country. We also have contacts at other distributors that can distribute films to the theater, TV, Cable, and DVD release. Investors receive 2.5% of VOD and DVD net profits for a 5 year period.

We will also look at foreign distribution deals, but we will negotiate these in the form of cash buyouts per territory. Signing a deal whereby a foreign distributor pays a percentage of sales could be problematic for collecting profits unless it's through a larger reputable US distribution company.

8

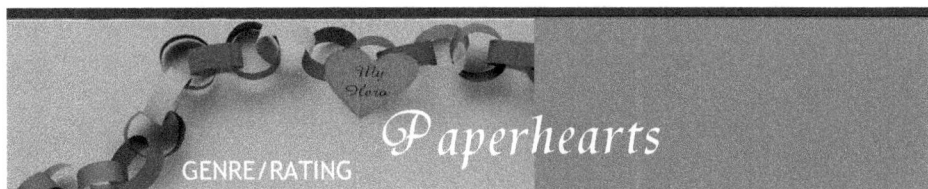

GENRE/RATING

Paperhearts

The genre of the film and the rating are equally important when considering distribution of a film. Studios have fought tooth and nail to get PG-13 ratings for films that were rated R by the MPAA because they know how important the rating is to profitability.

Our film will be rated as a PG or PG-13 (at most) since there is no violence, nudity, or harsh language that would offend. Our film will also fit into the Comedy and Drama genres. Note the top Genres and ratings below.

Top-Grossing Genres 1995 to 2012

	Movies	Total Gross	Average Gross	Market Share
1 Comedy	1,751	$44,792,158,044	$25,580,901	23.48%
2 Adventure	521	$38,199,674,469	$73,319,913	20.03%
3 Drama	3,132	$33,621,012,632	$10,734,678	17.63%
4 Action	570	$32,066,637,809	$56,257,259	16.81%
5 Thriller/Suspense	561	$15,495,734,985	$27,621,631	8.12%
6 Romantic Comedy	403	$11,286,883,357	$28,007,155	5.92%
7 Horror	329	$9,093,205,812	$27,638,923	4.77%
0 Documentary	1,076	$2,063,950,710	$1,918,170	1.08%
9 Musical	113	$1,865,013,970	$16,504,548	0.98%
10 Black Comedy	85	$781,440,299	$9,193,415	0.41%

Top-Grossing MPAA Ratings 1995 to 2012

	Movies	Total Gross	Average Gross	Market Share
1 PG-13	2,028	$85,955,147,762	$42,384,195	45.08%
2 R	3,575	$54,833,115,390	$15,337,934	28.76%
3 PG	986	$36,830,727,925	$37,353,679	19.32%
4 G	276	$10,634,593,071	$38,531,134	5.58%
5 Not Rated	2,279	$1,760,744,156	$772,595	0.92%
6 NC-17	21	$72,872,987	$3,470,142	0.04%
7 Open	5	$7,678,311	$1,535,662	0.00%

Data courtesy of Nash Information Services, LLC (www.the-numbers.com). Used with permission.

9

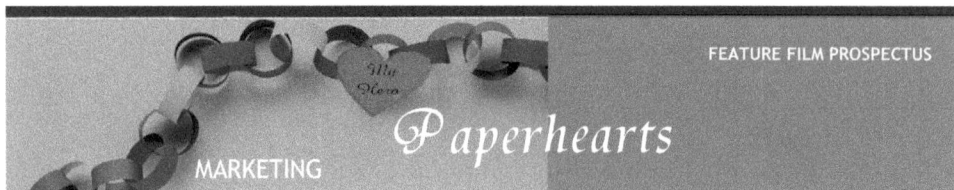

FEATURE FILM PROSPECTUS

MARKETING

Paperhearts

I DIDN'T KNOW YOU HAD A FILM SHOWING

Okay, here's the problem that we need to discuss. Young Films discovered during our limited release at the theaters that without spending an adequate amount of advertising funds on a release, nobody will know about the film or come to see it. It's a hard lesson to learn, but important. A film MUST be promoted in front of the general public or it will not have any success at the box office. The release MUST be preceded by national coverage to create interest in the film.

Studios spend millions of dollars in promoting big budget films. Naturally, we aren't budgeting millions, but are asking for over $ 400,000 in advertising budget to mount the best campaign that we can for those dollars. The intent is to negotiate with national broadcasters for prime time placement of trailers for the film, running them a week or two before the release of the film.

By attaching stars to the film, our Public Relations (PR) person (in budget) can push our stars to engage in national press coverage and TV shows to promote the film (included in budget). Any and all media markets will be pursued to include social media, You Tube, etc to promote the film. Young Films has also budgeted a dedicated web designer to build a dedicated web site for the film and work to interface it with other social media web sites.

Typically, the theater will schedule from 3 to 5 shows daily. The best audience attendance is usually on the weekends. If a show performs well, the theater has no issue with the film playing (they're making money) a couple or three weeks. Of course, if the film is a hit, it can run for a longer period. When our film was released, it ran for a couple of weeks at one theater and little over a week at the others.

Here's a scenario if the film does fairly well and fills 25% of the seats at 100 theaters, with a ticket price of $ 9.00 and us receiving 45% of the ticket price (typical theaters hold around 150=170) :

100 screens x (150 seats x 25% of capacity) x $ 4.5 ticket price x 3 weeks (4 showings x 21 days) = $ 1,417,500 revenue.

Box office is the key to making revenue from film. That's why it's important to fund the marketing and advertising with as much possible funding.

10

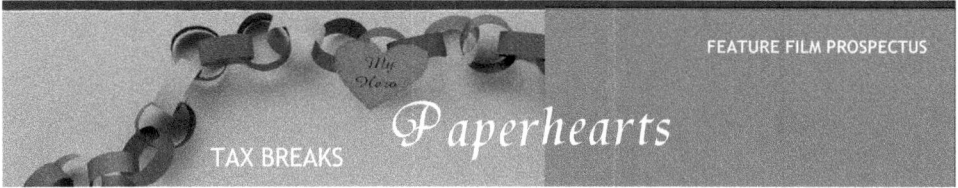

FEDERAL

Section 181 of the federal tax code was extended in January during the Fiscal Cliff bill through 2013. After, 2013, Section 181 will have to be extended again to be available after 2013. Section 181 states that investment in a motion picture shot in the US is 100% tax deductible for the investor in the same year invested. Under Section 181 an investor may deduct the money which is invested in a film or television production from his or her passive income earned in the same year. Productions with budgets below $15,000,000 (up to $20,000,000) which have at least seventy-five percent 75% of its production completed within the United States qualify under Section 181. Investors can be either individuals or businesses.

STATE OF ILLINOIS

In addition to the Section 181 tax deduction, if the feature film is filmed in a state with rebates or transferable tax credits. The film Producers can pass this subsidy onto the investors upon release of the rebate. As an example, if a $1,000,00.00 movie shoots in Illinois and spends every penny in the state, the state of Illinois will issue a 30% tax rebate, worth approximately $333,000.00. If shooting in a low income area, another 15% percent tax break is available through the state of Illinois. A total 45% tax break can be realized depending upon the geographic area that the film is shot. The Illinois tax break refund money can then passed onto to the investors. This is a considerable risk minimization for the Investor.

Depending on the investor's tax bracket and the percentage of the production funds spent in Illinois, investors can see a tax break anywhere between 50% and 65% on their investment.

VERIFICATION

Young Films LLC will verify the type and amounts of tax breaks available to investors with a Certified Public Accountant (CPA) and make this information available to investors.

11

SCHEDULE — *Paperhearts*

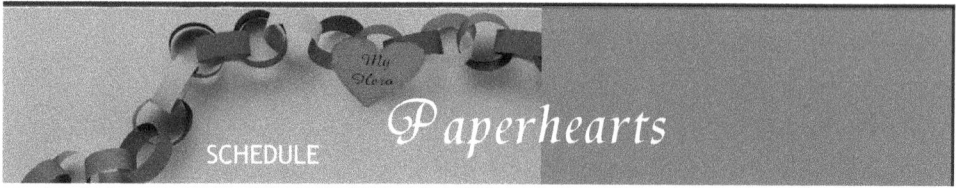

Young Films LLC develops a production schedule that details each and every day of production. Below is an example shooting schedule from our last film "The Darkening." The same type of detailed schedule will be developed for the complete 24 day shooting schedule of "Paperhearts".

Schedules that we develop not only identify actors and locations, but also identify when extras and vehicles are needed. They are an excellent tool for managing production resources and determining on an ongoing basis whether the production is on schedule.

The following figure shows the activities during each production phase and how funds are appropriated among those phases.

12

Pre-Production

- Star Attachments: $ 90K for 3 actors ($ 25K each) to lockdown contract
- Location Insurance/E&O Insurance = $ 20K
- Locations/Costumes/Props = $ 20K
- Young Films Studio Building/Rental office furniture/big screen for one month - $ 10K
- Film Web Page
- Design/Maintenance - $ 2.2K
- Pre-production activities $ 15K
  - Location Mmgt
  - Auditions
  - Contracts

Total $ 157.2K

Production

- Star Attachments: $ 90K for 3 actors ($ 25K each) balance of payment for work
- Star lodging – For 4 actors, 3 weeks = $ 16K
- Food for 20 people for 28 days = $ 16,800
- Crew of four for 4 weeks = $ 12,800
- Makeup for 4 weeks $ 3,200
- Young Films crew of 10 for 4 weeks = $ 20K
- DP (Rob) 4 weeks = $ 20K
- Tracking and dolly vehicle $ 7K
- Camera boom = $ 7K
- Red One/Lenses rental = $ 15K
- RV Rental - $ 3K
- Equipment truck - $ 3K
- Transportation - $ 3.5 k

Total $ 217.3K

Post-Production

- Song for soundtrack - $ 60K for 3 hit songs
- Editing of film - $ 20K
- Iain Kelso – Score = $ 20K
- Animation at beginning of film – $ 1,500
- Graphic Artist - $ 4K
- MPAA Rating - $ 3K

Total $ 108.5K

P&A Costs

- Printing costs – Posters for theaters - $ 10K
- DCP development - $ 12K
- VPFs for 100 theaters -$ 100K
- Advertising film release $ 400K (60K-trailers at Cinema, 5% on Web Advertising)
- TV Show Promotions $ 40K
  - Travel, Lodging, food for 2 or 3 actors
- PR Person $ 15K
- Develop Trailer for film $ 5K

Total $ 582K

Total Film Budget $ 1065K

13

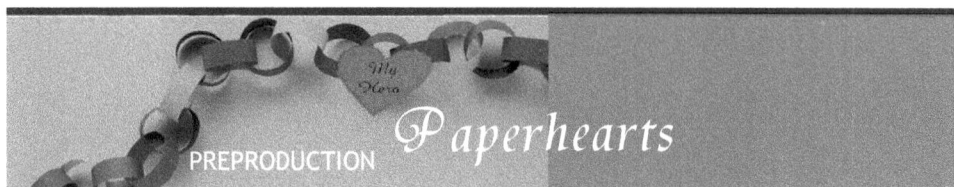

PREPRODUCTION *Paperhearts*

The pre-production phase includes all of the items required for us to go into film production and to actually start filming the movie. Everything required is locked down, to ensure that the filming schedule can be implemented. During pre-production, Young Films LLC will accomplish the following:

- Finalize screenplay
- Secure Star Attachments
  - Write actor agreements
- Secure Location Insurance and E&O Insurance
  - Using locations for filming requires a $ 1 Million dollars of liability insurance.
- Secure Locations
- Secure Costumes and Props for production
  - Includes vehicles
- Secure a building for the Young Films Studio Building
  - Requires rental of office furniture
  - Requires big screen for editing screening and dailies
- Develop Film Web Page for film
- Location Management
- Auditions of cast
- Conduct rehearsals
- Development and review of contracts
- Contracts – cast & crew, equipment, meals & transportation, etc.
- Permits – street closings, etc.

Young Films has experience with all of the pre-production elements and has done these activities on 3 films. Young Films is very professional when coordinating with owners of locations, whether it be personal locations (homes) or business owners (offices, restaurants, etc) and thorough when writing location agreements that lock down that location. We also ensure that the Producer performs to walk-throughs on locations to ensure no damage has occurred.

Young Films is also familiar with working with city and county government, whether we are securing resources from them or closing streets.

We have experience in all elements of pre-production and are confident in applying this experience for the pre-production activities required for this film. *14*

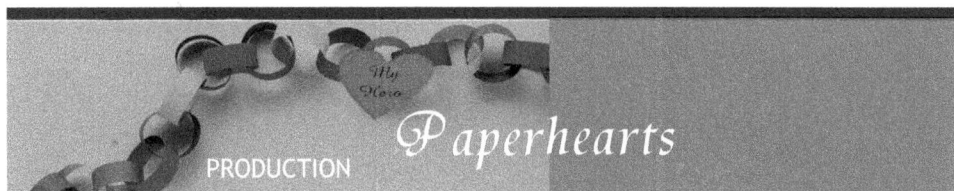

PRODUCTION

Paperhearts

The Production phase of film production is where the magic happens. This is where we film the principle photography, the major scenes that make up the film. We will schedule 24 days of shooting principle photography at locations to be determined in and around Rockford, Illinois. The production schedule will include one day off a week (Sunday). The following are some of the major budget items in production of the film:

- Star wages
- Catering
- Crew wages
- Makeup and special effects (sfx) makeup
- DP wages
- Film equipment rentals
  - Tracking and dolly vehicle equipment
  - Camera boom
  - Red One/Lenses rental
- RV Rental
- Equipment truck
- Transportation

During production, dailies (what was shot that day) are reviewed at the Young Films Studio temporary facility to assure the film's quality and that the required scenes for that day were picked up.

Daily production meetings in the morning and evening between the executive producer and the production crew help to review issues and the upcoming day's scheduled work.

Hour to hour and day to day production decisions about production resources and scheduling actors for daily principle photography are done by the Production Manager (PM). Young Films LLC will use the same PM that we used on "The Darkening." The PM will also have at least one assistant to assist in managing daily production activities. The PM reports to the film's Producer, who is responsible for making any major decisions regarding those resources and resolves production issues. The Producer reports to the Executive Producer (EP) at Young Films and maintains continuity between the EP and the PM. The film crew is directed by the Director of the film. The Director of "Paperhearts" will be the Director used on "The Darkening." *15*

POST PRODUCTION *Paperhearts*

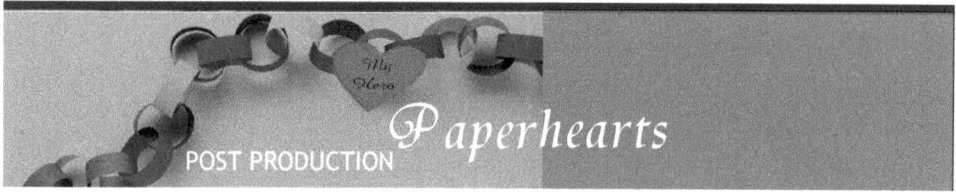

During Post Production, the principle photography along with location sound gathered during filming edited together to make a cohesive story. Scoring and music tracks are then added to round out the feature film.

Film Title credits and closing credits are also added along with the MPAA rating. The following are some big budget ticket items:

- Editing of film
- Songs for soundtrack
- Scoring
- Young Films Animated logo
- Film Poster Graphic Artist
- MPAA Rating
- Automatic Dialog Replacement (ADR)
- Foley Work

A professional editor will accomplish the editing of the film. The editor is required to have feature film editing experience. The editor will be supervised by Young Films, who edited their last feature film in-house. Young Films will discuss the possibility of having the editor available during shooting so that any shots not picked up and required for editing can be rescheduled. This will also help to drastically reduce the post production phase if the film can be edited during the production phase.

Young Films understands how the sound is such a major part of the final film and will hire an experienced musical composer to compose the score for the film. The composer also must have experience in composing scores for theatrical film. Young Films will make an offer to the composer that worked on Young Films previous film "Love Wine", a romantic comedy.

Young Films will also pursue licenses for at least 2 hit pop songs to fill out the films music tracks.

16

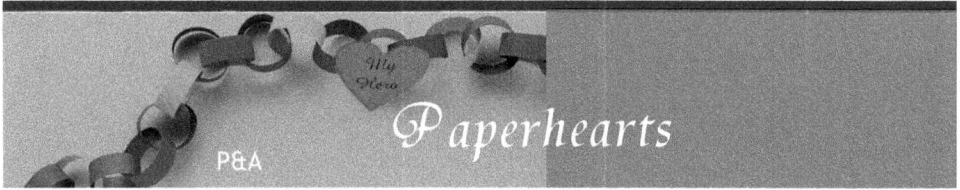

Paperhearts

P&A

P&A stands for Prints and Advertising. Young Films is not only the production company on this film, but will also act as the film distributor for theatrical release. Young Films has contacts with the major theatrical owners nation-wide. Young Films has accomplished a theatrical release previously with our last film, and will apply that knowledge and contacts to this film. The elements on page 13 are critical elements when releasing a film to a theater. Young Films developed contacts with individuals and companies that provided these services to major film companies in Hollywood.

Young Films will seek out a professional PR person and DCP developer in the Chicago/Illinois area. This will allow Young Films to work closely with them and will meet the Illinois Tax Break requirements. Young Films will also take an active role in promoting the principle name-recognizable actors to national TV talk shows to promote the film. We have allocated funds to fly 2 of these actors to New York (or elsewhere) to participate in several TV talk shows. Virtual Print Fees (VPFs) are fees assigned to each theatrical screen by third party vendors to collect fees that offset the cost of updating theatrical screens to digital. These are required to be paid to exhibitors by the distributor before exhibition of the film at the theater.

We will also seek out international release of the film and release markets overseas. The figure below shows the various markets for film distribution.

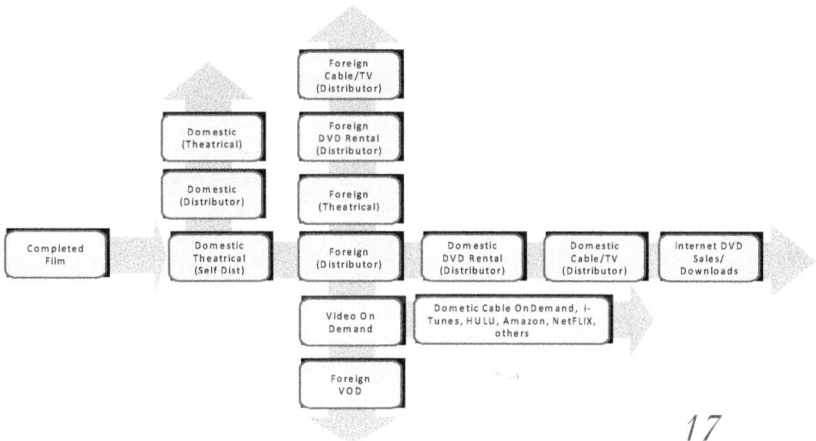

17

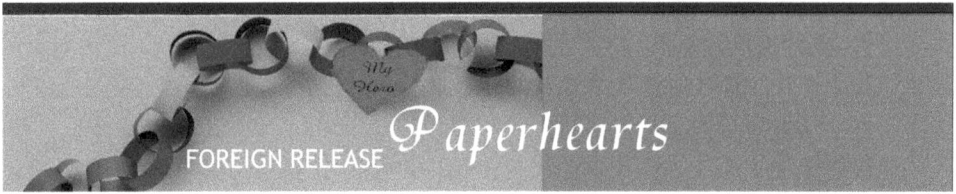

FOREIGN RELEASE *Paperhearts*

Domestic box office (U.S.) release can be a key to getting foreign release. A study performed by Texas A&M University titled "*The Determinants of Foreign Box Office Revenue for English Language Movies*" suggests that there are important determinates to consider in generating foreign box office revenues.

An important variable for determining foreign box office success is the domestic box office earnings. The results indicated that domestic box office has a positive and statistically significant impact on foreign box office revenue. Most English language movies are released in the U.S. domestic market before the foreign market. The results imply that the domestic box office serves as a good indicator of foreign box office success, with every dollar in domestic box office yielding slightly more than a dollar in foreign box office revenue. There are several possible explanations for the consistent relationship. Movies that perform well at the domestic box office may serve as a signal that a movie is good and builds positive momentum for the foreign box office.

The report also suggests that the addition of an Academy Award win has an impact on foreign box office success. The results indicated that the winning of an Academy Award is a statistically significant determinant on foreign box office revenue.

This study drives the reasoning that a domestic release is critical to overall film revenues and the reason that the budget has a significant amount of funding in the back end for marketing and advertising.

It is important when securing theaters for the film's release to ensure that a theater in New York and in Los Angeles are secured, because a film can't be considered for the Academy Awards unless it is shown in those two cities. Although hoping for an Academy Award is a long shot, if it qualifies for consideration, an Oscar nod can't hurt the film's profitability.

18

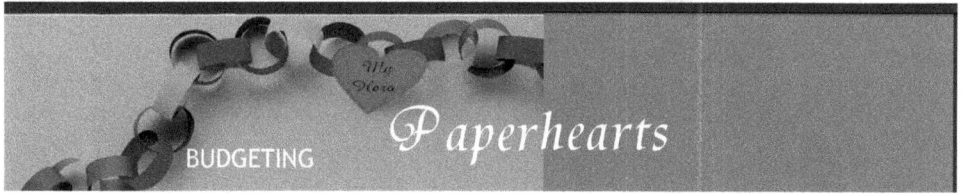

BUDGETING   *Paperhearts*

Young Films LLC will provide a complete and detailed budget that not only shows all expenses for the film but shows any deferred payments to actors or crew. Investors will be notified of budget overruns or shortages on a weekly basis via a production report. A complete detailed budget will be submitted for approval during the pre-production phase. The executive producer (Manager of Young Films LLC) of the film will make all budget decisions on the film. A "miscellaneous expenses" fund will be used for miscellaneous production items not noted in the budget but identified during production activities. Receipts for all expenses and miscellaneous purchases will be retained for the final production budget and overage/under-run report at the end of production. Below is an example of a budget.

	Young Films LLC			Title: Paperhearts		Producers: Jack Young		
3	Director: Jack Young			Writer: Jack & Dan Young				
6	Acct #	Description	Amount	Units	X	Rate	Subtotal	Total
7								
8	100-001	STORY		deferred		8,000	8,000	8,000
9	100-002	SCREENPLAY PURCHASE						
10		purchase		deferred		125,000	125,000	125,000
11								
12						Total for 100-001		133,000
13	110-00	PRODUCER						
14	110-01	EXECUTIVE PRODUCER						
15		Jack Young		deferred		12,500	12,500	12,500
16	110-01-01	Sales Agent / Distributor		deferred		0	0	0
17		TBA - @ negotiated % of sales						
18								
19	110-02	PRODUCER						
20		Jack Young		deferred		12,500	12,500	12,500
21		Dan Young		deferred		12,500	12,500	25,000
22								
23	110-03	ASSOCIATE PRODUCER						
24		TBD	0	contract		0	0	
25		tax	0			0	0	0
26								
27	110-04	Location InsuranceFees						
28		TBD		Allow		25000	25,000	
29								
30								
31						Total for 110-00		50,000

|◄ ◄ ► ►|\Sheet1 / Sheet2 / Sheet3 / Sheet4 / Sheet5 / Sheet6 / Sheet7 / Sheet8 / Sheet9 / She | ◄

19

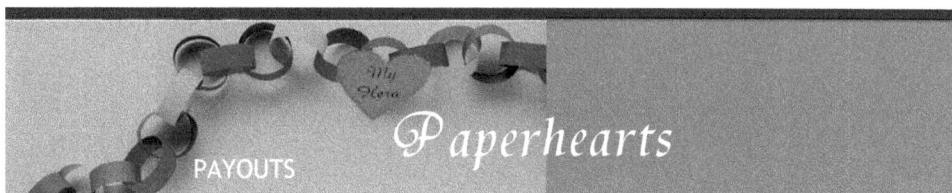

PAYOUTS

Paperhearts

Payouts during revenue is a tier-based scheme. The following shows the tiers and their position in the payout scheme:

Tier # 1 - Investors (Those contributing funding to the production of the film)
  (Invest funds only. Percentage of net profit is paid out under Tier # 3)
Tier # 2 - Deferred actors and crew
Tier # 3 - Investor percentage of net profits and principle actor percentage
Tier # 4 - Production company paid out from remaining percentage

Tier # 1 is paid out first. Tier # 2 is paid out second, and so on. The tier payout approach will be further detailed in the investor agreement.

Net Profits is defined as what remains from revenues after the investors have been paid out and all deferred payments for production have been paid out.

A note about deferred. Deferred is a method that allows the production company to bring aboard additional crew and actors without having to pay out wages from the production monies. Many aspiring actors and film crew will work for deferred monies to gain experience and to build a film production reel.

The film production will also utilize Apprentices from local colleges that have film courses. This adds production value at no cost at the same time providing film experience to those seeking it at local colleges. We expect to bring on at least 3 to 4 local students as apprentices.

20

IN CLOSING

Paperhearts

Young Films has, in the past, personally financed all of its film production activities but realizes to reach the next level needs the help of investors. We are a professional and experienced film production company that sincerely cares about telling a good story and making quality films.

We understand the requirements and tasks required from pre-production all the way to releasing a film at the local theater. We have established solid film industry contacts and relationships and never burn a bridge. We feel that we are on the road to broadening these relationships in attaining the next level of film production. The next level requires star attachments and enough investment in the back end of film production to make a run at a successful film release nation-wide.

With the help of investors, we will create a memorable family film, and provide a profitable return to investors.

Jack L. Young

Manager of Young Films LLC

21

APPX A - FILM SALES *Paperhearts*

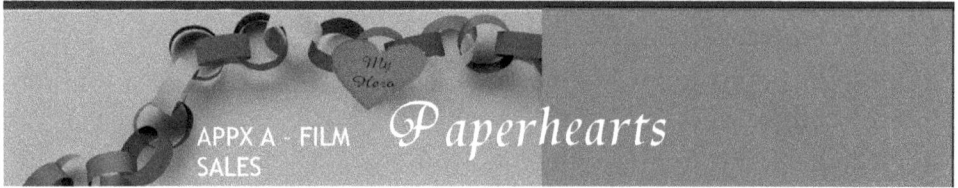

Independent films acquired at the Sundance Film festival in 2012. Sundance is a viable market for quality independent films. It's one of the few film festivals where independent films are actually shopped by distributors for acquisition. Young Films will consider a submission to the Sundance festival.

Film	Company	Deal Amount	Territories	Company	Box Office/Release date
2 Days in New York	Magnolia	N/A	North America	CAA	August 10th
28 Hotel Rooms	Oscilloscope	N/A	US	Preferred Content	
5 Broken Cameras	Kino Lorber	N/A	US	CAT&Docs	$22,787
About Face	HBO Doc	N/A	TV	Pre-Fest	July 30th
Ai Weiwei: Never Sorry	Sundance Selects	N/A	North America	Cinetic Media, Victoria Cook	July 27th
Arbitrage	Roadside	Over $3,000,000	North America	WME	
Bachelorette	TWC	Over $2,000,000	North America	CAA	
Beasts of the Southern Wild	Fox Searchlight	Almost $1,000,000	US	WME	June 27th
Black Rock	LD	Over $1,000,000	North America	Submarine	
California Solo	Strand	N/A	US	Visit Films	
Celeste and Jesse Forever	SPC	Almost $2,000,000	North And Latin America, Eastern Europe	UTA	August 3rd
Chasing Ice	Oscilloscope	N/A	US (Non TV)	Submarine	
Chasing Ice	National Geographic	N/A	TV	Submarine	
China Heavyweight	Zeitgeist	N/A	US	EyeSteelFilms	July 6th
Compliance	Magnolia	N/A	North America	Cinetic	June 20th
Detropia	DIY				
Escape Fire	Roadside	N/A	US	CAA	October 5th
Ethel	HBO Doc	N/A	TV	Pre-Fest	
Excision	Anchor Bay	N/A	North America	Preferred Content	
Filly Brown	Indomina	N/A	Worldwide	WME	
For a Good Time Call	Focus	$3,000,000	Worldwide	Cinetic	August 31st
For Ellen	Tribeca	N/A	North America	CAA	Sept 5th
GOATS	Image	Almsot $1,000,000	US	WME and Cinetic Media	
Grabbers	IFC Midnight	N/A	North & Latin America	Gersh	
Hello, I Must Be Going	Oscilloscope	N/A	North America	WME	
How To Survive a Plague	Sundance Selects	High Six Figures	North America	Submarine	September 21st
Indie Game: The Movie	HBO And Scott Rudin (Remake Rights)	N/A	TV	Film Sales Company	B.O. Gross not Reported

22

APPX A - FILM
SALES (Cont'd)

Paperhearts

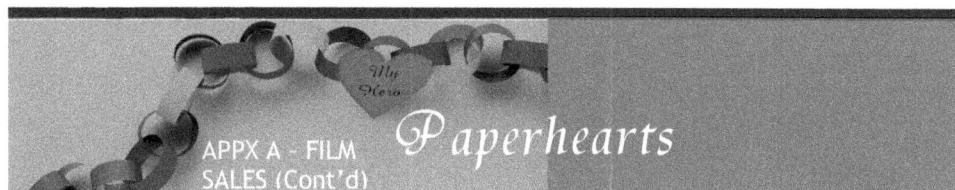

Film	Company	Deal Amount	Territories	Company	Box Office/ Release date
Keep the Lights On	Music Box	N/A	North America	Preferred Content	
Lay the Favorite	TWC	Over $2,000,000	US	CAA	
Liberal Arts	IFC	Over $1,000,000	North America	Gersh	
Luv	Indomina/BET	Over $1,000,000	North America/TV	ICM/Cinetic	
Marina Abramovic	HBO Doc		TV	Pre-Fest	July 2nd
Marina Abramovic	Music Box	N/A	US	Submarine	June 13th
Me @ The Zoo	HBO Doc	Mid Six Figures	TV	Submarine	June 25th
Middle of Nowhere	Participant and AAFFRM	Mid Six Figures	US	Paradigm	
Mosquita Y Mari	Wolfe	Low Six Figures	North America	The Film Collaborative	August 3rd
Nobody Walks	Magnolia	Mid-high Six Figures	North America	Submarine	
Payback	Zeitgeist	N/A	US	N/A	$12,962
Predisposed	IFC	N/A	North America	ICM and UTA	August 17th
Putin's Kiss	Kino Lorber	N/A	North America	N/A	$3,872
Red Hook Summer	DIY/Variance/Image	N/A	North America	N/A	
Red Lights	Millennium Entertainment	Under $4,000,000	US	UTA	July 13th
Robot & Frank	Sony & Samuel Goldwyn	Over $2,000,000	North America and select territories	ICM, CAA	
Room 237	IFC Midnight	N/A	North America	Betsy Rodgers	
Safety Not Guaranteed	Film District	Over $1,000,000	US	ICM	$97,762
Save the Date	IFC	N/A	North America	CAA	
Searching for Sugar Man	SPC	Mid Six Figures	North America	Submarine	July 27th
Shadow Dancer	ATO	$1,000,000	North America	CAA	
Shut Up and Play the Hits	Oscilloscope	N/A	North America	WME	
Simon Killer	IFC Films	N/A	North America	UTA, Caa	
Sleepwalk With Me	IFC	N/A	North America	UTA	August 24th
Smashed	SPC	$1,000,000	Worldwide	UTA and CAA	
Something From Nothing: The Art of Rap	Indomina	Over $1,000,000	Worldwide	UTA	
Teddy Bear	Film Movement	N/A	North America	Visit Films	August 22nd
That's what she said	Phase 4	N/A	US and Canada	Submarine	
The Comedy	Tribeca	N/A	North America	Submarine	

23

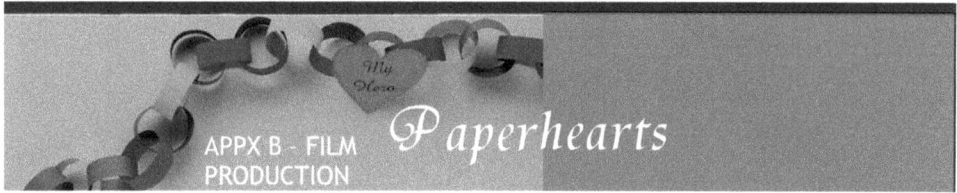

APPX B - FILM PRODUCTION — *Paperhearts*

The MPAA has not released statistics for 2012. Below are general box office numbers for 2011.

Global
- Global box office for all films released in each country around the world reached $32.6 billion in 2011, up 3% over 2010's total, due entirely to the increase in international box office ($22.4 billion). Each international region experienced growth in 2011. Chinese box office grew by 35% in 2011 to become the 2nd largest International market behind Japan, experiencing by far the largest growth in major markets.
- International box office in U.S. dollars is up 35% over five years ago, driven by growth in various markets, including China and Russia.

U.S./Canada
- 2011 U.S./Canada box office was $10.2 billion, down 4% compared to $10.6 billion in 2010, but up 6% from five years ago. Despite strong second and third quarter box office performance, 2011 box office did not fully overcome the slow start in the first quarter. 3D film releases increased, yet 3D box office was down $400 million in 2011 compared to 2010, which contained Avatar's record-breaking 3D box office performance.
- The decline in U.S./Canada box office was due to an equivalent decline in admissions (-4%) compared to 2010, as admissions reached 1.3 billion, while average cinema ticket price stayed relatively flat (+1%).
- More than two-thirds of the U.S./Canada population (67%) – or 221.2 million people – went to the movies at least once in 2011. Males and females went to the movies at similar levels. As in past years, Hispanics and 12-24 year olds are the most frequent moviegoers among their respective demographic categories.
- Ticket sales continue to be driven by frequent moviegoers, who represent only 10% of the population but purchase half of all movie tickets. In 2011, more 25-39 year olds were in the frequent moviegoer category, particularly males.

24

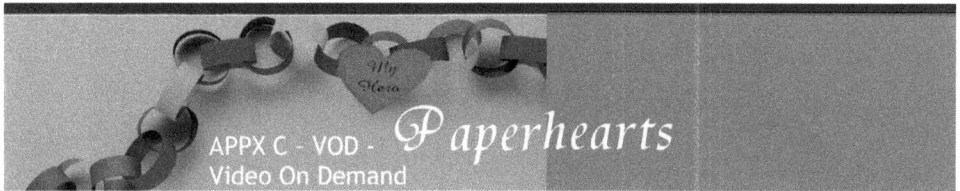

APPX C - VOD - *Paperhearts*
Video On Demand

Probably the hottest prospect for marketing independent film today is the latest Video on Demand (VOD) distribution for films that is blowing away DVD film distribution and in some cases rivaling theatrical release in sales. Young Films is securing a deal with Gravitas Ventures, the largest VOD distributor in North America, for its last production "The Darkening" and will pursue this as a secondary market to theatrical release for "Paperhearts". With a successful theatrical run, VOD is a perfect secondary market to follow with. For VOD, Young Films gets 70% of the returns as opposed to 45% on DVDs and theater Box office receipts. However, the 70% is the net profit from the VOD vendor. The cable companies take their 50% cut from the film's OnDemand download price (between $ 5.00 and $ 7.00). There is also upfront costs associated with VOD (About $ 3K), which is addressed in the budget, for lab fees associated with formatting the film for all VOD formats for download. Overall, VOD can generate considerable profits for a film if properly promoted.

Below are some insightful comments from Filmmaker Magazine.com on VOD. The first comment makes a point that the title determines the film's position in the catalogue of films and therefore may have an effect on being chosen by the VOD viewer. The second comment notes how well a low budget film did on VOD.

"It may sound facile or crass, but with Video-On-Demand an increasingly important segment of the business, recent indie movies like The Answer Man, A Quiet Little Marriage or Bart Got a Room will advantageously sit atop the catalogue of cable operator's On-Demand listings, while movies like World's Greatest Dad and What Goes Up will sit at the bottom."

FilmmakerMagazine.com

"Pablo Proenza's Dark Mirror, a low-budget supernatural thriller, for example, was released on VOD in early May as part of IFC's Festival Direct Midnight slate and has become one of the company's top-selling titles, with an estimated 110 to 120,000 buys priced at $7 a pop. After cable companies take somewhere around 50 percent and IFC takes its cut, the film's sales agent Josh Braun expects the filmmakers to take home $200,000 to $250,000 in back-end revenue. (The revenue split for filmmakers tends to be noticeably more beneficial with VOD than theatrical exhibitors.)"

FilmmakerMagazine.com   *25*

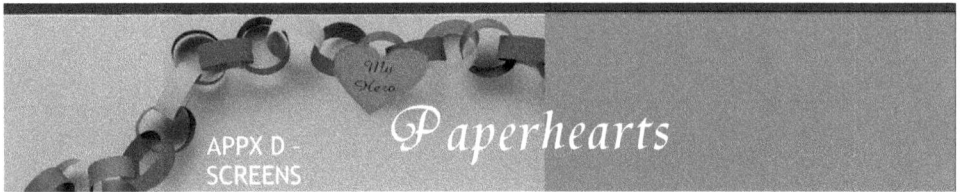

APPX D -
SCREENS

$\mathcal{P}$ *aperhearts*

The growth of digital screens continues to be strong both domestically and internationally. Digital screens make way for the independent filmmaker since analog screens depend upon an analog print of the film. Analog prints can costs as much as $ 1,500 per screen, while the Digital Content Package (DCP) can costs as little as $ 900 per screen. Larger theatrical chains also use network servers to house the digital print, thereby reducing the cost of having to deliver DCPs to each theater. The VPFs still apply to each screen (until the costs of digital conversion has been recouped. This is still in debate) but DCP delivery (Usually $ 100 to $ 350 per DCP) costs can be reduced by dealing with larger theater chains. The chart below shows the growth of digital screens.

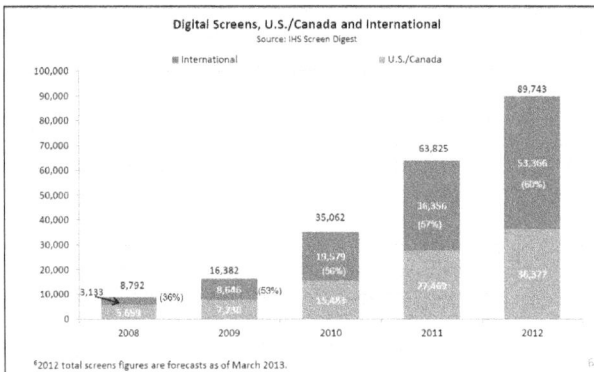

Digital Screens, U.S./Canada and International
Source: IHS Screen Digest

◼ International   ◼ U.S./Canada

$^{€}$2012 total screens figures are forecasts as of March 2013.

Worldwide Digital 3D Screens
Source: IHS Screen Digest

	2008	2009	2010	2011	2012	2012 % of digital
U.S./Canada	1,514	3,548	8,505	13,490	14,734	41%
EMEA	594	3,510	8,143	11,570	13,963	53%
Asia Pacific	344	1,584	4,659	8,590	14,219	62%
Latin America	84	362	1,104	2,142	2,629	63%
Total	2,536	9,004	22,411	35,792	45,545	51%
% change vs. previous year	96%	255%	149%	60%	27%	--

26

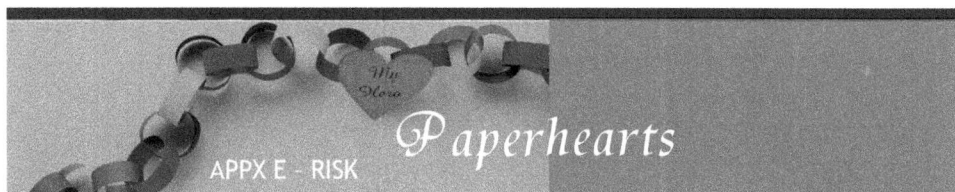

APPX E - RISK

Paperhearts

Investors should be aware that investing in film is a risky business. Because of the advances in digital camera technology and the available of sophisticated editing software and high-end computers for the desktop, more independent films are being created today than anytime before.

However, the landscape for motion picture distribution and exhibition (Digital deliveries and presentation) has been drastically changing over the period of the last four years. It has become possible for independent filmmakers to bring their films to the theater along side major motion picture distributors (Young Films has proven this).

Along with the digital revolution, came the Internet and the video-on-demand (VOD) method of film delivery. This instant method of downloading and viewing a feature film has exploded recently with VOD available from hundreds of delivery services to include NetFLIX, HULU, Amazon, and most cable TV broadcasters.

Young Films shot its first film (a short) in 1997 and learned film production using a 16 MM analog camera. Our next venture (in 2001) was inspired by George Lucas when he shot a portion of Star Wars use digital photography on the set. We follow George's lead and shot our next feature (*Love Wine*) using the same model camera as George to shoot our first digital feature. Young Films was also there when the digital age brought high-end editing software and composing software to the desktop (wasn't there for Love Wine) and used the latest digital camera technology and editing software/hardware to shoot and edit our last film (*The Darkening*).

Young Films understands the risk with investing in film, but by understanding the latest tax laws and pursuing these for our investors, and by investing in not only the latest technology to develop the best possible product, but investing the time and effort into understanding film production models and processes and how the film industry infrastructure works, we have faith that we can drastically reduce the risk and make a profitable film for investors.

Investors should, however, be aware that film production is a fickle business, and is after all, risky business.

27

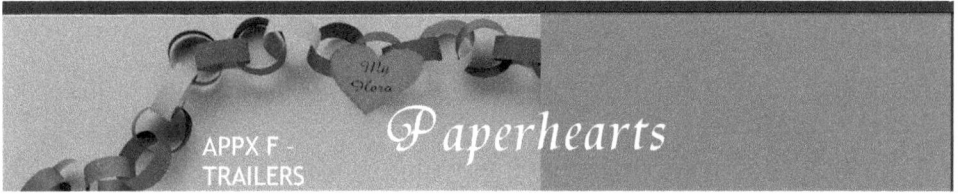

APPX F -
TRAILERS
Paperhearts

Trailers are essential promotions for films. Young Films will promote the trailer on the Internet (Film Home Page, YouTube, etc) as well as promoting the trailer on national TV and in theaters. Young Films will also budget and place movie posters in the theaters at least a month before the film premiers.

"Almost three-quarters of Americans who went to the movies in the last month arrived at the theater at least 10 minutes before the film's start time, with young Adults 18-24 and Adults 25-54 arriving 19 minutes ahead, on average".

This means that they are in the seats early and see the trailers for upcoming attractions (Trailers).

Not only do movie audiences like to see trailers, but they DO NOTICE movie posters in the lobby:

"Posters are noticed by cinema audiences and have high impact. The study found very high awareness rates for posters by last-month moviegoers: Eighty three percent remembered looking at posters in the lobby. Posters had an impact on all age groups. Eighty-four percent of Teens 12-17, 83% of young Adults 18-24 and 85% of Adults 25-54 remembered seeing or looking at posters. More than three out of every four Americans aged 55 and older was aware of posters in the lobby."

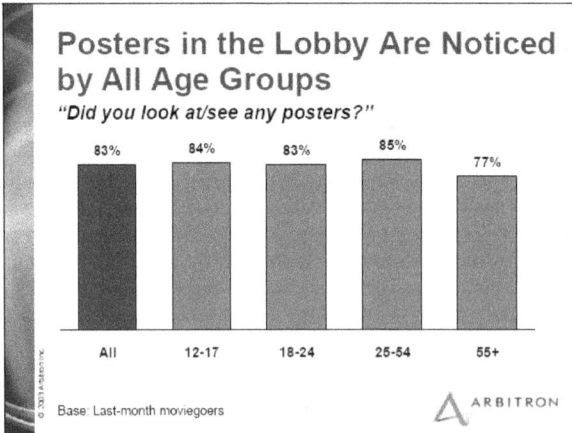

Data excerpted from the *The Arbitron Cinema Advertising Study*   *28*

Although Independent films normally lack "A" movies stars and are shot with less budget, movie goers appear eager for fresh stories from independent filmmakers. Below are some past independent films that did well at the box office.

Most Profitable Movies, Based on Return on Investment

	Release Date	Movie	Distributor	Budget	Worldwide Gross	Percentage Return
1	9/25/2009	Paranormal Activity		$15,000	$196,681,656	655,505.52%
2	3/21/1980	Mad Max	Filmways	$200,000	$99,750,000	24,837.50%
3	5/7/2004	Super Size Me	IDP/Sam Goldwyn	$65,000	$29,529,368	22,614.90%
4	7/14/1999	The Blair Witch Project	Artisan	$600,000	$248,300,000	20,591.67%
5	2/26/1993	El Mariachi	Columbia	$7,000	$2,041,928	14,485.20%
6	10/1/1968	Night of the Living Dead		$114,000	$30,000,000	13,057.89%
7	11/21/1976	Rocky		$1,000,000	$225,000,000	11,150.00%
8	10/17/1978	Halloween		$325,000	$70,000,000	10,669.23%
9	8/11/1973	American Graffiti		$777,000	$140,000,000	8,909.01%
10	10/19/1994	Clerks	Miramax	$27,000	$3,894,240	7,111.56%
11	5/16/2007	Once	Fox Searchlight	$150,000	$18,997,174	6,232.39%
12	7/25/1969	The Stewardesses		$200,000	$25,000,000	6,150.00%
13	6/11/2004	Napoleon Dynamite	Fox Searchlight	$400,000	$46,140,956	5,667.62%
14	8/6/2004	Open Water	Lion's Gate	$500,000	$55,116,982	5,411.70%
15	5/9/1980	Friday the 13th	Paramount Pictures	$550,000	$59,754,601	5,332.24%
16	12/15/1939	Gone with the Wind	MGM/UA	$3,900,000	$390,525,192	4,906.73%
17	2/8/1915	The Birth of a Nation		$110,000	$11,000,000	4,900.00%
18	1/6/2012	Devil Inside The		$1,000,000	$99,661,944	4,883.10%
19	1/1/1925	The Big Parade		$245,000	$22,000,000	4,389.80%
20	10/29/2004	Saw	Lion's Gate	$1,200,000	$103,096,345	4,195.68%

Note: The profit and loss figures are very rough estimates based on the assumption that 50% of box office receipts were returned to the studio. They don't include ancillary (video, TV etc.) earnings; and serve only as a guide.

Data courtesy of Nash Information Services, LLC (www.the-numbers.com). Used with permission.

APPX G - Indie Sales

Paperhearts

29

APPX H - Track Record — *Paperhearts*

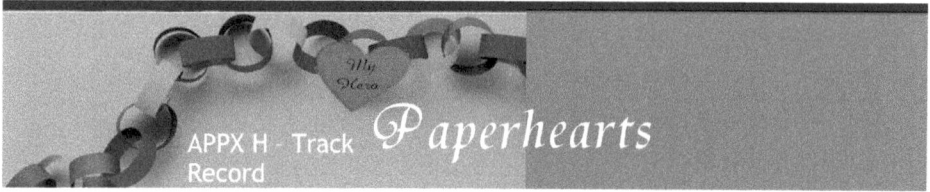

Young Films has a track record of producing low budget quality films and following standard processes to ensure completion and production quality.

In 2012, we finished completion of our latest film, "The Darkening" a suspense/horror film.

30

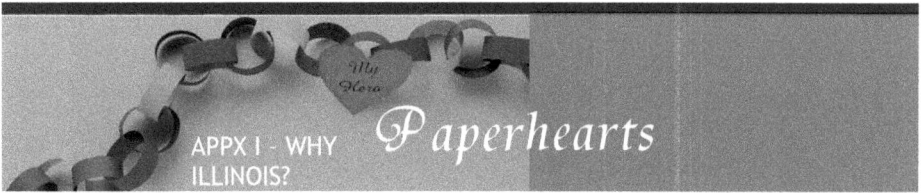

APPX I - WHY *Paperhearts*
ILLINOIS?

Young Films chose to shoot in Illinois because we are familiar with the local area and the fact that Illinois offers such great incentives for film production in the state. Not only does the incentives encourage filmmaking in the state, which creates additional revenue for the state, but creates jobs in the local area.

Economic Impact of the Industry on Illinois

The motion picture and television industry is responsible for 20,946 direct jobs and $969.2 million in wages in Illinois, including both production and distribution-related jobs. Over 6,100 of the jobs are production-related.

- 2011: During the course of 2011, 9 movies and 10 TV series filmed in the state. Movies include Man of Steel, Lincoln, A Fonder Heart, Just Like a Woman, Valley of the Sun, A Green Story, and Call Me On Tuesday. TV series include The Rosie Show, The Playboy Club, Boss, The Chicago Code, The Oprah Winfrey Show, Judge Jeanine Pirro, and Cold Case Files.
- 2010: During the course of 2010, 25 films and 9 TV series filmed in the state. Movies include Source Code, LOL, The Vow, The Dilemma, Contagion, Bad Teacher, and Colombiana. TV series include The Oprah Winfrey Show, The Chicago Code, Cold Case Files, Judge Mathis, Giuliana & Bill, Future Food, and At the Movies.

Production Incentives:

The Illinois Film Production Tax Credit entered into effect on January 1, 2009. The tax credit has no sunset and consists of: (1) 30% of the Illinois production spending for the taxable year; and (2) 30% credit on Illinois salaries up to $100,000 per worker. Another 15% is available for low income areas.

31

APPENDIX G

DIY Film Equipment Projects

DIY Sun/Wind Screen

We rented one of these on our first feature film and it came in handy with blocking out the sun for one of our scenes. It's not something that you'll want to drag out of the equipment truck unless you really need it, but it's very handy to have in times where you need more control of the environment. My brother Dan and I got together and made our own out of parts you can get at most hardware stores. I had to order the tarp online but you can shop around for tarps to see if you can find some on sale.

The sun/wind screen can be to any size that you need but depends upon the tarp sizes available. For PVC pipe, use 1.25 SCH 40 (about 2 inches outer diameter). Here's the parts list:

- PVC piping - Four (4) 6-foot lengths of 2 inch diameter
- PVC piping - Two (2) 10-foot lengths
- PVC 90-degree elbows to fit 2-inch diameter PVC
- 10 x 12 tarp with eyelets (Wholes around edge)
- Eyelet bolts (Or called "eye" bolt. See picture below), washers, and nuts.
- Nylon Rope (enough to feed through the tarp eyelets and through the eye bolts - figure at least 60 feet)
- PVC pipe glue
- Tools: Hacksaw to cut the PVC pipe

PVC 90
degree Elbow

8 Foot PVC

10 Foot PVC

Clothesline
rope

This end of the
sleeve fits over the
PVC and can be
glued

8 Foot PVC

This end is not glued
but is held together
with a bolt.

Removing the bolt
and pulling the half
from the sleeve
allows the unit to be
folded in half.

10 x 12 Foot
canvas tarp
with eyelets

10 Foot PVC

Eyelet Bolts with washer
and nut (Long enough to
go all the way thru the
PVC pipe)

NOTES: 1) Pre-drill the PVC pipe for the eyelet bolts 2) Glue all PVC elbows into place.

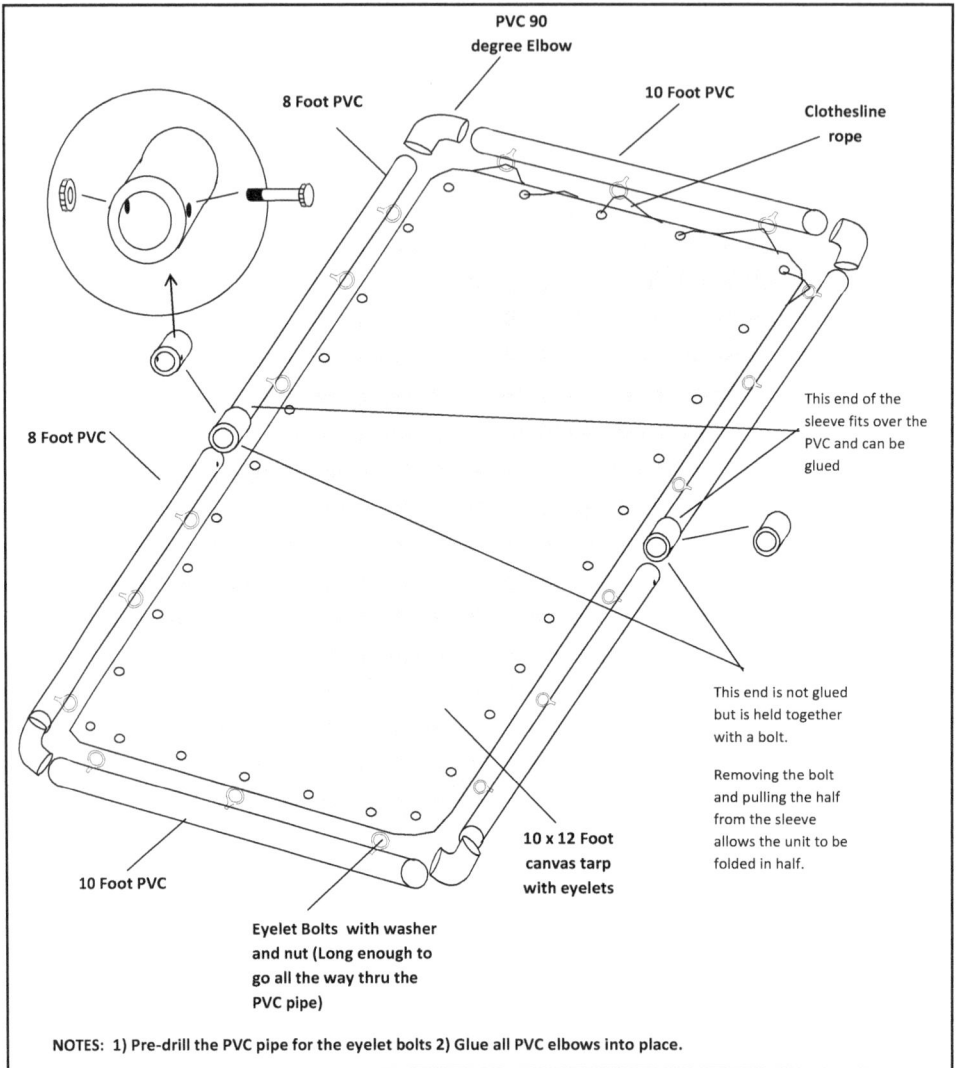

Picture of an Eye Bolt

DIY Tripod Dolly

Before we started filming our last film, we looked around for a good solid dolly that was sturdy and of course cheap. We didn't have much luck so Dan, my brother, and I came up with a design that would meet our needs. Since Dan worked at a plastics factory, he had access to scrap plastic that was very thick. The design should be narrow enough to move through doorways and have good quality casters to make movement with it fairly smooth. Needless to say, on our film we used "Dan's Dolly" a LOT! Here's the design.

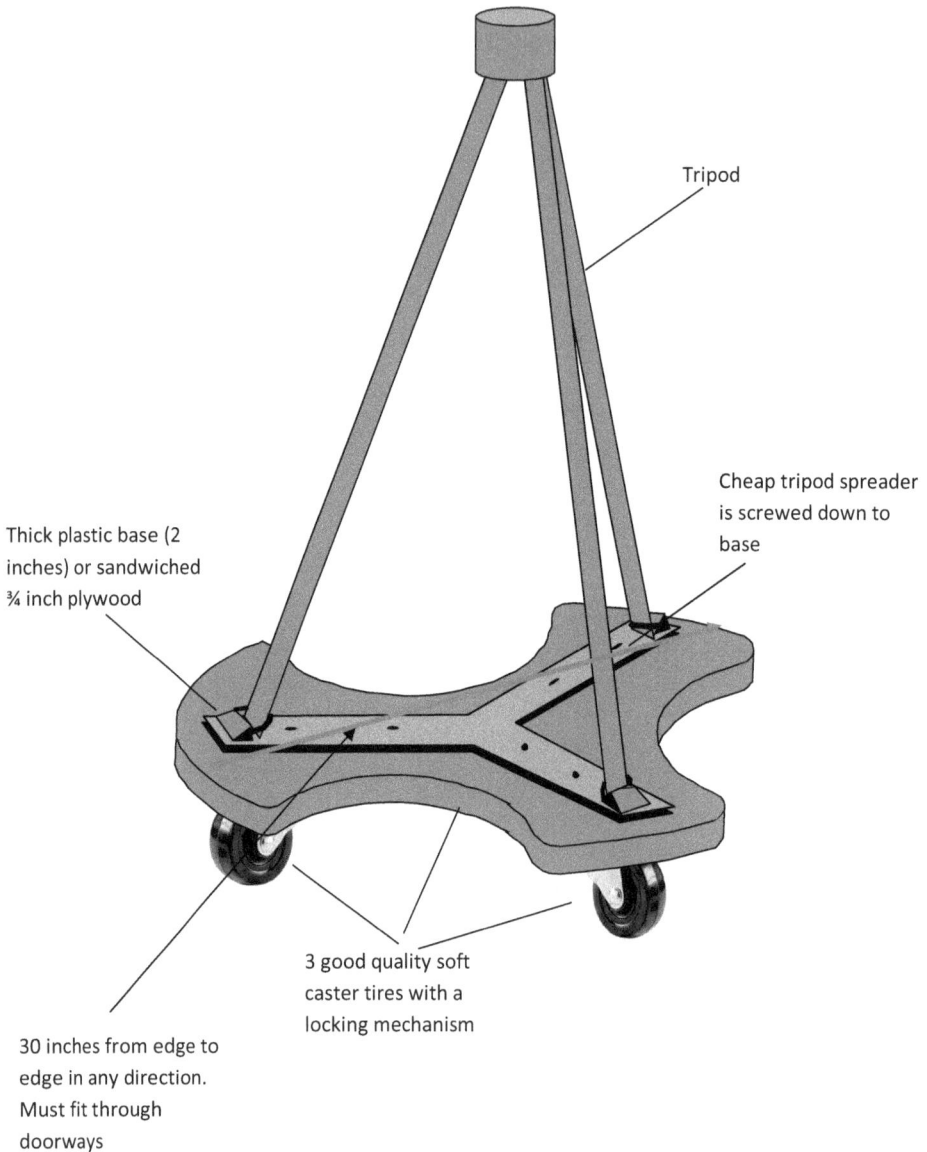

"DAN'S DOLLY"

Tripod

Cheap tripod spreader is screwed down to base

Thick plastic base (2 inches) or sandwiched ¾ inch plywood

3 good quality soft caster tires with a locking mechanism

30 inches from edge to edge in any direction. Must fit through doorways

The most important pieces of the design are the wheels and the tripod spreader. The base is laid out as a circle with cuts out on three sides (See figure above). The caster wheels (Get a locking mechanism with the wheels or your dolly will want to slide away) are plate mounted on the bottom of the base. The spreader (Where your tripod lock down) is mounted to the top of the base. Below is an example of a plate mounted caster wheel and a tripod spreader. You can buy the cheapest spreader since you just need a way to lock down your tripod, but try and buy some quality wheels because that will make a difference.

Plate-Mounted Wheel and a Tripod Spreader

If you can't find scrap plastic from a local plastic factory, you can use 3/4 inch plywood sandwiched together (glued in the middle) to make a solid 1 1/2 inch base.

I hope these designs work out for you and it adds some long-lasting tools to your film equipment inventory.

APPENDIX H
Links

Acting:
http://www.cothespians.com/LeeStrasberg.htm

Acting - Working with actors:
http://www.filmmaking.net/articles/show_article.asp?id=30

Arbitron Inc. cinema advertising study:
http://www.natoonline.org/Cinema%20Advertising%20Study.pdf

Film rating (CARA) and Motion Picture Association of America (MPAA):
www.filmratings.com www.mpaa.org

Adding production value to your film:
http://www.cinemaadvanced.com/producing/adding-production-value-to-your-film/

Adobe Audition 5.1 surround sound:
http://help.adobe.com/en_US/audition/cs/using/WS2bacbdf8d487e582474d57d512e2c5496d1-8000.html

Adobe Premiere Pro CS5 third party plug-ins:
http://www.adobe.com/products/plugins/premiere/

AF100 user info:
http://af100central.com/?page_id=2#comment-109

Audio equipment:
http://www.trewaudio.com/

Audio - Mapping audio channels:

http://help.adobe.com/en_US/PremierePro/4.0/WS1c9bc5c2e465a58a9
1cf0b1038518aef7-7f46a.html

Blank firing guns:
http://replicaweaponry.com/9mmf92sifi.html

BMI music rights:
http://www.bmi.com/licensing/entry/533606?link=footer

Boom - How to operate a microphone boom:
http://www.brighthub.com/multimedia/video/articles/60015.aspx

Camera car mounts:
http://www.youtube.com/watch?v=eXplMdHQLAc&feature=related

Camera mounts:
http://www.filmtools.com/mewecarmo.html

Camera work – how to:
http://www.ehow.com/video_4992202_learn-basics-good-camera-
work.html

Chicago SAG:
http://www.sag.org/branches/chicago

Chicago filmmakers:
http://chicagofilmmakers.org/cf/classes

Cinedigm acquisition and distribution:
http://cinedigm.com/marketing.shtml

Cinema equipment:
http://www.jbkcinequipt.com/PRODUCTS.htm

Cinema Gadgets:

http://www.cinemagadgets.com/product/dollies__tracks/dollies

Cinematography – shot design- video:
http://www.youtube.com/watch?v=IZA9r0iWbdw&feature=fvw

Cinematography:
http://www.youtube.com/watch?v=iDMRB5cCrzY&feature=related
And http://www.youtube.com/watch?v=3JFQ9a3Qo8k&feature=related

Cinematography:
http://www.cinematographers.nl/THEDoPH2.htm

Cinematography:
http://www.mvscnmtr.tk/page/28

Cinematography:
http://www.lightsfilmschool.com/articles/cinematography/index.html
and http://classes.yale.edu/film-analysis/htmfiles/cinematography.htm

Cinematography – shot design- video:
http://www.youtube.com/watch?v=IZA9r0iWbdw&feature=fvw

Closed captioning service:
http://www.closedcaptionservice.com/

Contact Lenses:
http://www.coastalcontacts.com/halloween-lenses/cHalloweenLenses-p1.html

Contracts - Free film contract examples:
http://filmmakeriq.com/2009/04/588-free-film-contracts-and-forms/

CS5 - Exporting in CS5:
http://www.adobepress.com/articles/article.asp?p=1661113&seqNum=2

CS5 tutorial-Making a rough cut:
http://tv.adobe.com/watch/learn-premiere-pro-cs5/gs04-making-a-rough-cut-in-adobe-premiere-pro/

Day for night - Shooting day for night:
http://www.youtube.com/watch?v=4MaC44MU4iw&feature=related

DCP info – Wikipedia:
http://en.wikipedia.org/wiki/Digital_Cinema_Package

DCP-= Making a DCP:
http://www.dvxuser.com/V6/showthread.php?249664-Making-a-DCP-(Digital-Cinema-Package)

Digital solutions for cinema:
http://www.dcipllc.com/Home

Distribber – indie film distributor – fee based:
http://www.distribber.com

Distrify – independent film distributor:
http://www.distrify.com/pricing

Dolly track:
http://www.cartala.com/track.php

Doorway dolly:
http://www.blackbearstudiosystems.com/doorway_dolly.html
and http://wn.com/doorway_dolly_and_track

Duclos lenses:
http://www.ducloslenses.com/Duclos_Lenses/Cinemod.html and
http://ducloslenses.com/Duclos_Lenses/Main.html
Dutch angle – Wikipedia:

http://en.wikipedia.org/wiki/Dutch_angle

Entertainment insurance:
http://www.filmemporium.com/ and http://www.fracturedatlas.org/
site/liability/Equipment?gclid=CMyx4eDFu60CFUhgTAodfkfA_w

Error & Omissions Insurance:
http://www.frontrowinsurance.com/sectors/e-o-insurance/

Fake newspaper: http://www.trixiepixgraphics.com/scanshtm/c-115.
html

Fight scene tutorial:
http://www.youtube.com/watch?v=IsLDt2iaOBk&feature=related

Film crew info – Wikipedia:
http://en.wikipedia.org/wiki/Film_crew

Film distribution:
http://www.newfilmmakersonline.com/opportunity.
aspx?opID=214&source=rss

Film equipment:
http://www.zacuto.com/

Film equipment insurance (Floater):
http://www.filmins.com/programs/entertainment-equipment-floater.
htm

Film equipment:
http://www.cineultima.com

Film equipment - Used film equipment:
http://prodcentral.com/used-video-equipment-for-sale.html
Film insurance:

http://www.ifilmalliance.com/business.php?bid=1343

Film insurance:
http://www.filmins.com/contact-movie-insurance.htm

Film look:
http://library.creativecow.net/articles/maschwitz_stu/red-giant-blockbuster-film-look.php

and http://library.creativecow.net/articles/maschwitz_stu/red-giant-blockbuster-film-look/video-tutorial.php

Film scoring:
http://www.filmscoremonthly.com/cds/composers/index.cfm

Film tools:
http://www.filmtools.com/dolliesandjibs.html

Flickering lights:
http://www.horrorseek.com/home/halloween/wolfstone/Flicker/flktch_FlickerTechniques.html

Flolight lighting:
http://www.flolight.com/

Follow focus:
http://www.cinevate.com/catalog/product_info.php?products_id=215

Follow Focus lever:
http://www.cinevate.com/catalog/product_info.php?products_id=203

Forensics props:
http://copstopshop.com/forensics

Gravitas Ventures – VOD distribution:

http://www.gravitasventures.com/

Green screen supplies:
http://www.tubetape.net/servlet/the-Green-Screens--fdsh--Backdrops-
cln-Chromakey-Green/Categories

Green screen tape:
http://www.filmandvideolighting.com/chkeygrscta2.html

Guns - Safety precautions using blank guns:
http://www.a2armory.com/blank-safety.html

Holomatrix software: http://www.redgiantsoftware.com/products/all/
holomatrix/

Horror film festivals:
http://www.biglistofhorrorfilmfestivals.com/

How to shoot a low budget film:
http://indiemoviemaking.com/the-ultimate-low-budget-blueprint-for-
shooting-a-scene/

LCD monitors:
http://www.lcd4video.com/products/LCD4Video-7%22-HD-LCD-
Monitor-.html

Lighting equipment:
http://www.thecinecity.com/eshop/product.php?productid=390&cat=2
81&page=1

Lighting equipment sales:
http://www.eoslightingllc.com/cm/filmmakers/tungsten/tungsten-
fixtures-accessories/

Lighting instruction:

http://www.studio1productions.com/dvd-651.htm

Lightning machines:
http://www.i-zombie.com/pages/st2401-lightning-controller.php

Locations:
http://www.studiosystemnews.com/how-to-save-big-on-location-your-starter-guide-to-state-by-state-tax-incentives/

Location Insurance info: http://www.aivf.org/magazine/07/2009/filmmakerinsurance

Master shots and coverage:
http://www.brighthub.com/multimedia/video/articles/22842.aspx

Michael Weiss web site sample budgets:
 http://www.mwp.com/filmschool/resources.php?partner=mwp&resource=budgets

Microphone windshield:
http://www.rycote.com/products/full_windshield_kit/

Miller Tripods:
http://www.millertripods.com/product_details.html?id=175

Movie lens:
http://www.planet10studios.com/movie-camera-lens/

Music Composers:
http://freelancemusiccomposers.com/job-submission/

Music cue sheet:
http://derekaudette.ottawaarts.com/cuesheetfaq.php and http://musicinfilmreview.blogspot.com/2010/12/cue-sheet.html

Police uniforms:
http://www.chiefsupply.com/faq/index.asp

Production Boards - How to complete a production board: http://www.ehow.com/videos-on_5993_make-script-production-board.html

Production Boards: http://filmtvworkshops.com/film_resources/film_production_strip_boards.html

Red Giant Magic Bullet:
http://www.redgiantsoftware.com/products/all/magic-bullet-suite/

Red Giant software. This is the studio quality software for special effects, coloring, etc: http://www.redgiantsoftware.com/

Red Giant Tutorials (Cool stuff): http://www.redgiantsoftware.com/videos/tutorials/

Russian Cinema Lenses:
http://rafcamera.com/info/movie_lenses.htm

Screen Actors Guild (SAG):
http://www.sag.org/theatrical-0

SAG info:
http://www.suite101.com/content/sags-ultra-low-budgets-producer-beware-a124716

Scheduling: http://www.ehow.com/how_2127353_schedule-independent-film-shoot.html

Scoring info:
http://www.robin-hoffmann.com/dfsb/daily-film-scoring-bits/

Slamdance film festival:

http://showcase.slamdance.com/#Film-Festival

Sound:
http://www.soundonsound.com/forum/showflat.php?Cat=&Number=7
95548&Main=790232

Smoothing your video:
http://www.youtube.com/watch?v=sFW0UTLcZJw

Surround Sound - Making a 5.1 sound track from stereo – video:
http://www.youtube.com/watch?v=sPc2KZ9xDbw&feature=related

SV2 Studios – DCP creation:
http://www.sv2studios.com/dcp/dcp-services-pricing/

Tarps - Link to white tarps (have eyelets): http://www.tarpsplus.com/
suheducata.html

Thunder and lightning:
http://www.horrorseek.com/home/halloween/wolfstone/
ThunderAndLightning/clsbuy_CommercialLightning.html

Uniforms:
http://www.uniformswarehouse.com/prostores/servlet/-strse-Gun-
Holsters/Categories

Vertigo shot - How to do the "Vertigo" shot:
http://www.youtube.com/watch?v=Ag4ucx3wYoU

Zeiss Cine lens:
http://cinematechnic.com/resources/zeiss_cinematography_lens.html